MW00333752

Spiritual Formation
in Local Faith Communities

Spiritual Formation
in Local Faith Communities

A Whole-Person, Prompt-Card Approach

Neil Pembroke

Ewan Kelly

Theo Pleizier

William S. Schmidt

Jan-Albert van den Berg

RESOURCE *Publications* · Eugene, Oregon

SPIRITUAL FORMATION IN LOCAL FAITH COMMUNITIES
A Whole-Person, Prompt-Card Approach

Resource Publications
An Imprint of Wipf and Stock Publishers
199 W. 8th Ave., Suite 3
Eugene, OR 97401

www.wipfandstock.com

PAPERBACK ISBN: 978-1-6667-1375-6
HARDCOVER ISBN: 978-1-6667-1376-3
EBOOK ISBN: 978-1-6667-1377-0

FEBRUARY 3, 2022 8:52 AM

Contents

Acknowledgments

WE OWE A HUGE debt of gratitude to the fifteen ministry agents and forty-five parishioners across Australia, South Africa, Scotland, the Netherlands, and the USA who gave so generously of themselves and their time in participating in the pilot and the focus group evaluation process. It was our enormous privilege to share with them in the challenges and joys of the spiritual formation journey. We learnt so much from our coresearchers. The final chapter of the book is testament to this. To these wonderful human beings, we say a big thank-you.

INTRODUCTION

THERE IS BOTH ANECDOTAL and empirical evidence that regular, ongoing, and structured spiritual and pastoral guidance by ministers and
priests (hereafter we use the term "ministry agents," interchanged with
"pastor") is very rare.[1] When ministry agents do spend time with their

1. There is limited, but significant, empirical evidence available. We turned up
findings from a recent survey of Reformed and Evangelical pastors indicating that 81%
of those questioned indicated that a primary reason for deep frustration and disap-
pointment is the fact that there is "no regular discipleship program or effective effort of
mentoring their people or teaching them to deepen their Christian formation at their
church." See Krejcir, "Pastoral Ministry."

We also found a 2007–2008 survey of 758 Australian pastors in which it was reported that fewer than 20% of those surveyed indicated that they spent greater than 5
hours per week on average engaged in pastoral or spiritual counseling. See Beaumont,
"Pastoral Counseling Down Under."

Finally, we came across a report by Dr Gladys Ganiel of the Irish School of Ecu-
menics, Trinity College, entitled, "21st Century Faith Results of the Survey of Clergy,
Pastors, Ministers and Faith Leaders." Retrieved from http://www.ecumenics.ie/
wp-content/uploads/Clergy-Survey-Report.pdf, August 4th, 2020. Ganiel provides a
summary of the responses to the open-ended question put to Irish clergy about opportunities for them and for the Christian Church. While many very important issues
are nominated, we note that spiritual formation, pastoral care, or discipleship training
do not feature: "[Some] identified opportunities in the ending of the Troubles, which
they saw as opening the way for deeper engagement with others; or they identified
opportunities in immigrants coming to Ireland and Northern Ireland, who they felt
could invigorate the faith of Irish Christians. Other opportunities included greater
involvement of laypeople and women . . . the Credit Crunch/recession/collapse of the
Celtic Tiger, which was seen as prompting people to re-think their values and turn to
faith; the collapse of traditional church structures and the chance for new forms of
church to be developed; a post-modern, post-Christian and secular humanist public
milieu that is open to spiritual questions; an innate spiritual hunger within people
in Ireland; increased interest in Celtic spirituality; the decline in church attendance
creating communities of Christians who are really committed; youth with a passion
for justice; the opportunity to use modern technologies; the chance for the church to
lead the way on green/ecological issues; and the chance to bring lesbian, gay, bisexual

people, their pastoral work most often involves informal conversations that lack structure and intentionality. We developed this model of spiritual formation in the local church, taking as it does a holistic and formalized approach, because of our conviction that it would bring significant benefits to parishioners and invigorate pastoral ministry. A pilot project was conducted in a variety of cultural contexts—namely, Australia, the Netherlands, Scotland, South Africa, and the USA. The institutional affiliations of the research team are as follows: Associate Professor Neil Pembroke, University of Queensland, Brisbane, Australia; Professor Jan-Albert van den Berg, University of the Free State, Bloemfontein, South Africa; Professor William Schmidt, Institute of Pastoral Studies, Loyola University, Chicago, USA; Rev Dr Theo Pleizier, Assistant Professor of Practical Theology, Protestant Theological University, Groningen, Netherlands; and Rev Dr Ewan Kelly, Lecturer in Chaplaincy, Glasgow University, Scotland. All of us have a background in pastoral ministry and in teaching pastoral theology and practice. None of us are trained spiritual directors. What unites us is a shared interest in, and commitment to, the integration of spirituality, psychology and personal/social ethics in theological education and in pastoral practice.

Each research team member engaged three ministry agents who each in turn recruited and worked with three parishioners. The spread of Christian traditions included mainline Protestantism, the Anglican (Episcopal) Church, and Roman Catholicism. At the conclusion of the six-week long pilot, a local team member conducted focus groups with both parishioners and ministry agents. The feedback was almost universally extremely positive. Though we thought we had a good program to offer, we were quite taken back at just how affirming the participants were. Here are some typical comments from the focus group sessions:

> Well, this is quite a dramatic one, so I'll just get it out of the way. Maybe about twenty years . . . For the first time in about twenty years I've started praying. So that's pretty dramatic (nods from others in the focus group). You know. It's amazing! ("Rachel," Scottish female, age 60)

> I'm exactly the same as "Rachel." I've been a member of the church . . . well . . . since I was christened. And then you begin to doubt things. You get into a doubting frame of mind. And like Rachel was saying earlier on, a vicious circle. Well that can't be

---

and transsexual (LGBT) people into the church."

right, because that doesn't happen there. If God does this, why does this happen? Ahhhh! So what now? But [after this] I've been more willing to accept faith, and just let things happen. As opposed to worrying at it. And the conversation has definitely helped that, and a bit of reading as well . . . What it made me do . . . what you were talking about before. Noticing . . . wondering . . . realizing. Things we thought about from the previous session. Ah . . . keeping a journal. Well, I've never in my life kept a journal (laughs). I just don't write things down. But actually I started doing it. But since the COVID thing started, every day I've been writing something. And it's been a bit like the conversations . . . um . . . doing that is a release of worries. Writing it down . . . it's like talking to someone. But it's private. And it's the same every night. I do a little prayer course of my own . . . a little prayer meeting. And I would never have done that before . . . before the conversations. So it opened up a whole new world to me. ("Kate," Scottish female, age 70)

Look, the whole thing was . . . was . . . fantastic, you know. I enjoyed it . . . You get an hour with "Jane" [the pastor]. But I've spent a lot of time with Jane in the last 18 months and she's like my mate . . . There's nothing she doesn't know about me. I was totally honest and she didn't blink an eyelid . . . Just another good time for me to be myself and . . . I just really loved it. Just to spend the hour . . . Mate, I wouldn't change anything. 100%. It was great to just dump all the crap, you know. And to think about things you could do better. A bit like Emmaus [a weekend spiritual retreat experience]. Fantastic. ("Jack," Australian male in his 50s)

So, just putting the questions and going through the questions. It gave me time to reflect and to self-evaluate. What am I really doing? How am I doing this? It made me realize I want to pray more, I wanna meditate more, I wanna get closer to . . . um . . . God's presence. I wanna read the Bible more and look for the message that applies to me. That changes as I change. Our lives change and the message is different and that is so rich. So many important things included, depending on where we are in our lives. We read the same part of Scripture but the message is different. There's a depth to . . . ah . . . ah . . . the Bible . . . to the message. The ability to gain perspective on life. To think about what I wanna do with the rest of my life . . . how I wanna live it. ("Hanna," Polish-American female, aged in her 50s)

We wanted a whole-person approach; we therefore incorporated three domains: spirituality, positive psychology, and personal and social ethics. These domains are expressed in four areas: spirituality is split into "spiritual practices" and "spiritual character." The structure is provided in the following way. The parishioner and the ministry agent work together over six sessions. The first of these sessions is an orientation to the approach and the process. Then there are four sessions on each of the following areas: spiritual character, spiritual practices (domain 1), psychological well-being (domain 2), and personal/social ethics or moral character (domain 3). The areas can be covered in any order. The final session consists of a closing conversation and prayer or ritual. Another structural aspect is that the parishioner is invited to work with sets of prompts (printed on cards of playing card size) covering the four areas indicated above. Each set has a "wild card." This symbolizes an invitation for the parishioner to bring an issue or issues of interest or concern not covered in the prompts provided.

We offer a pastoral resource to ministry agents. Beyond that, *we present a challenge to rethink and rejig the nature of pastoral ministry.* We expect that a typical reaction to our proposal will be something like this: "Well, it looks like it might be useful, but there's no way I can fit anything else into my busy week." True to a point, but the shape of pastoral ministry, like that of virtually every other professional vocation, comes down to priorities. In the contexts that we operate in, we observe ministry agents prioritizing certain ministry and mission areas. Many dedicate a considerable amount of time to action for social inclusion, peace, justice, and ecological sustainability. Others dedicate themselves to equipping and inspiring disciples for evangelization. We also recognize that these and other missional activities are important. But we want to issue this challenge to those who need to hear it: The pastoral functions that have been accorded an absolutely central place in the history of the Christian church—healing, sustaining, guiding, and reconciling[2]—should not simply be squeezed in if time allows. Spiritual companioning needs to be placed right at the center of pastoral ministry. We recognize that in order to take up this challenge, restructuring of the ministry week and of pastoral priorities is required. Such a realization came to one of the ministers based in Scotland:

---

2. See Clebsch & Jaekle, *Pastoral Care*, 4.

No, actually, they were looking for more from me [he is indicating that the parishioners wanted the six-week long process to continue]. But I was thinking, "How would my energy cope with this if there were more people in this?" And that puts a real challenge over the mutual journey, over my journey. Because there's a feeling of . . . of not wanting to leave them in a hiatus of expectations of what I could offer and be there. *Unless I reconfigured my whole ministry and nature of ministry.* If I was to do that then I could see how this could happen more. And it might be that this is something I might want to do out of this process. To reconfigure ministry and have a totally different outlook. ("Peter," aged in his early 60s; emphasis added)

We think that changing up priorities and making time for ongoing work on spiritual formation would look roughly like this. A ministry agent—in small congregations probably the pastor, in large congregations a pastoral team member—would dedicate six to eight hours each week to working with parishioners across the four areas in our model. That would mean working with six people every eight weeks (allowing for a two week break). Over roughly forty weeks—taking out time for a vacation and the busy periods such as Advent, Christmas, Easter and downtime over the summer—that's five blocks of eight weeks and therefore a ministry agent could work with thirty people per year. If a small group approach was implemented, obviously many more parishioners would be able to benefit. A number of the parishioners and pastors we interviewed also made this observation (more on this in Chapter Ten). While we were aware of the possibility of taking a small group approach—and indeed the team coordinator, Neil Pembroke, has in fact done this—we made the judgment that on balance a one-to-one approach would be better for the pilot. In particular, we recognized that individuals are usually less likely to be fully honest and to truth-tell in a group setting. As Jack indicated above, he felt free to dump "his crap" and he was confident that Jane would not "bat an eyelid." It is unlikely that he would feel as free and confident in a group setting. Of course, we could have trialed both approaches. But we simply did not have the resources available to run a bigger project.

The rest of the introduction to the model is set out as follows. First, in recognition of the fact that some readers may have little understanding of one of the domains we include, positive psychology, a brief overview is provided. Second, the genesis of the project is discussed. Finally, the model in outline and the evaluation process we used are presented.

BRIEF OVERVIEW OF POSITIVE PSYCHOLOGY

As mentioned above, we are not assuming that readers of this book have an understanding of positive psychology. Let us therefore provide a sketch of it. One of the pioneers in this new psychology wave was Martin Seligman. Seligman became increasingly dissatisfied with the way in which his field devoted so much attention to psychopathology and methods of treating it. Whether it is unconscious conflict (psychoanalysis), or an identity crisis (Erikson), or the destructive effect of "Parent" or "Child" dominance (Transactional Analysis), or faulty cognitive schemas (CBT), or dominance of the problem-story (Narrative Therapy), the message is the same: psychology is primarily concerned with mental dysfunction. He tells a personal story that was pivotal in his switch to a concentration on emotional well-being and human flourishing.[3] The event happened a few months after Seligman was elected president of the American Psychological Association. At the time, he was weeding his garden with his five-year-old daughter, Nikki. Seligman confesses that while he writes books for children, relating to them doesn't come naturally. He is too task-oriented. While he is focusing on getting the garden weeded, Nikki is playfully throwing weeds into the air and singing and dancing around. At one point, she had something she wanted to say to her father: "Daddy, do you remember before my fifth birthday. From the time I was three to the time I was five, I was a whiner. I whined every day. When I turned five, I decided not to whine anymore. It was the hardest thing I've ever done. And if I can stop whining, you can stop being a grouch." The moment was an epiphany for Seligman. He remarks: "I was a grouch. I had spent 50 years mostly enduring wet weather in my soul, and the past 10 years being a nimbus cloud in a household full of sunshine." The journey of research on "authentic happiness" was launched.

In his book with this title, he explains why this is so crucial for human beings: "[F]eeling positive emotion is important, not just because it is pleasant in its own right, but because it *causes* much better commerce with the world. Developing more positive emotion in our lives will build friendship, love, better physical health, and greater achievement."[4] In this focus on psychological well-being, attention is given to character strengths, optimism, life-satisfaction, self-esteem and self-confidence.

3. See Seligman & Csikszentmihalyi, "Positive Psychology," 5–15, at 5–6.

4. Seligman, *Authentic Happiness*, 76.

A helpful overview of the approach is found on the website of the Positive Psychology Center at the University of Pennsylvania (Seligman's home institution):

> Positive Psychology is the scientific study of the strengths and virtues that enable individuals and communities to thrive . . . This field is founded on the belief that people want to lead meaningful and fulfilling lives, to cultivate what is best within themselves, and to enhance their experiences of love, work, and play . . . Positive Psychology has three central concerns: positive emotions, positive individual traits, and positive institutions.[5]

Clearly, there is a great deal more that could be said about positive psychology. Indeed, an extended treatment is provided in Chapter Eight. Perhaps enough has been offered to give a good general sense of the theory. We want to make it clear that *we are not advocating uncritical borrowing.* While we are advocating a whole-person approach and we therefore consider that pastors need to support the psychological wellbeing of their parishioners, there are elements in positive psychology that theological interrogation will either reframe or reject entirely. To give just one example here, whereas positive psychology identifies accomplishment as a cornerstone, Christian theology posits service as the primary value. In Chapter Eight, we give sustained attention to critical engagement with this new school of psychological thought.

The ten strengths advocated by positive psychology that we incorporated into the model are these: self-acceptance, capacity for love in relationships, autonomy, skill in everyday living, purpose in life, personal growth, optimism, intellectual curiosity and imagination, conscientiousness, and being in the moment (flow). The other domains incorporated in our model— spirituality and moral virtue—will be very familiar to the reader and therefore need no introduction here. They are discussed in detail later in the book. At this point, we turn to a consideration of how this project originated.

---

5. Seligman, Positive Psychology Center homepage. Retrieved from http:// www. ppc.sas.upenn.edu, July 24th, 2020.

THE GENESIS OF THE MODEL

The story begins with the fact that in an early stage in his pastoral ministry Neil Pembroke, the team's coordinator, read with appreciation Eugene Peterson's book, *Working the Angles*.[6] Peterson makes the claim that too many pastors have turned away from their primary calling and taken on the role of "shopkeeper" instead. The vocation of the congregational minister involves three basic pastoral acts—namely, prayer, reading Scripture, and giving spiritual direction. This way of referring to the essential calling of the pastor made a deep impact on Neil. The genesis of this project can be traced back to that experience.

Peterson used his shopkeeper metaphor to call out a widespread tendency in American Protestant pastors to construe their ministry as offering the newest and the best in the ecclesial range of goods with a view to satisfying the customer's tastes and desires. He lamented the fact that such pastors have "gone whoring after other gods."[7] Thirty years later, the context for pastoral ministry has changed quite a bit. Many ministry agents now give a high priority to working for inclusion, peace, justice, and ecological sustainability. Others have formed the view that the major focus today needs to be on forming disciples passionate about, and equipped for, the task of evangelization. Some devote quite a bit of time to pastoral counseling. Other ministry and mission foci could be mentioned. While we support the view that the scope of pastoral work needs to be broader than what Peterson advocated for, we do think that he was on to something important. Spiritual formation needs to be pushed up the list of priorities many pastoral agents work with. While it is common to marginalize this important ministry, this pattern, thankfully, is far from universal.

A decade after his encounter with Peterson's thought, in 2004, Neil was invited to be the keynote speaker at a national conference of the Center for Religious Development (CRD) in Adelaide, Australia. In one of the addresses, a holistic model of spiritual companioning was presented, featuring the three domains of psychology, spiritual practice, and personal and social ethics.

The approach in the CRD sessions, in turn, was shaped by teaching the "Formation for Christian Ministries" course at the Adelaide College of Divinity in 2001–2002. Not long after, Neil had a book published entitled

6. Peterson, *Working the Angles*.

7. Peterson, *Working the Angles*.

Moving Toward Spiritual Maturity.[8] In this book, he gave the ideas he had been developing a comprehensive biblical and theological grounding.

A WHOLE-PERSON APPROACH

It is important to recognize that the three domains in the approach we offer—spirituality, personal and social ethics, and positive psychology—are inextricably linked. In our view, it is not possible to be optimally helpful in companioning an individual on their journey of spiritual growth without addressing both moral character and psychological strengths. Certain influential pastoral theologians have been arguing for some time that it's necessary to move past the "silo approach" to pastoral ministry; the contention is that it is not helpful to separate out and isolate psychological, spiritual, and moral issues.

For example, quite a long time ago now Don Browning started a movement to restore the moral dimension of pastoral care.[9] Others have expanded on his seminal work.[10] Bill Schmidt, a research team member, explored the contribution of the spiritual practice called "pilgrimage" in facilitating healing and recovery for persons suffering from grief and loss.[11] Also significant is the argument mounted by Jean Stairs that a comprehensive approach to caring for others requires the integration of theological and psychological insights with wise teaching on the spiritual life.[12] Stairs discusses the nature of the close relationship between pastoral care and the ministry of spiritual direction. More recently, this theme has been developed in two important collections edited by Peter Gubi, entitled *Spiritual Accompaniment and Counselling*[13] and *What Counsellors and Spiritual Directors Can Learn from Each Other.*[14] The contributors in these volumes present a psychologically informed approach to spiritual companioning and a spiritually attuned method for pastoral counseling. Highly significant issues such as building an effective relationship

---

8. See Pembroke, *Moving Toward Spiritual Maturity.*

9. See Browning, *The Moral Context.*

10. See Noyce, *The Minister*; Capps, *Life Cycle Theory*, 33–54; Miles, *The Pastor*; Graham, *Moral Injury.*

11. See Schmidt, "Transforming Pilgrimage."

12. See Stairs, *Listening for the Soul.*

13. See Gubi, *Spiritual Accompaniment.*

14. See Gubi, *What Counsellors and Spiritual Directors Can Learn from Each Other.*

in spiritual companioning, prayer in counseling, and dialogue between counselors and religious pastoral carers are discussed, along with topics that stretch across the moral and spiritual domains such as forgiveness, spiritual abuse, and sexual abuse.

In his pastoral theology, Daniël Louw develops this integrated line of thinking in his own unique and deeply insightful way.[15] Louw construes the work of pastoral counseling as helping people correct unhealthy personal schemas.[16] He points out that the categories that make up a schema are moral, psychological, and spiritual in nature.

A theorist and practitioner that has been especially influential in terms of developing the model is Len Sperry. When the project coordinator was putting the finishing touches on his own book, he came across Sperry's (2002) fine contribution entitled, *Transforming Self and Community.*[17] Sperry offers a new model for the dedicated ministry of spiritual direction that encompasses the three domains identified in the research team's model. What is offered is the same three-domain approach, but the focus has been shifted to the pastoral work of ministry agents in a congregational setting. Moreover, the approach of Sperry has been developed by us through the incorporation of four sets of prompt cards (discussed below).

The thread tying together all the important scholarly contributions discussed above is the conviction that supporting people in Christian formation requires working with them on personal psychology, spiritual practice, and personal and social ethics. However, these domains are not three water-tight containers standing side-by-side; they leak into each other. For example, a lack of self-awareness and psychological integration in a person often results in destructive and hurtful interpersonal behavior rather than that which is good, right, and up-building. Or to flip this around, we note that the positive psychology movement views psychological strengths as the processes or mechanisms that define moral virtues. For example, the virtue of humanity is enacted through love, kindness, and social intelligence. It is also very evident that spiritual practice informs and shapes our personal psychology and moral life.

While it is clear that there is both interaction and overlap between the three domains, it is also true that each of them has its own specific

---

15. See Louw, *A Mature Faith*; Louw, "Philosophical Counselling."

16. See Louw, "Philosophical Counselling."

17. See Sperry, *Transforming Self and Community.*

focus. In the psychological domain, we are concerned with intrapsychic and interpersonal dynamics. The spirituality area involves us in reflection on prayer and meditation on God's Word, sacramental life, images of God, and the God-relationship. Finally, in the moral category we concentrate on virtue and character, on moral principles and rules, and on what is right and good.

This holistic aspect of the approach that we have developed is vitally important. It's crucial that the ministry agent discusses this with the parishioner in the orientation session; it will set the scene for the process that is about to unfold. A significant feature of the closing session is an invitation for the parishioner to do some integrative thinking. Let us now develop these and other features of the model more fully.

THE MODEL AND THE RESEARCH PROCESS

Before we get to a description of the model and how it was tested, it's worth mentioning that there was a significant change in relation to the how the self-reflection by the parishioner prior to each session was structured. The initial intention was that the parishioner would complete a series of self-evaluation sheets. A sample is presented below:

Spiritual Character Self-Assessment

Key: 1 = Strongly disagree; 2 = Moderately disagree; 3 = Mildly disagree; 4 = Mildly Agree; 5 = Moderately agree; 6 = Strongly agree

Gifts of the Spirit	Definition	Statements	1	2	3	4	5	6
Faith	Trust in the love and grace of God that has been made known to us by Christ.	"I understand that times of doubt are normal, but generally my trust in the love and grace of God is secure."						

Hope	Confidence that God is at work in our world bringing good out of evil; that no matter what happens in life God loves me and I have the hope of eternal life.	1. "I have an abiding hope that God is at work overcoming evil in the world." 2. "I have assurance that in Christ I am right with God and have the hope of eternal life."	1	2	3	4	5	6
Love	Love of God and love of neighbour. Loving God with all my heart, mind, and soul. Giving of myself to advance the well-being, dignity, freedom, and peace of others.	"In the follow-up sessions with my pastor, I would like to make time to reflect on love of God and love of neighbor in my life."	1	2	3	4	5	6

As a result of input from a team member, Theo Pleizier, a decision was made to change from the self-evaluation sheets to the use of small cards. We used playing-card sized prompts like this one (though we changed the expression "How am I doing with . . . " after the focus group feedback came in):

> How am I doing with PEACE?
> Serenity flowing from resting secure in God's
> unconditional love, sustaining grace,
> and gift of Christ and the Holy Spirit.

Now to the process we followed in our pilot project. The first task given to the participating pastor was recruitment of three parishioners to work with over a six-week period. Obviously, a potential participant needs a sense of what the process entails. In the broadest terms, it's an opportunity to do some reflection on their journey toward Christian maturity through attending to spiritual practices, psychological wellbeing and moral character. Advice was given to the ministry agents to show a potential participant a selection of the cards to be used as part of the process. Each ministry agent was also instructed to inform an interested parishioner about the focus group at the end and to indicate that the evaluations will be used to refine and improve the model, which will then be written up for publication as a book. Ministry agents were told to assure participants that confidentiality will be respected: in the write-up for the book, no names of participants would be included; it's only their thoughts and evaluative comments that will be incorporated.

The process we trialed consists of six sessions (each approximately one hour) conducted, ideally, over six weeks. The first session is an orientation and has the following aims. The first is to give an opportunity for a conversation about expectations, hopes, and concerns. The parishioner is invited to reflect on questions such as: What would you like to see come out of this process and our conversations? What are you hoping for? What is it about what we are about to embark on that excites you? Are there things about it that you feel a bit anxious or uncertain about?

The first session is also the time, obviously, to talk about how the process will unfold over the next five weeks. This is laid out just below.

Finally, at the first session the parishioner is invited to select a set of cards to work with at the next session. The set can be any one of the four.

The process is as follows. After the first session, the parishioner reflects on the set of prompts (covering spiritual character, or psychological well-being, etc.) that they have chosen. They then bring one or two of these cards to the second session. The cards form the basis for the conversation.

The form of the conversation is pastoral and informal in tone. The approach is not that of formal spiritual direction. It needs to have the feel of companioning, guiding, and facilitating. The ministry agent is not cast in the role of the expert, though they clearly have quite a bit of expertise to bring. Mutuality in the work together is appropriate.

At the close of the session, the ministry agent invites the parishioner to consider doing some journaling as a way of reflecting further on what was talked about. This is an invitation only; the parishioner needs to feel totally free not to take it up. If they do opt for journaling, the minimal guidance set out below is offered. It's shaped around three levels of "seeing" (on the model of John 20 and the relevant Greek words):

> In reflecting on the session just past ...
>
> What do you notice? What feelings and thoughts arise for you as you reflect on the conversation?
>
> What are you wondering about? What are you feeling curious about?

Is there a "light bulb" moment for you? Is there an insight that seems especially important right now?

If the parishioner wants to reflect on what came to them in the journaling process at the start of the next session that is fine, but it is not expected. That is, there's no need to offer an invitation to do so.

At the conclusion of the second session, the parishioner is invited to select their second set of prompts to take away. They will bring one or two cards to the third session to form the basis of that conversation. And so it goes on.

The sixth session is a wrap-up. It is a time for both reflecting back and projecting forward. The pastor might ask questions such as: What was most significant for you along this journey? What did you learn? What are the questions and issues that will stay with you? Where to from here?

The final session, lastly, is an opportunity to reinforce the holistic dimension in the process. At this point we indicate that in setting up the trial, we instructed the pastors to remind their parishioners in this final session that a team member would contact them about participation in a focus group to evaluate the process. A list of the questions we used in these evaluation sessions can be found in Appendix B at the end of the book.

Getting back to the holistic element, we note that though each session has its particular focus, humans are whole beings; they cannot be carved up into three sections. Personal psychology, spiritual character, and moral character are all inextricably linked. To promote integrative reflection, the ministry agent may ask questions such as: What connections have you noticed between the conversations in the four sessions? After our times together and your own reflection, how are you seeing your psychological life, your spiritual life, and your moral life as linked?

A full listing of the four sets of prompt cards is provided in Appendix A at the end of the book. What we provide in the Appendix is a revised version; we made some minor changes after receiving the focus group feedback. One comment we heard a number of times was that the connection with Christian values and principles needs to be made explicit in the moral character and emotional wellbeing prompts. Small changes were made to accommodate this. There is also a revision of the introductory sentence ("How am I doing with . . . ") and the addition of a short explanation on what was previously a blank card. To give you a sense of the prompts we used at this point, here are three examples. From the Spiritual Practices domain: "How am I doing with SABBATH-KEEPING? God's gift of a regular routine of rest. A time given to us to celebrate life and the world around us and to simply be with God. A time for *being* in the midst of a life of *doing*." In the Moral Character domain we offer: "How am I doing with PEACEABLENESS: A way of life in the spirit of Christ involving the refusal to use force to protect yourself, to use coercion to get your own way, or to violently resist evil when it is done to you." Finally, from the Spiritual Character domain: "How am I doing with GENTLENESS? Mild and gentle friendliness; relating to others and to self in a non-judgmental and nurturing manner; speaking a hard truth in a gentle manner."

It will be evident that there is a certain arbitrariness around the choice of ten prompts for each area. Why not seven, or twelve, or fifteen? The simple answer is that we decided that ten is "the goldilocks" number. Presenting, in turn, ten psychological strengths, ten moral virtues, ten spiritual practices, and ten spiritual character traits gives enough scope for reflection without overloading the parishioner.

There is also a degree of arbitrariness associated with the selection of virtues and traits. There *is* a logic operating, though. In relation to positive psychology, we simply selected ten that are regularly discussed in books and articles on this new approach in psychology. The traits in the spiritual character domain are largely the fruits of the Spirit in Galatians 5:22–23. For the spiritual practices area, we chose ten out of a long list that we take to be of vital importance. Finally, in the moral character domain you will find the cardinal virtues plus others that we have gleaned from our reading of leading moral theologians who opt for a virtue ethics approach.

Now that you are familiar with the process, let us offer a map of the territory covered in the book. In Chapter One, we identify the way in which the identity and character of the pastor as spiritual, psychological, and moral guide is grounded both in ancient traditions and in contemporary developments. Quite apart from the historic links, we show how the three areas are inextricably bound up together.

At the start of Chapter Two, we distinguish between the specialized ministry of spiritual direction and that of pastoral care. We point out that what we are interested in is a general ministry we refer to as "spiritual guidance." In a brief overview, we hit some highlights in the story of spiritual guidance over the past 2000 years. We look to Jesus, the Desert

Elders, Aelred of Rievaulx, Ignatius of Loyola, and Teresa of Avila for inspiration and guidance. Further, while it is acknowledged that spiritual guidance benefits from an interdisciplinary orientation, with psychology at the forefront, we make it clear that it is spiritual formation and not pastoral psychotherapy we are attuned to with our process.

In Chapter Three the model is placed in transcultural and contextual perspective. Insights from various disciplines (e.g., postcolonial analysis, cultural studies, and contextual theology) highlight the importance of culturality. Spiritual care is a situated practice: it concerns unique persons in specific socio-cultural circumstances. The model we introduce in this book has been used in five different global contexts. In this chapter we connect our model of spiritual formation to intercultural theology on the one hand, while raising the question of whether spiritual care in the local church has transcultural traits, on the other. Two theological concepts are especially relevant here: apostolicity and sanctification.

The theme of Chapter Four is the pastoral capacity and spiritual character of the ministry agent. A method ultimately is only as good as the individuals who work with it. With this in mind, we offer theological reflection on the personhood and spirituality of the ministry agent. The topics covered are these: wisdom, availability, integrity (virtues), attentiveness and embrace of weakness (personal attributes).

The topic for Chapter Five is spiritual perspectives on formation. Our lives flourish when they are centered in prayer. Our ever-changing lives need living water, and intentional spiritual practices can give access to that water. The spiritual disciplines of contemplation/listening, seeing, relating, and discernment together form a conduit for the living water, perhaps not in equal measure all the time, but taken together they make for a reliable pathway to deepen the immersion of our lives in God. When we avail ourselves of these resources our engagement with life becomes centered and unified. Our head, heart, and hands when unified in this way find the nourishment needed for sustained loving in our complex worlds.

In Chapter Six the concentration is on vital spiritual practices serving as a conduit to the Sacred. Christians throughout the ages have found certain disciplines and practices to be profoundly helpful on their spiritual journey. This chapter offers reflection on specific practices that have proven themselves over time in practicing the presence of God. These practices provide guidance and nourishment and help us find a unity of purpose in weaving together our heart, head, and hands in the service of an integrated Christian life.

In Chapter Seven, the focal question is this: How do spiritual practices shape the human soul? Spiritual companioning and spiritual practices guide the soul in the journey of life. In helping people to integrate the story of God with their life stories, pastoral attentiveness and spiritual practices shape the human soul. This shaping has both spiritual and moral dimensions. This chapter draws from Scripture and the Christian tradition to develop a deep understanding of the pastoral shaping of the soul. The question of whether we become "better" persons through Christian faith is explored with help of the imagery of Fruits of the Spirit. The metaphor of growth contributes to a holistic understanding of the shaping of the soul in relation to other people (relationally), in relation to God (spiritually) and in relation to the world (ecologically).

In Chapter Eight, we take up the challenge of showing why it is appropriate to include positive psychology in a spiritual formation process. Topics covered are these: the theme of happiness in the Bible; the concept of a positive theology; communion (giving and receiving love) as the ideal for *agape*; and lastly, the theological rationale for including optimism in the psychological well-being domain and hope in the spiritual character field.

The task that we turn to in Chapter Nine is demonstrating that there is a natural fit between virtue ethics and spirituality. We consider two other candidates—deontological ethics and utilitarianism—and show why a moral character approach is the best option for our purposes.

The final chapter is dedicated to presenting the main ideas and themes that emerged in the focus group conversations. The team met to discuss these and made decisions around revisions. The revised model that we agreed on is presented.

1

A Contemporary Paradigm with Historical Roots

The Pastor as Spiritual, Psychological, and Moral Guide

In this opening chapter, we discuss the pastoral functions of spiritual, psychological, and moral guidance. With this chapter we establish the foundation for the project and present important markers that anchor further perspectives presented in the ensuing chapters.

Key to the description of the project is the view of the pastor as guide on the believer's holistic journey of formation in the Christian life.[1] The research project not only identifies the spiritual, psychological, and moral dimensions of pastoral care, but also how these integrated fields are directly associated with spiritual growth and development in the Christian life.

This first chapter not only serves as background to the research project, but also as an introduction to the various chapters in the book that focus in more detail on specific aspects of the proposed method.[2] In this chapter and as background orientation, we present the following: a brief sketch of the development of pastoral care, perspectives on the identity of the pastor, and the nature of spiritual, psychological, and moral guidance.

1. Pembroke et al., "Toward a Structured," 105.
2. Pembroke et al., "Toward a Structured," 109.

Against this background, the philosophy behind the project differs from the common understanding of pastoral care as associated with crisis and assistance in dealing with different existential issues in life.[3] From the start, the project focuses on how pastoral care can create room for facilitating the development of the Christian life, with the emphasis on the pastor as spiritual, psychological, and moral guide. It must be understood that this chapter's focus, and indeed also that of the entire book, is precisely *not* on the professional task of the pastoral therapist dealing with the healing of life in all its dimensions. The concentration is rather on the task of the local pastor who facilitates pastoral care with the aim of the positive development of the spiritual and personal life of the members of the community of faith.

To further specify this aim, we believe that in pastoral care the Bible and the Christian spiritual and moral heritage in general need to be integrated into the ministry. Further, we affirm that pastoral work is the joint responsibility of the pastor and the community of faith; the faith community supports the individual's spiritual journey of healing, growth, and transformation.

Consonant with the aim of this chapter of orientation to the project and its undergirding philosophy, a concise history of the development of pastoral care is presented in the following sub-section. We aim to point up clear resonance with elements in our own approach.

SKETCHING THE DEVELOPMENT OF PASTORAL CARE

To begin, we present a couple of orienting perspectives. The word "pastoral" in the term "pastoral care" derives from the Latin *pastorem*, the shepherd, with the connotation of caring for the defenceless and their needs.[4] In addition, this care has a communal orientation. The chief meaning of "care" in "pastoral care" implies the care and guidance of the congregation on all levels, originally specifically referring to Jewish and Christian communities of faith.[5] We provide here a short overview of the history of pastoral care as a primary task of religious leadership. This is followed by a concise reflection on the recent development of pastoral care as a discipline.

3. Louw, "Philosophical Counselling," 2.

4. McClure, "Pastoral Care," 269.

5. Schuhmann and Damen, "Representing the Good," 405.

A (Very) Brief Historical Overview

The practice of pastoral care, of course, is not restricted to the Jewish and Christian faiths; it also refers to designated care in the context of other traditions, including the Muslim, Buddhist, and Hindu faith traditions.[6] It is important, however, for the introduction to this project to highlight the Christian orientation, as clearly pointed out in both the First and Second Testaments, with Jesus' ministry significantly portrayed through the metaphor of the Good Shepherd.[7]

Pastoral ministry can be traced back to earliest Christianity.[8] The Apostle Paul is clearly practicing pastoral care when he writes to his faith communities to offer theological, pastoral, and spiritual guidance and support. Gregory of Nazianzus views pastoral ministry, the cure of souls, as "the art of arts and the science of sciences."[9] For Gregory, pastoral work is inextricably linked to God's dealing with humankind in and through Christ. The foundation of the pastoral ministry is the virtue and sanctity of the priest, the mediator of Christ's grace. This idea was shared by other Church Fathers such as Ambrose of Milan and John Chrysostom. The character of the priest is absolutely central in his pastoral work, which is focused on both the spiritual and the moral dimensions of the Christian life.[10] Gregory observes that in seeking to cure the sick souls in his care, the priest needs to "diagnose" each one's condition and administer the appropriate remedy, just as a physician diagnoses a bodily sickness in order to prescribe the correct treatment.[11] John Chrysostom also uses a medical metaphor in discussing pastoral care. The pastor is the "physician of the soul": "Bestowing attention and tender care, by trying every means of amendment, in imitation of the best physicians, for neither do they cure in one manner only, but when they see the wound not yield to the first remedy, they add another, and after that again another; and now they use the knife, and now bind up. And do thou accordingly, having become a physician of souls . . . "[12] Augustine's pastoral ministry was of a different order. His doctrinal theology can be viewed as a form of

---

6. Schuhmann and Damen, "Representing the Good," 405.

7. Gerkin, *Introduction*, 23–28.

8. Oden, "Historic Pastoral Care," 137.

9. Beeley, *Gregory of Nazianzus*, 235.

10. Greer, "Pastoral Care," 566.

11. Beeley, *Gregory of Nazianzus*, 245.

12. Chrysostom, Homily 29.

pastoral care. He offers perspectives for a moral, righteous, and worthy Christian life.

Barbara McClure helpfully reviews different epochs in the development of pastoral care. [13] After surveying the early periods as we have done, she notes that in the Middle Ages pastoral care acquired a strong sacramental character, with baptism, the Eucharist, confession, and the last rites providing spiritual uplift, inspiration, healing, challenge, and comfort. This changed during the Reformation, with the emphasis on reconciliation rather than on the sacramental dimension of pastoral care. During the age of Enlightenment, pastoral care acquired a strong supportive function, with believers being led from "the corrupted world" to a new pilgrimage of the soul. Within Reformed thought, pastoral care is directly linked to the message of the Word and to a strong kerygmatic hypothesis and approach. Changing perspectives, accompanied by a scientific point of view, led to a systematic and wide-reaching shift in pastoral care in the late 20th and early 21st century, with a more individualized character emphasising personal experience and a constructed spirituality, personal fulfilment, and self-actualization.

Some Recent Developments in Pastoral Care

During the 20th century, there were a number of significant developments in pastoral care. We refer to a kerygmatic, a therapeutic and, since the 1970s, a hermeneutic phase, in which theology and therapy are in a bipolar relationship.[14] Different paradigmatic movements can also be pointed out in the development of the formation of a pastoral theory.[15] The first shift, then, is from a unilateral model based on preaching to a participatory model of pastoral care. In the kerygmatic model, a specific church identity strongly informs and orients the pastoral task of the minister, in order to express a specific understanding of Scripture. From the European and Reformed context, the nouthetic reaction model is a specific example of this pastoral orientation. In the participatory approach, on the other hand, the pastor is instrumental in guiding individuals to discover God's involvement in their lives.

13. McClure, "Pastoral Care," 270–274.

14. Louw, *Pastoral Hermeneutics*, 23.

15. Louw, *Pastoral Hermeneutics*, 23–30.

A second movement is from a therapeutically- to a hermeneutical-ly-oriented pastoral care, with the emphasis in the latter on the search for meaning. The strong emergence of psychotherapy in Western culture, especially in the USA, inevitably drove the development of therapeutic pastoral care. On the other hand, the pastoral ministry took a significant turn to interpretation as a result of the hermeneutic revolution in the social sciences. The American experience model, in which phenom-enological and empirical descriptions are key, has made an important contribution to this development. Therapeutic pastoral ministry assigns an important place to insights from psychology, whereas hermeneutic pastoral care seeks less for psychologically informed knowledge and intervention and more for understanding and clarifying what is going on for a person in the emotional, interpersonal, and spiritual domains. For example, narrative pastoral care reads signs of God's presence within people's stories.

The above clearly shows that pastoral care has developed dynami-cally over a number of historical epochs. With the historical development of pastoral care as background, we can distinguish the following impor-tant and bigger changes in the nature of pastoral care.

THE IDENTITY OF THE PASTOR AS CAREGIVER

It is commonly stated that four central functions of pastoral care, namely healing, sustaining, guiding and reconciling, are intimately linked to its history and phases of development. The South African pastoral theolo-gian, Daniël Louw, presents specific metaphors to add thickness to this basic description of the functions of pastoral care.[16] These are summa-rized below.

The Shepherd. With the emphasis on the dimension of sensitivity, atten-tion is paid specifically to the emotional and physical needs of others, as expressed in, for example, relationship problems, stress in the workplace, and loss and grief.

The Servant. The emphasis on therapy as pastoral identification highlights the dimensions of empathy and compassion. The role acquires further

---

16. Louw, *Mechanics of Soul*, 123–150.

room and meaning in the development of the general pastorate to a more professional, qualified pastoral therapy.

Wisdom. Seeking to provide insight into the will and presence of God, despite paradoxes. There is an emphasis here on a spiritual understanding of life.

Paraclesis. Emphasis on consolation as pastoral agent of salvation. The aim is to support and empower, especially when trauma and loss are experienced. Pastoral involvement with individuals and families affected by the COVID pandemic is a particularly salient example at this time.

The Guide. The primary focus is on caring for those who are trapped in need, but also with the view to developing spiritual growth. This metaphor is strongly linked to the metaphor of wisdom that inquires about the discovery of specific spiritual truths that support spiritual growth.

The Dutch practical theologians, Ruard Ganzevoort and Jan Visser,[17] unsurprisingly perhaps, have developed an understanding of pastoral identity that overlaps heavily with Louw's proposal. However, we note that the metaphor of witness is new. The metaphors they use are as follows.

- *The Witness*: Relates to a kerygmatic, church-sacramental pastorate. The charismatic pastorate could also provide room for the pastor as witness.

- *The Helper*: Connects to a therapeutic pastoral ministry.

- *The Partner*: Journeys along with interlocutors, using existential philosophical models.

- *The Interpreter and Guide*: Interprets the person's story in dialogue with the Scriptural story.

In relation to the research project, it is important to point out that the pastor acts as a guide only. The word "guide" suggests a person who has specific knowledge of the process, but who does not necessarily know the content of the process. Just as a capable tour guide leads the tourist from a specific field of knowledge and experience to discover new sights, the "pastoral guide" leads the co-traveller in making new discoveries in

17. Ganzevoort and Visser, *Zorg*, 33–41.

the areas of emotional well-being, spirituality, values and character. Mutuality is highly significate here; the pastor is a fellow-traveller.

In the context of the method and theory we propose, it is useful to highlight two other roles identified by these pastoral theologians—namely, the interpreter and the partner in care. Throughout the 20th century, the shifts in interpretation of pastoral care had a significant influence on the understanding of the identity of the pastor. Although several influential figures played a role in this evolution, the American pastor, Anton Boisen, can rightly be viewed as the father of modern pastoral care. He suffered from mental illness himself and was instrumental in developing the Clinical Pastoral Education movement. It is significant that he viewed a person as a "living human document", whose stories beg to be interpreted.[18] This hermeneutic task connects the human story, the pastor's story, and biblical narrative. While on the one hand we have seen the professional development of the pastor's identity, especially with the establishment of postgraduate programs in pastoral therapy, the corporate nature of pastoral care has also been increasingly acknowledged. Though the pastor has a high level of theological and, in many cases at least, also therapeutic training, for a long time now it has been strongly affirmed that the pastor is not the only one who is responsible for the well-being of individuals and families. The pastor leads a community of faith. All the faithful, by virtue of their baptism, are called to ministry. Other persons and members of congregations are increasingly empowered to render pastoral services in communities and congregations.

This understanding of the pastoral role orients and guides the further development of the project. As researchers, we use the specified functions of pastoral care to describe the identity of the pastor. As mentioned earlier, the functions of pastoral care play a direct role in determining the multilevel identity descriptions of the pastor.[19]

With these pastoral role descriptions as background, we now pay attention to their significance for this research project on spiritual growth and development. The project focuses on the spiritual, psychological, and moral dimensions associated with spiritual growth and development. With this meaning as background, linking up with original description, we want to use Campbell's pastoral metaphors[20] to describe the identity

---

18. Gerkin *Introduction*, 38.

19. Pembroke, *Spiritual Maturity*, 23.

20. Campbell, *Rediscovering Pastoral Care*, 48–60.

and task of the pastor in terms of each of the dimensions, namely "wise folly" (spirituality), the "wounded healer" (psychology), and "the Shepherd" (the moral domain) to introduce the research project described in this book.

SPIRITUAL, PSYCHOLOGICAL AND MORAL DIMENSIONS OF PASTORAL MINISTRY

The spiritual, psychological, and moral dimensions of the pastorate are for us vitally important and constitute the theoretical perspective of the proposed method for spiritual growth. This also links up with a more recent development in practical theology that acknowledges the significance of "lived religion," where the everyday becomes the space for concrete expressions of spirituality. Those who come to a pastor for support and guidance commonly tell stories of conflict, confusion, and pain as they engage the spiritual, the emotional, and the moral domains in their everyday world.

The Pastor as Wise Fool: Spiritual Guidance

Spirituality is essentially about the life of the spirit under the influence and empowerment of the Spirit. The heart of the spiritual life is an encounter, in and through love, between God and humans and between human persons (Deut 6:5; Mark 12:30–31). It goes without saying that spirituality is not about a withdrawal from life; it is about doing and living faith (*praxis pietatis*). Spirituality truly has to do with providing meaning as an expression of a wisdom that is lived daily, and where one must attune to God's presence and love. Spirituality is not the outcome of any particular process; it is truly part of the process of life. It describes the quality of the art of living in the Spirit and interpreting life experiences in a context of prayer, sacramental life, and Scriptural meditation. Riding the wind of the Holy Spirit implies dynamic growth, change, and development. The pastor inevitably plays an important facilitating role in this process. In this project, we describe concrete possibilities in relation to this exciting and, at the same time, daunting journey.

While lacking the high-level expertise and wisdom of a spiritual master, pastors nonetheless draw from personal experience and knowledge to skilfully engage the parishioner in exploration of deep life questions. Like the clown, who appears to have no particular circus expertise, they have mastered their subtle art and express their own brand of professionalism.

The basis for any confidence the parishioner has is not that the pastoral agent has all the answers, but rather that they have already stumbled along the road and learned a few things along the way. Liebert puts it nicely: "The guide has already traversed the terrain, and knows from experience what the spiritual phenomenon actually means."[21]

In spiritual guidance, the basic human question and search for meaning is addressed in recognition of God's presence.[22] Spiritual companioning is an interpersonal relationship, in which a person leads the other to reflect on experiences "… in the light of who they are called to become in fidelity to the gospel."[23] The person who is receiving spiritual companioning seeks insight into the presence and action of God. The pastor who provides the spiritual companioning guides the other person, albeit sometimes in an almost bumbling way, as they reach for spiritual insight and new discoveries.

Spiritual guidance concerns the link between the most personal and the search for God's presence in one's life. In this instance, the spiritual guide is mindful of pointing out potential blind spots to the person when tracing God's presence and interpreting God's character and ways. The practice of spiritual companioning is thus based on the assumption that we cannot on our own clearly and distinctly perceive the things of God. The wise fool and the seeker move together toward insight and growth. Sometimes the movement is smooth and assured; at other times it is more the fumbling, comedic style of the clown. The pastor in the mode of wise folly frames the spiritual journey around our laughable humanity. The joke is in the way we take ourselves far too seriously, take sin far too lightly, rate ourselves much too highly, and look everywhere else but in the direction of our shadow side. The pastor as wise fool knows this about humans and gently reminds the parishioner, as well as her- or himself, about it from time to time.

In light of the process described in this book, it is also important to understand that spiritual guidance is not only about the individual. The individual's spiritual growth and transformation has a direct and positive

21. Liebert, "Practice," 511.

22. Nouwen, *Spiritual Direction*, 28.

23. Liebert, "Practice," 528.

influence on the congregation. Aspects of public significance related to spiritual companioning can clearly be noted in the moral-ethical component of the proposed project.

The Pastor as Wounded Healer and Psychological Guide

The recognition of autobiographical and biographical descriptions of human lives is important. The ebb and flow of daily life shapes human stories that describe the pain of life.

In describing the pastor as wounded healer, it is assumed that in acknowledging and understanding our wounds, and then finding the path to healing, we have something very real and precious to bring to those we minister to. In approaching the emotional or psychological dimension of the method, a clear decision was made to steer away from a heavily psychotherapeutic approach. The method's reference to the psychological field reflects our understanding that growth in that domain is inextricably linked to spiritual growth. In this case, psychological growth is viewed against the background of the relatively recent development known as positive psychology[24] and its potential to support the flourishing of the individual. The primary aim, then, is precisely *not* to act as amateur psychotherapist. Rather, the focus is on the virtues and strengths required for human flourishing and ways to establish these more firmly. Links with spiritual maturity are also suggested in the prompt cards. More than this, the correlation between the two domains is developed fully later in the book.

The Pastor as Shepherd: Moral Guidance

In describing the third field, the pastor is portrayed as the shepherd. The divine shepherd leads his people on the right path (Ps 23:3b); his undershepherds share in this ministry. The pastor offers a lead as the parishioner seeks to grow in virtue. In our integrative process, the shepherd supports the parishioner as they seek to personally appropriate the truth that "spiritual practices are the link between the story of Jesus and the Christian moral life . . . Under the grace of God's Spirit, these embodied convictions of faith become virtues."[25] In our view of pastoral

24. Seligman, *Authentic Happiness*, 20–44.

25. Spohn "Christian Spirituality," 275.

ministry, the focus needs to be on both ethics and spirituality; the two are inseparable. William Spohn has perhaps done the most in developing this notion:

> There is an ethical dimension intrinsic to the Christian life because the experience of following Jesus Christ includes elements that are not optional but obligatory . . . The Scriptures have moral authority for Christians because the texts are believed to contain the normative self-revelation of God in Jesus Christ as well as the appropriate ways to respond to Christ . . . At the same time, the Christian moral life is founded on spirituality, the experience of God in Christ. [26]

The work of the highly influential practical theologian, Don Browning, is also very significant in this regard. Browning had a long-term interest in showing how pastoral ministry needs to weave together the ethical and the spiritual. [27] For him, the church is a community that continually approaches moral issues and points of conflict in both thought and action. Moreover, it is at the intersection of moral reasoning and spiritual teaching that this task is executed. There is thus a continuous and circular movement between the development of spirituality and specific moral commitments that, in turn, determine both the individual's and the faith community's moral character and concrete action.

In understanding the pastor as moral guide, the space within which the journey occurs is created not only by our responsibility to others. Existential questions as to how to lead a meaningful life also give direction to the pastor's task. In this respect, it is important to understand that an orientation to the good also contributes toward both facilitating and creating sense and meaning and creating identity and capacity for change. The challenge for the pastor is to support movement toward a moral habitus. The moral person possesses a way of being that is guided by a sensitive conscience and supported by virtue.

SUMMARY

In this chapter, we identified the way in which the identity and character of the pastor as spiritual, psychological, and moral guide is grounded both in ancient traditions and in contemporary developments. Quite

---

26. Spohn "Christian Spirituality," 269.
27. Browning, *The Moral Context; Fundamental Practical Theology*, 58.

apart from the historic links, we aimed to show how the three areas are inextricably bound up together.

We also used the metaphors of wise fool, wounded healer, and shepherd to suggest a vision for holistic spiritual formation. In part, we sought in this way to hold the tension in pastoral ministry between assuredness that comes from identifying clear directions in Scripture and in the Christian heritage more generally, on the one hand, and the tentative, unsure, and almost comedic nature of pastoral work, on the other. The other aspect we attempted to highlight is the power and authenticity in healing as a wounded human being. The pain one experiences and interrogates, and finally moves through, touches the other and forms a point of deep connection. The ensuing chapters further describe the possibilities for pastoral support of spiritual, psychological, and moral growth.

2

SPIRITUAL GUIDANCE

THERE IS A STORY about a little boy attentively watching a sculptor who was chiseling away systematically at a marble block. Weeks later, the little boy returned and was stunned to see this marble block, which the sculptor had turned into a beautiful maned lion. The little boy asked the sculptor how he knew that there was always a lion in that rock. The sculptor calmly answered that he had seen the lion in the rock for a long time . . . " The art of sculpture is, first of all, the art of seeing; and discipline is the way to make visible what has been seen."[1]

The story tells of the expectation hidden in the process of spiritual guidance and sits behind the method described in this book. God is present in all places and in all situations; a wise spiritual guide helps others to look out for that: "At the heart of spiritual direction . . . is becoming aware that God is everywhere, and learning to practice his presence and yield to his transforming grace."[2]

All of the members of the research team specialize in pastoral care. It is our view that spiritual guidance is an essential element in such care. There is a ministry specialization called spiritual direction (later in this chapter we discuss how it is related to, but also distinct from, pastoral care). What we refer to in this book is not this specialized ministry, but rather a more general practice that is usually called spiritual guidance or spiritual companioning. We construe the role of the ministry agent, in essence, as supporting others as they discern God's presence and calling

1. Nouwen, *Spiritual Direction*, 17
2. Moon, "Spiritual Direction," 265.

in the realities of daily life. Such discernment goes to the depths of human existence; "... spirituality defines a person's way of being [and] leads to fundamental questions of human purpose. Spirituality has an implicit transcendent dimension because it engages ultimate questions."[3] The privilege and responsibility of the pastor is to companion a parishioner on this journey. Our process asks not for spiritual mastery and extraordinary expertise (the pastor is a wise fool in this regard!), but rather authenticity, integrity, and fidelity. It is these traits that engender trust and confidence in others. Lamontagne captures this well when he says that the spiritual guide is a person who, in practicing the disciplines of the Bible and the church, is perceived by others as someone to whom they are willing to be accountable for their lives in God's presence. [4]

The chapter is structured around the following markers. First, there is a brief discussion on how and why pastoral care and spiritual direction both correlate and differ from each other. Second, the practice of spiritual guidance is investigated historically, starting with earliest Christianity, and then moving to more contemporary expressions. Third, perspectives on the interdisciplinary nature of spiritual guidance are offered. Lastly, descriptions of theory and method of spiritual guidance are presented.

SPIRITUAL DIRECTION AND PASTORAL CARE: DIFFERENTIATION REQUIRED

As mentioned above, we are concentrating on a general ministry we are calling spiritual guidance. [5] We do recognize, however, that there is a ministry speciality known as spiritual direction. Although both this ministry and pastoral care take place within the domain of faith-based orientations to life,[6] there are clear differences between them. Identifying both the overlap and the distinctiveness is useful in clarifying what is involved in the pastoral care and spiritual formation aspects of the process we offer.

In seeking to highlight the distinguishing marks separating spiritual direction and pastoral care, it is necessary to first refer to their similarities. Both pastoral care and spiritual direction are situated in the field

3. Haight, *Christian Spirituality*, xx.

4. Lamontagne, "Inner Sharing," 103.

5. Cf. Van Dam, *Dicher*, 23.

6. Louw, "Philosophical Counselling," 6.

that prioritizes spiritual growth and the development of human life. Such growth is supported by practices such as prayer, meditation, silence, and ritual. Important in this regard is looking to God; but the gaze up is also the gaze down. Hoenkamp-Bisschops confirms this when she says that both pastoral care and spiritual direction "have long been helpful in travelling the road inside oneself, in looking at oneself, instead of losing oneself in activities, or losing oneself in others: in the care for others, fear of others, anger with others . . . "[7] It is important to note also that both pastoral care and spiritual direction operate in relationships built on trust and empathy, and both involve a strong focus on the community.

There are at least three main points of differentiation.[8] First, the agendas of pastoral care and spiritual direction are different. In pastoral care, the care seeker often draws the pastor's attention to a current crisis or urgent need, with the aim of securing specific concrete outcomes. For example, a married couple asks the pastor to help them address the conflicts in their relationship. On the other hand, the agenda in spiritual direction is not determined by a problem that the person experiences, but rather by a call to listen to the other's life story, to reflect on aspects of their faith and God-relationship, and to share in prayer, ritual, and meditation on Scripture. Most often, the search for God's presence is focused on daily life. For example, a person in spiritual direction tells the story that she received an offer of a new job, but she is not certain of God's will for her in considering this offer.

Second, the methods in pastoral care and spiritual guidance differ. Pastoral care primarily addresses the problem that the person experiences. The strategic handling of problems, the pragmatic management of crises, and addressing wounds from the past are often part of pastoral care; the aim always is to facilitate the establishment of more functional patterns of living, inner healing, and personal growth. Taking the example of the married couple's conflicts, in pastoral care one would make use of, among other things, interdisciplinary marriage therapy models to address the cause of the conflicts, and to facilitate establishment of better communication, greater compassion and empathy, and more constructive ways of relating. On the other hand, spiritual direction attends to the daily experience of the directee, listening sensitively for the shape of the God-relationship and style of spiritual practice; it is not necessarily driven

7. Hoenkamp-Bisschops, "Spiritual Direction," 54.

8. Hoenkamp-Bisschops, "Spiritual Direction"; Lamontagne, "Inner Sharing"; Moon and Benner, "Spiritual Direction."

by a presenting problem. This listening process facilitates moments of discernment that are primarily embodied in meditation on Scripture and prayer. For the woman who is seeking God's guidance when considering the offer of a new job, this would, for example, mean listening to her current experiences of the work environment, the possibilities that a new opportunity could offer, but especially listening for the presence of God in those spaces. During this conversation, God's presence will be traced through turning to the Word, prayer, and ritual.

Lastly, the outcomes of pastoral care and spiritual guidance differ. In pastoral care, the outcomes of pastoral intervention and involvement are often concrete. A tangible outcome is achieved when the married couple, caught in destructive conflict patterns, is led by a process of pastoral involvement to an alternative, more constructive handling of conflicts in their relationship. These outcomes aim to establish healing and health where there has been pain and pathology. On the other hand, the aim of spiritual direction is not necessarily to reach concrete outcomes. Rather, it is to realize a specific understanding of calling that is, by nature, spiritually anchored. When considering the possibility of a new job, the process is about considering and discerning where God wants to use this person and how the image of Christ could be more clearly visible in a specific environment.

For a very long time there have been spiritual guides who have practiced the interventions outlined above with great skill, wisdom, faith, and love. Clearly, we have an enormous amount to learn from them. In the next section, we provide an overview of the history of spiritual guidance, before moving to consider some contemporary expressions. We begin the story, appropriately enough, with the ministry of Jesus.

A BRIEF OVERVIEW OF THE HISTORY OF SPIRITUAL GUIDANCE

The history of spiritual guidance is of course a very long and complicated story. We have necessarily been heavily selective in our choices of subjects to treat. It is our hope that we can provide *some* insight, at least, into the main ideas and practices of the great spiritual directors in the Christian tradition.

The overview is shaped around the stages that are commonly acknowledged as particularly significant—namely, Jesus's ministry, the

Desert Fathers and Mothers, late medieval spirituality, and sixteenth century European spirituality.[9] Our aim is to give a general introduction to the most important concepts and practices. The material we are working with is so rich, however, that we expect the reader to find even this basic overview inspiring and challenging.

The foundation for Jesus's ministry of spiritual guidance is his intimacy with God, his Father/Mother.[10] The ultimate source of the wisdom and knowledge that Jesus shares is this relationship. However, Jesus's particular understanding of the nature and character of God, on the one hand, and the characteristics of life in the Realm God was initiating in and through him, on the other, was formed through his participation in the Jewish covenant community and his knowledge of Scripture and *Torah*.

A central feature of Jesus's spiritual direction, it goes without saying, was pointing others to God. In particular, he exhorted others to take up the style of worship that is required for a proper relationship with the Father/Mother. When he encountered the Samaritan woman at the well, he offered this counsel: "The hour is coming, and is now here, when the true worshipers will worship the Father in spirit and truth, for the Father seeks such as these to worship him" (John 4:23).

Finally, Jesus used a characteristic form of teaching, namely teaching in parables, to communicate his message about life in God's realm. Jesus artistically shaped metaphors to arrest, startle, and nudge his listeners in the direction of a God-honoring life. Teddi Chichester captures this beautifully: "[T]he metaphors that Jesus weaves, in his poetic parables, discourses and aphorisms require of those listeners who long to move beyond aesthetics not simply a leap of faith, but a willingness to reach toward each thread of Jesus' tropes and trace its heavenly message into the intricate earthly tapestry of human life, human art."[11]

The desert elders[12] followed the pattern of Jesus's desert sojourn. They were monks living in the Scetes region of the Egyptian desert from

---

9. Lamontagne, "Inner Sharing," 38-78; Van Dam, *Dicher*, 10-45; Moon and Benner, "Spiritual Direction," 10-54.

10. We recognize that the nature of God is Mystery. Humans, in their finitude, lack the language and intellectual power to capture and express Infinite Being. The best that we can do is employ adequate metaphors to talk about that which is beyond words and beyond intellection. We use gender-neutral metaphors throughout.

11. Chichester, "The Word as Poet," 36.

12. For helpful overviews, see Dunn, *Emergence of Monasticism*; Wortley,

the 3rd century CE. These holy ones were escaping from the chaos and persecution of the reign of the Roman emperor, Diocletian. In 313CE, the recently converted Roman emperor, Constantine, made Christianity the official religion of the empire. The large-scale persecutions stopped, but in the eyes of these holy men and women the Church was corrupt; they chose to separate themselves physically and to establish the space where they might find God in the depths of their hearts. They adopted a life of prayer and self-discipline, following in the footsteps of Jesus and John the Baptist, both of whom spent time in the wilderness fasting and praying.

They lived in caves, or they built small huts. They lived alone, or with a few companions. At first, they did not wear any monastic garments, but instead donned the ordinary clothes of the working man of Egypt. They earned their living through simple tasks such as rope making or basket weaving. In this way, they did not have to leave their cells.

After receiving counsel and guidance from experienced monks, they adopted their own individual practices. They didn't conform to an established Rule of Life, as we find in the later monastic communities. However, gradually some of the Fathers wrote down their practices and others joined with them to form a little community. Here we have the beginnings of cenobitic or community monasticism (as opposed to the earlier form of eremitic monasticism).

At the center of the life of the desert elders was the spirituality of the cell. As Benedicta Ward so aptly puts it, "The first teacher of the monk was God; the second was his cell."[13] In the cell, a monk learns to be patient. It is the place of encounter with God. In silence, one watches, waits, and listens.[14] The world is full of distractions. People get caught up in all the business of life and neglect the inner journey. This is the journey into the cave of the heart where God is to be found. Silence is absolutely central in the life of prayer sponsored by the desert elders.

Silence is a way of countering sinful tendencies. The desert elders recognized that a great deal of damage can be done with the tongue. The first duty of love is to not say anything that will do harm to others. Keeping silence helps a person to discipline his or her tongue. This latter discipline is very commonly advocated. Sayings such as the following are

---

Introduction to Desert Fathers.

13. Ward, "Spiritual Direction," 64.

14. Ward, "Spiritual Direction," 62–3.

everywhere to be found in available collections: "One of the Fathers said: 'If our inner man is vigilant it is capable of protecting the outer [man] too. If it is not so, then let us keep guard on the tongue as far as is possible.'"[15]

In the dark night of the soul, the monk opens himself to God and God exposes his sin.[16] In the distractions of everyday life, we tend to forget who we are and what we are. Christ teaches that a person is made for a relationship of love with God and neighbor. This is what gets forgotten. The drive to compete with others, to establish one's status in the world, to achieve, and to accumulate material things clouds a person's vision.

In the Christian tradition, pride is often thought to be the ultimate sin. The classic statement on the human tendency to *hubris* comes from Augustine. He identifies pride as the root cause of all human failings. Pride is a perverse form of exaltation, according to Augustine, in which the mind is fixed on the standard of the self rather than on the standard of God. Here is found the falsehood that characterizes all sin.

The desert fathers, however, said that while pride is certainly a cause of sin, it is not the ultimate sin. The ultimate sin for them is forgetfulness of who and what we are. One elder put it very succinctly: "The root of all evil is forgetfulness."[17] Another shows how the fall into sin begins with forgetfulness and then progresses to desire by way of negligence: "There are three powers of Satan that precede all sin: forgetting, negligence and desire. When forgetting comes, it begets negligence and from negligence comes desire: a person falls as a result of desire."[18] We fall as the result of desire, but it all starts with forgetfulness. Divine grace is active in the world and in our lives, but we fail to notice it. Silence allows the monk to open his eyes so that he can see properly. He learns to see himself as he really is; moreover, he attunes himself to God and God's grace at work in him and everywhere in the world.

In the silence, the monk is sometimes confronted by the dark night of the soul. It is at this point that he feels like he is hitting rock bottom. In what feels like an assault from God, he experiences the depths of his brokenness. He knows that his relationships with others and with God are marked too heavily by mistrust, selfishness, and failures in love. In the dark night, monks were commonly literally brought to tears. Tears in

15. Desert Fathers, *Anonymous Sayings*, 167.

16. Sittser refers to the monk's "struggle" and "battle within." See his "Battle Without and Within."

17. Desert Fathers, *Anonymous Sayings*, 55.

18. Desert Fathers, *Anonymous Sayings*, 183.

this case are an outward manifestation of inner feelings of weakness and vulnerability. The spiritual masters have always known that a person who is in touch with their brokenness is close to God.

In the dark night of the soul, the monk is confronting what was referred to as his "passions." It was said that a monk must "know" his passions. The word "know" has a sexual connotation in biblical usage. To know a woman in the Bible is to have sexual relations with her. It follows that some monks believed that to know one's passions is to love and embrace them. Others, however, were convinced that passions such as the sex drive, the desire for food and strong drink, and anger were sent from the devil and must be killed off. This reflects the Stoic tradition in philosophy. The passions are seen as disorder or infections that must be eradicated. This saying is typical of this line of thought:

> In the same way that nobody can do wrong to one who stands close to the emperor, neither can Satan do anything to us if our soul is close to God. "Draw close to me and I will draw close to you" [Zec 1:3]. But since we are continually distracted, the enemy easily snatches our wretched soul away towards disgraceful passions.[19]

As indicated above, this is not the only view amongst the desert elders. Some took a more Aristotelian line. Aristotle thought of the passions as neutral forces; for him, they are natural impulses that need to be embraced. The monks that took this view contended that they come from God, not the devil. It is a matter of knowing one's passions and then of seeking God's grace to put them to a good use. One simply notices the desire and then looks up to God, calmly trusting in God's empowerment:

> OLD MAN: "Whenever you contend against [a thought of vainglory], it will become exceedingly strong against you . . . You will not, as you imagine, be strengthened by the Spirit of God, as it is better able to contend against you than you are to contend against it. You will [not] find yourself, apparently, sufficient of yourself to resist the passions of your thought. For as it is with the man who has a spiritual father, that gives to him every desire, and who is without any care whatsoever, and who has, therefore, no judgment with God, so also is it with him who has committed his soul to God. It is . . . unnecessary for him to in any way fall into care concerning thoughts, or to allow a thought

19. Desert Fathers, *Anonymous Sayings*, 183.

to enter his heart. If it should happen that a thought has entered,
lift up strenuously towards your Father . . . "[20]

The desert elders did not rely on their own resources to get in touch with God and God's ways; they also regularly consulted a spiritual guide. The director helped them to become more attentive. They would lead them to focus on every detail in their lives. The spiritual guide—the *abba* or *amma*—has him- or herself made the journey through the desert and has much wisdom and knowledge on the one hand, and love and compassion on the other, to share.

A feature of the approach of these spiritual guides is that they were hard on harshness. That is, they saw very clearly that a harsh, judgmental, condemnatory approach to one's brothers and sisters is contrary to the spirit of Christ.

At the heart of the spirituality of the desert elders is silence and solitude that leads to greater attentiveness to God and neighbor. Ascetic practice such as fasting, going without sleep, loading the body with chains, and perching atop a pillar for hours is not the central feature. Asceticism is just one element in a purification of vision. Holiness for the desert elders is about learning to see with new eyes. One must see God, others, self, and world with a clear vision. This is a vision that sees as Jesus sees. Just as Jesus dedicated his life to helping others be reconciled to God, so to with the desert elders.

As stated above, we need to paint the story of spiritual guidance with broad brushed strokes. We shift now to the Middle Ages. There is a number of very important figures in late medieval spiritual direction. One need only think of Anselm of Canterbury (1033–1109), Bernard of Clairvaux (1090–1153), and Aelred of Rievaulx (1109–67). Given the limited scope of this historical overview, we have selected just the last of these for attention. Our reasoning is that Aelred offers a view on an aspect of the Christian life that speaks very directly to the contemporary orientation to spirituality in the everyday. We refer to his thought on spiritual friendship. Aelred was a 12th century English Cistercian monk. He developed the theme of life in Christ as the ultimate expression of intimacy and friendship. In and through this close relationality, monks guide each other in the way of Christ.

---

20. Desert Fathers, *Paradise of Fathers*, 296.

Friendship in the community of faith, Aelred tells us, has its origin in Christ, is sustained by Christ, and reaches its *telos* in Christ.[21] A perfect spiritual friendship, one that is grounded in the Lord, is one in which two persons unite as one spirit and the "two form one."[22] This union in love is expressed through bearing one another's burdens gladly, trusting each other implicitly, and having the confidence to correct each other when it is needed.

In a Christian community, brothers must guide each other into deeper union with Christ. This is the deep meaning of their spiritual friendship. In becoming one in heart and soul with our friends, we are made one spirit with Christ: "[F]riend cleaving to friend in the Spirit of Christ is made with Christ but one heart and one soul, and so mounting aloft through degrees of love to friendship with Christ, he is made one spirit with him in one kiss."[23]

That a medieval writer on spiritual friendship should emphasize unity of spirit is entirely understandable. Aelred's thinking was influenced in no small way by ideas that were commonly promoted in the Greco-Roman world. In Plato and Aristotle, and in Cicero and Seneca, the same notions concerning friendship appear regularly.[24] Friends are one soul. The friend is another self. Friends live in harmony and are of one mind. Friendship is fellowship (*philia koinonia*) and "life together" (*symbios*). Cicero's classic definition in his *De Amicitia* draws all these elements together in a succinct fashion: "Friendship is nothing else than an accord in all things, human and divine, conjoined with mutual goodwill and affection" (6.20).

With Ignatius of Loyola (1491–1556), spiritual direction took a new turn.[25] He broke the shackles of restrictive medieval spiritual theology. Aelred did this also, but in quite a different way. Ignatius "still [identified] with the medieval Church, but now with a new mobility, both geographically in no longer being tied to monastic life, as well as in moral sophistry around the sacrament of penance."[26] Ignatius was the founder of the So-

21. Aelred, *Spiritual Friendship*, 1:9.

22. Aelred, *Spiritual Friendship*, 2.11.

23. Aelred, *Spiritual Friendship*, 2.21.

24. For a brief survey of the Greco-Roman philosophical approaches to friendship, see Johnson, "Making Connections," 160.

25. For an introduction to Ignatian spirituality, see Fleming, *What is Ignatian Spirituality?*; Haight, *Christian Spirituality*; and Manney, *Simple Life-Changing Prayer*.

26. Houston, "Seeking Historical Perspectives," 93.

ciety of Jesus, the Jesuit order. His *Spiritual Exercises* were designed as a guide for a long period of intense spiritual reflection.

Most systems of prayer and contemplation grow out of personal experience. This was certainly the case with Ignatius. It was his own spiritual awakening to the challenges presented by the gospel message that stimulated his work in the *Spiritual Exercises*. His aim was to develop an instrument that could assist others in the all-important task of finding the divine will and thereby finding the way to salvation.

The Exercises are divided into four "weeks." These "weeks" constitute the stages that a person must pass through as they search for God's will and the path to redemption.

The first week involves an intense examination of conscience and confession of sin. This prepares the retreatant for the next three weeks during which they embark on a journey with Christ through the events of the incarnation, the passion, and the resurrection. The person making *The Exercises* is invited to enter fully into the gospel narratives through an act of active imagination. Through the "prayer of the senses" the retreatant attempts to see, hear, taste, and smell the biblical story they are contemplating. Ignatius asked the retreatant to contemplate Christ in the Gospels by projecting himself into the scene. Through participating in the conversation and the action, he places himself in a space where God can reveal God's self in fresh ways.

We have translated this aspect of the *Exercises* loosely to illustrate how this method of spiritual guidance works. The movements in composing the place of a scriptural text are as follows.

Prepare yourself for prayer. Still your mind. Ask God to reveal more of God's truth and love to you.

Talk to Jesus. Ask him to speak to you through the scripture passage you are about to engage with.

Choose a story from the Gospel. As an example, let's reflect on the story of James and John asking Jesus for places of honor (Mk. 10:35-45). The other disciples are angry upon hearing that James and John want to grab the glory for themselves. Jesus responds by teaching them that the greatest of all is the servant of all.

Imagine yourself in that Gospel scene. What sort of day is it? Bright sunshine? Cloudy? What smells are you picking up, what sounds are you hearing, as you place yourself back in Palestine 2000 years ago? Sense the atmosphere. Pick up on the emotional charge in the dialog. Talk with James and John. Perhaps you will ask them why they are so desperately grasping for honor and glory. Or you might inquire about their reaction as Jesus rejects their request and instead confronts them with the way of suffering and service. Talk with the other disciples. You might be interested in why they are getting so hot under the collar about the request from James and John. Perhaps you want to know what they think being a servant of all really means.

Become aware of what you are feeling. Is there someone in the story that you identify with? Is there someone that really turns you off? Is there something that you see or hear that makes you uncomfortable or brings you joy? What are you feeling as you are confronted by raw ambition, on the one hand, and the call to suffering and service, on the other?

Some suggest that what Ignatius offered is essentially a mystical spiritual practice.[27] We turn finally in our historical overview to a great exponent of this type of spirituality—namely, Teresa of Avila. For Teresa, union with Christ is the telos of the spiritual life. She uses bridal imagery to described oneness with the Lord. Teresa de Ahumada was born in 1515 in the Castilian town of Avila. She entered the Carmelite convent of the Incarnation in Avila when she was twenty. Shortly after her profession of vows in 1537, she became extremely ill. Two years later, Teresa nearly died; she was partially paralysed for three years following the illness. Right throughout her life thereafter, ill health was a prominent feature.

During most of her nineteen years as a religious, Teresa showed very little in the way of spiritual giftedness. Indeed, she thought herself lax and lukewarm, and even gave up praying altogether for two years out of "humility." In 1554, however, she had a profound conversion experience while praying before a graphic depiction of the wounded Christ. From that time onward (she was 39), until her death in 1582 (at age 67), she made stunning progress in the mystical way. Spiritual visions began to feature in her prayer life, and she described the ecstatic and loving union with Christ in terms of "spiritual betrothal" and "spiritual marriage."

Teresa wrote her most well-known work toward the end of her life. *The Interior Castle* captures her best spiritual guidance for her Carmelite sisters and all those who seek after union with Christ.[28] In this classic work, Teresa talks about the spiritual journey in terms of a series of different ways of dwelling with God interiorly. While there is a great diversity of images cropping up in the book, the organizing principle is the

27. See Sheldrake, "A Mysticism of Practice."

28. Teresa of Avila, *Interior Castle.*

allegory of the human soul as a castle, with God dwelling at the center. In the center of the castle, there are "very secret exchanges between God and the soul" that take place. Since the castle is the soul, we already live in it, but in a variety of ways. The range includes those who dwell in the outer courtyard with the guards and the vermin, right through to those who live at the very center with God.

Around the basic image of the castle, Teresa builds her theological anthropology. She likens the senses and faculties to people who live in the castle as vassals of the soul, and ultimately of the Lord. The higher faculties are the higher-level servants who keep guard over the castle and direct the lower-level servants. As one moves to the rooms away from the center, one comes under the sway of various distractions and temptations. These she compares to poisonous creatures or little lizards who may get as far as the fourth dwelling place (there are seven of these in total). The Lord in the center is depicted as a brilliant sun or a crystal-clear fount. The light, or the fount, is always there, but can be darkened or muddied by mortal sin.

In the Fifth Dwelling Place, the castle allegory drops away into the background, and two new images appear. The first is the silkworm that builds a cocoon from which a beautiful white butterfly emerges. This image depicts the movement from prayer as our work to prayer as God's work in us. The "worm" must work to build the cocoon, but transformation is the act of God. The second set of images that is added is that of courtship and marriage. Here the purpose is to indicate that intimacy and wholehearted love are the features of mystical transformation.

While Teresa does not intend the seven dwelling places that make up the interior castle which is the soul be thought of as constituting a "stage theory" of mystical transformation, it seems clear that the last four dwelling places taken together do refer to a higher level of experience. That is, while it is not a matter of moving through the dwelling places one by one and in sequence until one arrives at spiritual transformation, there is definitely an upward movement involved. The higher dwelling places represent an advanced level of spiritual experience.

Those in the First Dwelling Place have only made a start on the spiritual path. They are trying to be attentive to God, but their hearing is not very acute. There are major problems in their spiritual lives that need sorting out.

In the Second Dwelling Place, a person has the capacity to hear God speaking through sermons, devotional books, personal struggles, and more, and responds by attempting to overcome the disorder in the exercise of their faculties. By the time a person reaches the Third Dwelling Place, they have largely got their life into good spiritual order. But herein lies a hidden danger. They may think that they have already achieved maturity in the spiritual life. The twin problems are, on the one hand, becoming self-satisfied and self-righteous, and, on the other hand, becoming bored and taking leave of prayer and religion altogether.

When referring to the Fourth Dwelling Place, Teresa says, "Supernatural experiences begin here." Here a person really hears the voice of God calling. They go beyond their own powers and open themselves to God and to God's message. There is both activity and passivity in this phase. It is a transition between active meditation and infused contemplation. The person who has entered this dwelling place experiences the spiritual delight that comes when God speaks.

When it comes to the Fifth Dwelling Place there is a jump up into union with God. In the other places, a person concentrates on being attentive to God. In this new experience, there is entry into union with the Divine. There are no spiritual techniques needed here. The faculties are "asleep"; it is necessary to take leave of the world and all its temptations and distractions in order to enter into union with God.

We also find Teresa's nuptial imagery coming to the fore here. In the Fifth Dwelling Place, the soul's communion with God is like a woman who has started a relationship with a man, but there is no betrothal contract. When this state of the love affair comes, the person is already in the Sixth Dwelling Place. Over one third of the *Interior Castle* is given to describing this stage of mystical transformation.

Having reached this deep stage of spiritual union, the soul experiences rapture. This rapture Teresa relates to betrothal. In the state of rapture, the faculties are out of commission. In this passive state, they are totally receptive to the things of God. In being enlightened in an intense way by God, the soul is overcome with delight.

The rapturous experience of the Sixth Dwelling Place is so intense that a person does not know whether it has taken place in the body or out of it. In the Seventh Dwelling Place the spiritual intensity wanes. The faculties operate in a more "normal" manner. Raptures are very rare and not nearly so intense.

Visions are part of this mystical union. But they are grounded in the everyday. Teresa says over and over that in this dwelling place one's energy for, and commitment to, practical service reaches new heights.

We would simply comment that while this form of high mysticism is not something that every Christian will quest after, St Paul reminds us that all of us are called to what might be called Christ mysticism. Through faith and the grace of God we are bound in a spiritual union to the Lord. In his letter to the Galatians Paul has this to say: "I have been crucified with Christ; it is no longer I who live, but it is Christ who lives in me. And the life I now live in the flesh I live by faith in the Son of God, who loved me and gave his life for me" (Gal 2:19b-20).

From the time of Paul, through the middle epoch of Aelred, Ignatius, and Teresa, and right on into the 21st century, the true self, the self that conforms to Christ under the grace of God, sits in the center of descriptions of a faithful spiritual life. This authentic spiritual self is the thread that runs through the next section on contemporary perspectives.

A CONTEMPORARY UNDERSTANDING OF SPIRITUAL GUIDANCE

At the present time, it is common for theologies of spiritual guidance to draw on the wisdom of different Christian traditions. The general aim that is expressed, and what draws the various approaches together, is support of the spiritual life of the whole person (encompassing spiritual practice, spiritual and moral character, and emotional life) and guiding a process of personal transformation. Transformation is usually expressed as conversion to the true self. Spiritual guides such as Thomas Merton, Henri Nouwen and Eugene Peterson, each in their own way, develop models for supporting this fundamental goal.[29]

Spiritual guidance is an interpersonal relationship in which one person guides the other in reflection on experiences in the light of the true self, the self that is hidden with Christ in God. The spiritual guide is a faithful companion who wisely engages with the quest for new insights in the presence of the Lord. Spiritual formation requires a commitment to discover where God is present in one's life. The companion is mindful of pointing out blind spots; this action opens up other perspectives, and perhaps even revelations from God. Seeking after the presence and calling of God is ultimately seeking after mystery. Spiritual formation is a process involving "the cooperation of two people, standing before God, prayerfully grappling with the mysteries of the soul in response to God's

---

29. Cf. Liebert "Perspectives," 50.

initiative. It is not so much the analysis of life to propose solutions to its problems, as it is the exploration of a beautiful, ongoing mystery."[30]

Helping another explore the mystery of life and of the divine presence requires narrative listening. A person's spirituality is embedded in their personal narrative. Haight captures this well: "Because spirituality has been defined as the logic or pattern that organizes a human life, its character is explicitly narrative. In other words, a person's spirituality both reflects and describes the story of his or her life."[31]

Listening well to the other's story requires a certain way of being-with. It is important, first, not to try to rush the story. The guide clearly needs good listening skills; they need to listen attentively, trusting that they will discern the truly important facets in the personal narrative. The listening needs to manifest responsiveness of soul and proceed with gentleness and kindness.[32]

There is a need for a guide to listen to personal narratives and to support discernment because individuals do not see clearly on their own. Here, living into the true self is the central focus. A guide helps with discerning where and how the true and false selves are expressing themselves. The false self is drowning in egotism. "Whichever conception of spiritual development and spiritual direction we use, letting go of the ego, of our egotism is central."[33] Spiritual guidance aims to support individuals in moving beyond egoism, to reach out to others in love, living in the face of God.[34]

In supporting others in the journey into the true self, a spiritual guide draws on expertise from a number of disciplines. We turn our attention at this point to the interdisciplinary mode of spiritual companioning.

The Interdisciplinary Nature of Spiritual Guidance

Pastoral care is traditionally more oriented to the human sciences, whereas spiritual direction is shaped around spiritual theology. We contend that these two need to be brought together. There is a spiritual–therapeutic dynamic involved in spiritual companioning.

30. Lamontagne, "Inner Sharing," 38.
31. Haight, *Christian Spirituality*, xx.
32. Moon and Benner, "Spiritual Direction."
33. Hoenkamp-Bischops, "Spiritual Direction," 258.
34. Perrin, *Studying Christian Spirituality*, 25.

For centuries, the disciplines of psychology and spirituality had the same objective; it was commonly assumed that there is "no difference . . . between mental health and spiritual welfare."[35] It is even reported that before the modern era "the languages of Christian spirituality and psychology were so intertwined that they were hardly distinguishable."[36] Since the eighteenth century Enlightenment, psychology has opted for a more independent perspective on the "life of the soul," defining itself over against religion and spirituality.[37] In the nineteenth century, psychology developed even more strongly as a discipline, and spirituality was jettisoned almost completely. Over the past few decades, however, these two disciplines have shown greater appreciation for each. Certain schools in psychology have expressed an interest in spirituality. Martin Seligman, the founding father of positive psychology, views spirituality as the central pillar in the new psychology and its quest for sources of human "flourishing."[38]

From the side of spirituality, there is also an embrace of psychology. This move has been going on for many decades now. Some even refer to "therapeutic spiritual direction."[39] While there has inevitably and regrettably been some uncritical borrowing, generally spiritual theologians are discerning when it comes to choosing a partner. They seek to establish a clear affinity with the Christian heritage. Some are also connecting with philosophy that is amenable for re-thinking the nature of spiritual guidance. Drawing on the method of philosophical counseling, Daniël Louw construes pastoral work as helping people correct unhealthy personal schemas.[40] His philosophical analysis indicates that the categories that make up a schema are moral, psychological, and spiritual in nature. There is not space here to discuss this and other important new moves in depth. It suffices to say that working with other disciplines in an integrative manner opens up new and important interpretations of the nature of spiritual companioning.

35. Hoenkamp-Bisschops, "Spiritual Direction," 262.
36. DeHoff, "In Search of a Paradigm," 335.
37. Miller, "Reciprocal Maturities," 100.
38. Seligman *Authentic Happiness*, 23.
39. Burton "Therapeutic Spiritual Direction."
40. Louw, "Philosophical Counselling."

We discussed above the method a spiritual guide uses in general and theoretical terms. In concluding this chapter, we turn to a brief consideration of the practicalities.

PRACTICAL ASPECTS OF METHOD

It is important, first, to structure the process by way of frequent meetings; these can be scheduled weekly, monthly, or *ad hoc*. It is also important, second, to monitor the words that are being used. In a psychology-driven environment, words such as "frustration," "conflict," "depression," and "stress" are used often. In spiritual guidance, the intention is to choose words with a spiritual connotation such as "sin," "resurrection," "grace," "forgiveness," and "reconciliation." We are clearly not excluding the psychological dimension from the process. The point is that we suggest pastors watch lest the process shifts from spiritual formation into pastoral psychotherapy. Third, the style of the conversation needs to be right. It needs to be pastoral and informal in tone. The approach is not that of formal spiritual direction. It will have the feel of companioning, guiding, and facilitating. The pastor in this process is not set up as "the expert," though those with formal theological training clearly have quite a bit of expertise to bring. Mutuality in the working together is appropriate. It is envisioned that the parishioner will likely contribute to the spiritual formation of the pastor along the way (though this is not a stated aim).

As part of our process, finally, we recommend the keeping of a journal. Commonly, questions such as the following are used in ordering the journaling: "What is God saying to me through this Scripture?" What is an image that comes to mind as I reflect on this biblical passage?" "Where have I discerned the presence of God in my life this week?" "In my relationships with others this past week, have I conformed myself to Christ?" The journal becomes an important source of information for reflection in conversations with the pastor during the personal meeting. We also suggest journaling to capture the insights and experiences in a session: In reflecting on the session just past . . . What do you notice? What feelings and thoughts arise for you as you reflect on the conversation? What are you wondering about? What are you feeling curious about?

Is there a "light bulb" moment for you? Is there an insight that seems especially important right now?

SUMMARY

In this chapter, we first distinguished the specialized ministry of spiritual direction from that of pastoral care. We noted that what we are interested in is a general ministry we, and others, call "spiritual guidance." In a brief overview, we hit some highlights in the story of spiritual guidance over the past 2000 years. We looked to Jesus, the Desert Elders, Aelred of Rievaulx, Ignatius of Loyola, and Teresa of Avila to inspire and inform us. Though there are so many other figures deserving of treatment, even our very select survey provides more than sufficient spiritual food to nourish a spiritual guide.

While it was acknowledged above that spiritual guidance benefits from an interdisciplinary orientation, with psychology at the forefront, we made it clear that it is spiritual formation and not pastoral psychotherapy we are attuned to in our process. The central aims in companioning that we identified are these. First, the spiritual guide summons faith, experience, and wisdom on the one hand, and trusts in grace on the other, in helping a person grow into their true self, the self that is hidden with Christ in God. Second, the companion, drawing on the same resources, supports the process of attuning to the mystery of life and of God's presence. The spiritual life is about learning to see that which is out of plain sight. There is a lion in the block of rock. Once it comes into view, one realizes that it was there all the time!

3

THE MODEL IN TRANSCULTURAL AND CONTEXTUAL PERSPECTIVE

ONE OF THE UNIQUE features of the experiment that the research team conducted with the model for spiritual formation is its international character. We have tested the model globally in five different geographical contexts. Each context has its own challenges. The physical distance between parishes in some regions was a lot greater than in other parts of the world where parishes were found within only a few miles of each other. Though the model works with individual meetings between a parishioner and a pastor, it highlights the relationship with community. Physical distance, something the world has experienced globally during the COVID-19 pandemic, challenges the experience of community. Further, in the case of South Africa and the Netherlands, language issues played a role, since the model was originally designed in English. What happens with a model when you translate its core ideas into another language? Perhaps even more significant is the fact that as members of the same research team we find ourselves in different theological schools and academic environments. Our theological and scholarly orientations differ and converge at the same time. The cultural and religious environments in which we teach and conduct research differ to a large extent. Yet we are convinced that the four domains of spiritual practice, spiritual character, moral character, and positive psychology transcend the different orientations and provide a common pathway to spiritual growth and a promising new approach to pastoral care and counseling.

With all this in mind, we ask the question: What does it mean to apply the same model for spiritual formation as a method for pastoral care and counseling in various cultural worlds? The ambition to present a model for spiritual formation to the worldwide Christian family is obviously challenged by the reality of diversity in spiritualities, denominational theologies, and cultural varieties. In this chapter we deal with the challenge from the perspective of both the global and the local.

In the first part of the chapter, we offer global, denominational, and local perspectives on the issue of cultural diversity. Globally, we must deal with cultural differences in ecumenical perspective. Denominationally, we need to reflect upon theological identity and its impact on the theory and practice of spiritual formation. From a Western perspective, the model also challenges the gap between individual spirituality and shared religious identity. Diversity is often used as a value that engages with differences between individuals to support individual spiritual freedom. We contend that the tension between personal autonomy and communal norms needs to be maintained.

In the second part of the chapter, we address the gap between individual spirituality and the mission of the Church as the body of Christ. A model for spiritual formation extends beyond the boundaries of individual lives. Its mission is to engage individual believers with the broader teachings and practices of the worldwide Church in becoming more hopeful, more forgiving, more conformed to Christ, and deepening the practices of faith that are inherently communal, such as caring for creation, celebrating the day of the Lord, and reading Scripture.

IS SPIRITUALITY TRANSCULTURAL?
THE GLOBAL AND THE LOCAL

As indicated above, our focus is both whole-world and regional. A helpful way into this discussion is through historical exemplars.

Exemplars

Gisbertus Voetius was a Dutch 17th Century Reformed theologian. Voetius began his vocation as a Reformed minister in the southern part of the Netherlands. He later made his way onto the pages of history as the first academic theologian of the new University that was founded in Utrecht in 1636. One of his major works was a large piece on spirituality, written in Latin, the accepted academic language of Europe from the Middle Ages to late Modernity.

In his work he extensively deals with spiritual experiences such as the lack of assurance of faith or the experience of being deserted by God. Further, he deals with a wide variety of spiritual practices such as meditation, prayer, fasting, and care for the dying.

Our first response might be to question the relevance of this ancient source for our contemporary spiritual practices in parish ministry. Can we learn anything from these centuries-old examples? Such a response is reasonable; especially when we recall that existential philosophers such as Heidegger teach us that we are thrown into existence and that we are thoroughly historical people, contextually situated within the bounds of time and space.

This very response, however, also highlights the importance of the topic of this chapter, illustrated by three questions that we ask ourselves as a research team and that we think are important for you to consider working with the model of spiritual formation that we propose in this book:

1. How do we spiritually relate to other Christians that live in a different cultural context, both with respect to space and time?

2. Can we apply spiritual and pastoral methods across cultures and contexts?

3. Can a model of spiritual formation bind together Christians from different historical periods?

The questions we posit really boil down to this: In what sense is Christian spirituality trans-cultural? Undoubtedly, your own pastoral ministry will be characterized by all sorts of diversity. The value of current theological work in postcolonial, contextual, and intercultural theologies lies in their sensitivity for diversity, variety, cultural expressions and values, and different aspects of human identity. These varieties should be dealt with from a normative perspective: not every value, attitude or behavior contributes equally to spiritual health or human flourishing.

The rise of the so-called "cancel culture" in the current Anglo-Saxon cultural realms radically demonstrates the downside of cultural relativism; there are positions that really should be excluded from discourse. However, the Christian understanding of sin, and the conviction that true

spiritual maturity manifested as Christ-likeness is an eschatological reality, lead us in a different direction. We should not "cancel" spiritualities.
Yet we also need to acknowledge the reasonable question of whether our
model privileges a certain spirituality. Are we guilty of excluding other
important types of spirituality? The normative question will be dealt with
in the second part of this chapter. First, however, we celebrate the variety
of Christian spiritualities and point to ways in which our model tries to
do justice to this spread.

Back to our 17th Century Dutch theologian, Gisbertus Voetius. In
his large volume on spirituality, he writes about, *inter alia*, "spiritual desertions." He describes the phenomenon as follows:

> An inner cross that the Christian has to bear or a spiritual ordeal
> through which the believer lacks the inner feeling of enjoyment
> of God and things divine. This flows from darkened assurance
> of faith in the personal appropriation of faith.[1]

It is striking that in his writing Voetius abundantly quotes the
Church Fathers, authors from the Middle Ages, and contemporary Roman Catholic scholars. The inclusion of the last category is especially
noteworthy. Engagement with Roman Catholic scholarship happened
only rarely in the context of religious wars. Yet Voetius did not accept
that truth is bound to a particular religious culture; rather he held that
spiritual experiences are equally shared by Christians in all cultures, eras,
and places.

It is important to note that what Voetius expressed as an academic
theologian in his concept of "spiritual desertions" has been confirmed
by many spiritual giants in and through their everyday ministries. One
prominent example is Mother Teresa. Her life-long ministry among people living in the slums of Calcutta was recognized by the awarding of a
Nobel Prize for Peace in 1979. After her death it became world news that
in her spiritual life she suffered a deep spiritual darkness. In her letters
she describes the spiritual wilderness that she had endured for several
decades because of a wrenching experience of the absence of God:

> The place of God in my soul is blank–There is no God in me.
> In the darkness . . . Lord, my God, who am I that You should
> forsake me? . . . The one You have thrown away as unwanted,
> unloved. I call. I cling. I want–and there is no One to answer, no

---

1. Voetius, *De Praktijk der Godzaligheid, [The Practice of Piety]*, 399.

One on Whom I can cling; no, No one. Alone. The Darkness is
so dark-and I am alone.[2]

Some will find it surprising that a profound spiritual experience
of a twentieth century Roman Catholic nun was so aptly described by
a Reformed writer from the seventeenth century. Christian spirituality
crosses boundaries, denominations, and times. While sharing similar
spiritual experiences, these voices point us to cultural variety on a global
level, to differences in denominational theologies, and to situated local
spiritualities. Let's unpack these three dimensions.

Cultural Variation across the Globe

In the *Nairobi Statement on Worship and Culture* (1996) the Lutheran
World Federation relates Christian practice to cultural diversity. The
statement is meant to bring together various global Christian traditions
on worship. This is something that Christian communities all over the
world wrestle with: how do our local, cultural expressions of worship
relate to the great truths of the Christian faith confirmed in the Church's
long history? Certainly, our cultural expressions do not determine Christian truth. Otherwise, other cultures would be excluded. Moreover, there
is the disturbing reality that equating Christian truth with a particular
cultural expression runs the risk of claiming a divine status for what is
simply a historical, human, cultural phenomenon, and thus fallible and
potentially sinful. The *Nairobi Statement* tries to do justice to the many
cultural expressions of Christian worship without becoming relativistic.

In order to approach the problem of one Christian religion with
many cultural expressions and contextual realities, the *Nairobi Statement* asks us to think about world-wide Christian faith in four modalities: transcultural, contextual, countercultural, and cross-cultural. This is
concisely expressed in article 1.3:

> Christian worship relates dynamically to culture in at least four
> ways. First, it is *trans-cultural*, the same substance for everyone
> everywhere, beyond culture. Second, it is *contextual*, varying ac-
> cording to the local situation (both nature and culture). Third,
> it is *counter-cultural*, challenging what is contrary to the Gospel

---

2. Mother Teresa, *Mother Teresa*, 187.

in a given culture. Fourth, it is *cross-cultural*, making possible sharing between different local cultures.[3]

Though the statement is on worship, its framework is equally helpful for the task of thinking about Christian spiritualities and cultural approaches to spiritual formation as a Christian practice. This becomes apparent when we change "worship" into "spirituality in the second article:

> 1.2 The reality that Christian spirituality (original: *worship*) is always lived (original: *celebrated*) in a given local cultural setting draws our attention to the dynamics between spirituality (original: *worship*) and the world's many local cultures.[4]

Spirituality is lived locally; it is expressed in the life of our communities of faith and churches. Pastors practice spiritual formation in a given cultural setting. Hence, the statement of the Lutheran World Federation on worship inspires us to think about the relationship between culture and spirituality. We are led to ask how the four modalities that are mentioned help us to think about the dynamics of spirituality and culture. More specifically, how does our method of spiritual formation reflect the transcultural, the cross-cultural, the countercultural and the contextual?

To start with the *contextual*, we note that our method is rooted in a pastoral context that has been thoroughly influenced by the movements of pastoral counseling and pastoral psychology. We consider this to be a gift from our parts of the world to the wider community of pastors. The therapeutic movement has taught us the importance of listening and the significance of the subjectivity of those who "receive" pastoral care. Our method, then, has incorporated the Western values of subjectivity and active listening. A great deal can be said—and even more has been written—about the relationship between positive psychology and pastoral care.[5] This is another contextual feature of our method. It is assumed that psychological theories and concepts contribute to the understanding of human well-being and that Christian soul-care greatly benefits from insights from human sciences. At the same time, we realize that this reflects our own mostly Western contextual valuation of non-theological

---

3. Lutheran World Federation, *Nairobi Statement*, 184.

4. Lutheran World Federation, *Nairobi Statement*, 184.

5. Moschella, *Positive Psychology as Resource*, 5-1–5-17.

sciences. Contextual aspects do not necessarily limit an approach; on the contrary they have the potential to enrich global Christianity. We offer our contextual approach to Christian pastoral practices with this hope.

There is also the *countercultural* relationship between culture and Christian spirituality. Our model of spiritual formation not only connects positively to the gifts of therapy and psychology; it also provides a critical perspective to human development and to human growth and transformation. We think that two aspects are especially important here. First, the central topics in our model reflect the Christian dynamics of sin and grace. For instance, the cards explicitly help the pastors and parishioners reflect on confession of sin and forgiveness. Positive psychology may teach that we have within ourselves the resources for flourishing, but we are ultimately beyond "self-repair" and we rely upon God's benevolence and mercy.

Second, our model of spiritual formation critiques cultural values such as self-dependency and an overweening emphasis on autonomy. It challenges pastors and parishioners to understand their lives in relation to God, the Source of calling and the One who holds us responsible for our lives. Theocentricity is a countercultural value, at least in the secularized contexts in the Western World. Given these examples from our own contextual positions, we challenge you to relate the model to values in your own context that are very commonly held but in need of transformation. Christian spirituality is countercultural as it moves us to confession of sin, opens us to God's forgiveness, and brings us into the sphere of the transformative work of the Spirit.

Most pastors have *cross-cultural* experiences. Even if you have always worked in the same general geographic location, you will have had quite a bit of experience with working with all sorts of people. Daily life is often very different for the various people in the parish; it is evident that they live in particular subcultures. Cross-cultural pastoral work involves contributing to binding together the various subcultures that make up the church. Crossing cultures means facing barriers. Groups of people that do not meet in everyday life meet at church and often this means having to overcome barriers and step over boundaries. The statement of the Lutheran World Federation uses the notion of "sharing" to understand the cross-cultural aspect: "The sharing . . . across cultural barriers helps enrich the whole church and strengthen the sense of the *communio* of the

Church."[6] In the use of our model of spiritual formation, the cross-cultural aspect carries with it three implications. First, we recognize that the model might feel strange in some of its aspects for some people; all that we have been able to do is to share one approach to spiritual formation formed from different perspectives and experiences (the research team is very diverse, both geographically and denominationally). Second, the experience of working with the model by pastors and parishioners demonstrates that pastors share their faith with parishioners and vice versa. Pastoral care is a sharing activity and the model stimulates the mutuality between pastor and parishioners. Third, parishioners from various backgrounds have used the model and they all take from the model what is beneficial for their individual spiritual lives. In brief, the pilot that we describe in this book shows that the model is helpful to bridge boundaries and to contribute to a sense of the communion of faith in the parish.

Finally, we consider the *transcultural* aspect. The example of spiritual darkness mentioned above pointed up transcultural features of Christian spirituality. The experience of the absence of God and the sense of darkness in the soul is recognized by Christians throughout the ages. Reformed writers in the seventeenth century reflected on experiences that twentieth century nuns recognize. A white male European Protestant pastor and theologian and a Catholic woman who spent her life in Christian service in India share a point of connection in their spiritual experience. We acknowledge that our model is very contextual in its theology and its pastoral methodology. Yet we also believe that our model has transcultural features. The statement on worship understands transculturality as follows:

> The resurrected Christ whom we worship, and through whom by the power of the Holy Spirit we know the grace of the Triune God, transcends and indeed is beyond all cultures. In the mystery of his resurrection is the source of the transcultural nature of Christian worship.[7]

The statement continues by discussing baptism, Eucharist, the Bible, and Sunday in terms of the "transcultural" times of the church's year. Across the nations there are cords that bind us together: "There is one Lord, one faith, one Baptism" (Eph 4:5). Besides these theological foundations, the statement on worship also mentions the elements of liturgy

6. Lutheran World Federation, *Nairobi Statement*, article 5.1.

7. Lutheran World Federation, *Nairobi Statement*, 185.

(creeds and prayers) and the contribution of worship to Christian unity. Let us unpack these three a little more with respect to spiritual formation and specifically in relation to the model that we present in this book.

TRANSCULTURAL FOUNDATIONS, PRACTICES, AND CHRISTIAN UNITY

When you meet with a parishioner for a pastoral conversation, you are very much aware that this is a unique situation. This parishioner is a particular person. The setting in which you meet and the community of faith that you both belong to represent context and locality. In pastoral care we can easily lose sight of the transcultural; we may forget that we engage in a practice that is not simply defined by this particular situation, but by the fact that it is "Christian" in the broadest sense of the word. You are both unique individuals, but at the same time you engage in a practice that binds Christians together both locally and globally. Like worship, pastoral care has transcultural features. Otherwise, it would not make sense to talk about pastoral care and spiritual formation as *Christian* practices.

We have seen that we may discern three transcultural aspects in Christian practices: theological foundations, such as the resurrection of Christ; elements in practices, such as the creed in Christian worship; and the contribution to Christian unity. The shared acts and practices point to the one church and the one faith and gives a local sense of the global church. For processes and practices of spiritual formation we can also distinguish between foundations, elements of practices, and Christian unity.

Theological Foundations

Three foundational doctrines help us keep the transcultural aspect of spiritual formation in view. These theological convictions also indicate the foundational ideas in the model for spiritual formation that we propose. They are as follows.

First, we note that the understanding of creation and the way in which humans are both new beings in Christ and always in the process of renewal is expressed in Christian theologies in different frameworks. Lutheran theology stresses that we are sinners and justified at the same time (*simul justus et peccator*). Reformed theology makes the doctrine of sanctification central in understanding the process of the renewal of human existence. Roman Catholic theology may be more open to the possibilities that are hidden in the image of God in which we are created. Yet all traditions combine the aspects that the apostle Paul mentions in his letter to the Ephesians, that we have to put off our old self and "put on the new self, created after the likeness of God" (Eph 4:20–24).

Second, there are different theological understandings of spiritual transformation. The transformation from the old self in Christian theology is understood as a spiritual transformation. This does not mean that only the heart and the inner life are transformed. It points to the working of the Holy Spirit. Again, Christian pneumatologies are all very different. However, the conviction that renewal is renewal by the Holy Spirit is a transcultural conviction that binds Christians together.

Last, we consider relational spirituality. In Christianity, spiritual transformation is a social process; putting on the new self makes no sense without reference to our relationships with others. The apostle Paul speaks about relational spiritual values such as forgiveness, honesty, love, kindness, and graceful speech (Eph 4:25–32). Spiritual formation is a relational process: pastors and parishioners meet and talk. We also note that it takes place in the wider spheres of the Christian community, the church, and the world.

These three foundational theological principles undergird our model for spiritual formation. We acknowledge the uniqueness of each person as a created being and at the same time we assume that renewal and transformation are at the heart of a Christian life. Though the model works with a relational process, the pastor cannot organize another person's spiritual renewal. The openness in the model acknowledges the role of the Holy Spirit in human lives and the subjectivity of the parishioner as agent in the process of transformation.

Elements in Spiritual Practices

Worship has transcultural elements, as we saw above when we attended to the Lutheran statement on worship and culture. Do spiritual practices also have transcultural elements? At first sight, it might not seem so. Spiritual practices are always very much contextually and culturally determined. Praying, fasting, singing, giving and sharing all belong to the practices of worldwide Christianity, yet they are also very much denominationally and contextually determined.

Renowned spiritual writer, Richard Foster, explains this very clearly in his book *Streams of Living Water* (2001). Foster writes:

> We are not the only ones from a different culture and age who have wanted to imitate the life of Christ. Others—myriads and myriads of them—have sought to imitate the way of Christ and to translate that way into their own setting and surroundings. We are helped immensely by looking at their efforts and learning their stories. Furthermore, it is a genuine act of humility to realize that we can learn from others who have gone before us.[8]

What Foster writes about the history of spirituality also concerns our present time; it is indeed a genuine act of humility to learn from others. For Foster, this learning from different types of spirituality entails learning various traditions in Christianity. He discerns at least six different spiritual traditions: contemplative, holiness, charismatic, social justice, evangelical, and incarnational. These traditions all have different approaches to spiritual formation, from meditative practices to social action. In our model we try to incorporate aspects of the various Christian traditions. Some of the cards focus on the outward life, such as ecological care and social justice; other cards call for a more inner spiritual practice such as prayer and meditation. Indeed, we believe that inner and outer practice need strong integration.

We suggest three transcultural elements to spiritual formation as a pastoral care practice. The first is the *pastoral conversation*. Spiritual formation is carried out in a relational context, in conversations between believers. The way these conversations are conducted is contextual (following local norms and preferences), yet the fact that we engage in relational encounters counts as a transcultural element in processes of spiritual formation (relationality is a universal phenomenon). The second element is the *caring relationship*. Spiritual formation takes place in a relationship of care. Within Christian communities we are responsible for each other's spiritual well-being and spiritual growth. In our model we assume that the role of care is taken by an ordained minister or a lay person with a high level of formal theological and pastoral training. This will not be possible in certain cultural contexts. However, care is a universal pastoral and Christian value. Engaging in a caring relationship

8. Foster, *Streams of Living Water*, 22.

may therefore be conceived as a transcultural Christian practice. The third and final transcultural element is the *orientation toward Scripture.* Christian pastoral care listens to the wisdom from the Scriptures; this is true no matter the cultural context. In our model we have incorporated a biblical frame in two ways. First, various cards point to Biblical images and use vocabulary that is grounded in the Scriptures, for example the fruits of the Spirit and the theological virtues of faith, hope, and love. Second, we encourage pastors and parishioners to pray but also to reflect upon the Biblical sources when engaging in a conversation about the topics suggested by the cards.

Contributing to Christian Unity

The third transcultural dimension concerns Christian unity. This is a particularly important transcultural aspect. The Christian faith aims to bind together believers from all ages, contexts, and regions.

On the one hand, it may be too presumptuous to think that our model could have ecumenical significance. It may be that it is fruitful in certain contexts and parishes, but contributes little, if anything, to advancing Christian unity across the various communities. This is a reasonable objection. We clearly need to respond to it. There are two aspects to Christian unity that we think our approach contributes to and that were in fact manifested in the pilot that we conducted in our own contexts.

First, congregations, parishes and Christian communities are often very diverse. Christian unity is commonly needed *within* a parish. We found that using a similar model for parishioners transcends the pastoral practice. It helps to move from being primarily adjusted to individuals toward a shared intention. Using the same model for parishioners of various ages and in various circumstances of life may run the risk of losing sight of individual needs. However, our experience was that it proved to be an opportunity to bind Christians together toward common goals of discipleship and spiritual growth.

At the same time, we need to acknowledge the fact that the model also has its limitations. It may not be suitable for all parishioners. The model is predominantly language-focused, both in its presentation (texts on cards) and its method (conversations). The model may be less fitting for parishioners with a learning style that requires images, or for those who find it difficult to put their experiences and way of being Christian into words in a conversation.

Despite this limitation, we found that pastors strengthened Christian unity within the parish through getting to know parishioners in greater depth and connecting through a shared language of faith.

The theme of Christian unity calls for deeper reflection on pastoral care as practice of the church. It is to this important theme that we now turn.

SPIRITUAL FORMATION AS AN ECCLESIAL PRACTICE

In our pastoral care practices, we often engage at the level of the individual. Commonly, pastoral care and counseling is viewed as helping individual parishioners to cope with their everyday problems and needs. It makes pastoral care perhaps one of the most situated and contextual religious practices: we meet with unique individuals and every encounter is unique. The client-centered approach has strengthened this. The agenda for pastoral care has been individualized; we talk about what the individual person indicates as relevant.

Our approach to spiritual formation may suggest that we work with an individualistic model; the use of themes that the parishioner takes and applies to their own unique situation suggests this. But pastoral care in the parish is an ecclesial practice; it concerns the community of faith. The church is shaped through a multitude of caring relationships and caring conversations. Spiritual formation takes place within a network of relationships, contributing to unity within a multitude of cultural and situational diversities. Our model of spiritual formation integrates the needs of the individual within a broader agenda of the Church, it builds upon the teaching of the Church throughout the ages (apostolicity), and it aims to connect Christians both within the one congregation and across congregations. Let's look at these aspects more closely.

Pastoral Care and the Agenda of the Church

Pastoral care and counseling are often based upon principles established by the influential therapist Carl Rogers. The starting point is the client. Pastoral care shaped by this tradition of counseling has adopted the principle that the situation of the parishioner leads the pastoral care conversation. The significance of this principle can hardly be stressed enough. Pastors should not overrule parishioners; they need to listen first, second, and third!

But you listen to your parishioner *as a pastor*. That means that you represent the wider Christian tradition, and more narrowly, the local church. The relationship between the pastor and the parishioner is ultimately defined by the relationship both have to the church and the Christian faith.

Taking the perspective of pastoral care as an ecclesial practice points up an important feature of care in Christian communities. We need to recognize that there is another agenda present in pastoral care conversations. We refer not to the hidden agenda by the pastor, but rather to a common agenda. The pastor and the parishioner meet within the body of Christ. The agenda of the church has had different expressions throughout the history of Christian pastoral care. It has had a missionary face in the Early Church when pastoral care was about preparing the newly converted for baptism; it had the face of forgiveness during the Middle Ages with its central confessional practice; and it had the face of congregational care in the Reformation. The variety of understandings of pastoral care in the history of the church is described in the influential study of Clebsch and Jaekle. They distinguish between the healing, sustaining, guiding, and reconciling functions of pastoral care.[9]

Our model of spiritual formation can be viewed as an "agenda" for pastoral care. The agenda is not something imposed on parishioners; rather, it involves sharing with them a common journey of living with God, a life of discipleship, and of spiritual growth. Two aspects deepen this: the notion of apostolicity and the function of serving the Body of Christ.

Apostolicity as a Feature of Pastoral Care

Apostolicity is about faithfulness to the Christian message throughout the ages. John Flett, who recently wrote a major book on apostolicity in relation to world Christianity, defines apostolicity as "faithfulness to origins expressed in the continuity of mission." Mission is about "being sent"; apostolicity concerns the continuity of the gospel in the church. Hence, according to Flett:

9. Clebsch & Jaekle, *Pastoral Care in Historical Perspective*.

> Apostolicity is identified first with the cultivation of the faith
> and so in relation to historical continuity, stability, order and
> office . . . [Cultivation] promotes a precise definition of witness,
> one contingent on growth in the faith and the practices deemed
> essential to such.[10]

Flett's book challenges apostolicity in the light of intercultural theology. Important for our model of spiritual formation are the theological connections between the gospel as message that is handed over through the ages and the spiritual practices that aim to cultivate growth in the faith.

Two features in our model demonstrate this connection. First, by using the same cards and topics for Christians in a variety of contexts, we express our belief that central tenets of the Christian faith are worth cultivating among Christians. Second, the model serves as an instrument to bind Christians of all places together in sharing similar directions toward growth in Christ-likeness and discipleship.

Spiritual formation is one of those practices that shape the life of Christians. In the context of pastoral care this is very much focused upon the individual, in her or his personal situation, location and denomination. Yet, like worship, pastoral care is also a practice that binds Christians together in the worldwide body of Christ.

Pastoral Care in View of the Body of Christ

The final aspect concerns the church as Body of Christ. In the pilot that we organized in five different geographic regions and involving three pastors, each with three parishioners, we discovered both diversity and continuity.

Our model of spiritual formation can be used by pastors as a tool to discover diversity in their congregations by engaging in pastoral relationships. In the pastoral conversations we often found that pastors and parishioners shared their experiences of faith in a natural way. Parishioners got to know their pastors quite a bit better and vice versa. Mary Clark Moschella makes the case that ethnography, a method of research used by academic researchers, can also be used for pastoral purposes.[11] She argues that in order to understand the parish better, pastors must

10. Flett, *Apostolicity,* 16.

11. Moschella, *Ethnography as Pastoral Practice.*

listen and hear the stories of parishioners and their longing for God. We think that our model of spiritual formation can be such an ethnographic tool to deepen the understanding of spirituality or spiritualities in the congregation.

In the pilot, the evidence was that the model helped to cultivate continuity of the faith, for individual congregants but also between congregants from various congregations. For the pilot we sometimes invited participants from various denominations to join in one focus group to evaluate the model (more often, congregants within the one congregation made up the focus group). It was a joyful experience to see people from different congregations who participated in the same process sharing significant insights and experiences. We discovered that the model is a promising approach to bridge differences between Christians and thus serving the unity of the Church.

SUMMARY

In this chapter, we have reflected on the process of spiritual formation that we offer in both local and global contexts. We also addressed the gap between individual spirituality and the mission of the whole Church. In the first part of the chapter, we offered global, denominational, and local perspectives on the issue of cultural diversity. Globally, we must deal with cultural differences in ecumenical perspective. Denominationally, we need to reflect upon theological identity and its impact on the theory and practice of spiritual formation. From a Western perspective, the model also challenges the gap between individual spirituality and shared religious identity. Diversity is often used as a value that engages with differences between individuals and supports individual spiritual freedom. Our view is that the tension between personal autonomy and communal norms needs to be held.

In the second part of the chapter, we addressed the gap between individual spirituality and the mission of the Church as the body of Christ. A model for spiritual formation extends beyond the boundaries of individual lives. Its mission is to engage individual believers with the broader teachings and practices of the worldwide church in becoming more hopeful, more forgiving, more conformed to Christ, and deepening the practices of faith that are inherently communal, such as caring for creation, celebrating the day of the Lord, and reading Scripture.

4

The Ministry Agent

Virtues and Attributes

The five members of the research team have all had considerable pastoral experience and are either currently teaching pastoral theology or have done so in the past. We know a wise, spiritually attuned and interpersonally skilled pastor when we see one. Further, through our teaching and pastoral engagements we have had the great privilege of getting to know quite a few individuals who fit into this category. It is not surprising, then, that when it came to identifying ministry agents to participate in the pilot program, we came up with a cohort well-endowed with gifts and graces for ministry. Though we made it very clear in the guidance we gave to parishioners participating in the focus groups that the feedback needs to be about the method and process, not about how helpful, supportive, and insightful their pastors were, many could not hold back on expressing their deep appreciation and respect. A method ultimately is only as good as the individuals who work with it. So as a team we decided that when it comes to writing this book, we need to not only offer theological reflection on the three domains, but also on the personhood and spirituality of the pastor.

With this in mind, we offer reflection on a set of virtues and personal traits: wisdom, availability, integrity (the virtues), attentiveness and embrace of weakness (the attributes). So why these five, you may be wondering? Who decided they were the important ones? Well, the team did. But we took a strong lead from the wonderful thinkers and spiritual guides that we have drawn on for inspiration and insight. Are there others that could, perhaps should, be included in the list? Most certainly. If there was more space available, the theological virtues of faith and hope (we cover love under availability), and the attributes of kindness, patience, gentleness, and humility, would all be included. We could also profitably discuss empathy, compassion, intellectual curiosity, and imagination. No doubt you can think of a few more yourself. The simple fact is that this topic, like so many in the field of pastoral theology and theology more generally, deserves a book length treatment. We've set the modest goal of hitting some of the highlights, so to speak.

A ministry agent companioning a person on a journey of spiritual formation necessarily encounters the complexities, subtlety, ambiguities, and confusion that accompany all such wayfarers. Recognizing this fact, wisdom seems like a good place to start our reflections.

THE VIRTUES

Wisdom

Wise pastors see life, the world, other people, and God for what they are: complex, multi-faceted, and elusive realities. They eschew simplistic interpretations of, and approaches to, the challenges of human existence and of loving and knowing God. Wisdom is clearly an important attribute for a ministry agent (and for all Christians) to possess. How, then, does one accrue it? Obviously, this is the big question. There are no simple answers (no surprises there). There are, however, some very helpful traditions available to us to guide our reflections. We have in mind the Hebraic, Greek, and New Testament communal stores of truth.

The ancients saw themselves as living in and being shaped by a tradition of understanding, knowledge, and insight. They learnt from both those wise ones they shared life with and those who had gone before them. This communal orientation stands in stark contrast to that of the modern Western world. We are the heirs of Descartes' *cogito, ergo sum* (I think, therefore I am). Note that Descartes' method of establishing a set of clear and distinct ideas is built on the foundation of the thinking subject. The individualistic stance that is endemic in Western societies today can be traced back to the *cogito*.

In the ancient Greek tradition, wisdom was viewed as a virtue, an excellence that contributes to the *telos* of human flourishing or happiness (*eudaimonia*). Happiness, however, is hard won. Plato and Aristotle realized that virtue cannot be established quickly; it is literally the work of a lifetime. A person is trained in the virtues. Through exercising a particular virtue time and time again, it takes hold. The virtuous person was said to have formed a habit. But this is not habit as we typically construe it. Rather, it is a readiness to act. When, for the example, the situation calls for courage, the person who has trained themselves in this virtue cannot but act courageously.

What kind of virtue, then, is wisdom? In general terms, the ancient Greeks split wisdom into the practical and theoretical types. Practical wisdom, or prudence, refers to knowing what to do, how and when to do it, and in a way that contributes to the overall goal for the human of flourishing and happiness. Prudence is the capacity to read aright the current situation and context you are faced with. The practically wise person sees the situation in the right way and on that basis makes a judgment about how and when to act.

For Plato and Aristotle, however, there is more to wisdom than simply grasping the good and right thing to do in a particular situation. It is also necessary to have a global sense of what is good. A person has access to this big picture of truth and reality through theoretical wisdom. For Plato, the attainment of theoretical wisdom requires a painful and long ascent toward the Good, the source of all that is good and beautiful—Being itself (he makes this clear in his famous allegory of the cave in the *Republic*). Aristotle, for his part, was cognizant of the fact that what we learn about the particular things we encounter via our senses does not help us answer the big human questions—the why questions. We naturally seek to understand how everything fits together, what causes things to be the way they are, and the ultimate meaning behind all that is. This particular quest for insight is ultimately aimed at understanding the Divine, which Aristotle construed as the Uncaused First Cause. "Theoretical wisdom, therefore, was an exercise of the most divine element in us towards the most divine object."[1]

The ancient Greeks recognized that human reason was not unlimited in power and that therefore it must contend with its own limitations. The ancient Hebrews also saw this, but their rationale was different.[2] It is the reality of God that sets the limits on human wisdom. We read, for

---

1. Davis & Wadell, "Educating Lives," 94.
2. On this, see Thiselton, "Wisdom," 168.

example, that "all one's ways may be pure in one's own eyes, but the Lord weighs the spirit" (Prov 16:2). God is perfect wisdom and therefore reads truth and reality infinitely more acutely and accurately than any human. God's wisdom is as high above ours as the heavens are above the earth. As Job puts it, "Do you think you can find out the depths of God's being, know the limits of the Almighty?" (11:7). It follows that the wise human is humble in heart. Such a one is always prepared to learn from others. The wise person listens to what others experience and thereby grows in understanding (Prov 1:8). Further, to be wise is to accept correction or reproof with alacrity (Prov 15:31).

Thomas Aquinas (1225–1274CE), as one would expect, also recognized the reality of human limitation and dependence on God when it comes to growing in the virtue of wisdom. For him, unlike the ancient Greek thinkers, accepting the constraints we must live within is not simply an unfortunate and regrettable fact. God is necessarily a mystery. Human life and the world we live in are also characterized by the mysterious and the impenetrable. Reason has its inherent limits, but this is not the end of the story. God gifts us with knowledge and understanding. In an act of sheer grace, God has revealed certain wondrous truths to us through the sages, prophets and, definitively, through the Son.

For the Greeks, human flourishing is pursued through human effort. A person must train themselves in the various virtues, employing practical wisdom (prudence). For Christians, however, true happiness— experienced through the beatific vision—is not something that sheer effort of mind and will can attain. Aquinas refers to what might be called Christian wisdom (as opposed to Greek wisdom) as "infused virtue."[3] What he means by this is that Christian wisdom is ultimately the result of divine grace. God acts in humans to move them in the direction of the perfection of their nature.

While for Aquinas the ultimate perfection of the human only comes with the *beatitudo* (the personal union of human beings with the Divine in the life to come), growth in virtue in the present existence is nevertheless very important. Training in each of the virtues requires the application of prudence or practical wisdom. In this way, Aquinas, like the ancient Greeks, recognized that wisdom and the moral life are very

---

3. Aquinas, *Summa Theologiae* II, Q. 45

closely linked. We find the same general understanding in the Book of Proverbs. Here are just a few of the many examples:[4]

> Humility and wisdom go hand in hand: "A person's pride will bring humiliation, but one who is lowly in spirit will obtain honor" (Prov 29:23).
>
> *Self-restraint and discretion* are vitally important: "Death and life are in the power of the tongue, and those who love it will eat its fruits" (Prov 18:21).
>
> The wise person has a *peaceable* spirit: "The beginning of strife is like letting out water; so stop before the quarrel breaks out" (Prov 17:14).
>
> *Charity to enemies* is advocated: "If your enemies are hungry, give them bread to eat . . . for you will heap coals of fire on their heads, and the Lord will reward you" (Prov 25:21–22).
>
> *Hard work and industry* are promoted: "Go to the ant, you lazybones; consider its ways, and be wise" (Prov 6:6).

Like everything else in the Christian life, growth in virtue and in wisdom begins with human seeking, striving, effort and discipline, but it ends with divine grace. God reveals truth to the wise; there are some things that reason alone cannot grasp. God infuses the virtue of wisdom into the soul of the faithful. Humans will only become truly wise in the *beatitudio* when, through an act of sheer grace, they are perfectly united to God forever. One day we will see God face to face and nothing will be hidden from us. For now, we must simply do our best to grow in wisdom through prayer and worship, meditating on God's word and the saintly spiritual guides in the Christian heritage, and learning from the insights and experience of the wise ones it is our privilege to know.

Availability

It is not much good having wisdom in spades if it is not shared with others. Indeed, to lock away one's wisdom is not the action of a wise person. God has made available divine wisdom through the sages, prophets and in a definitive way through the Son and the Spirit; our calling is to follow suit. Whatever we have learned that is of value about the complexities,

---

4. See Thiselton, "Wisdom," 167 for a more complete listing.

puzzles, frustrations, anxieties, joys and hopes of the Christian way and life more generally we need to make available to others. But the concept of availability goes much deeper and broader than this. It is not simply about making available wise insights; it is ultimately about self-communication or self-donation. The French philosopher and Catholic Christian, Gabriel Marcel, offers a rich and thought-provoking take on what it means to make oneself fully available to the other. Ultimately it takes us to the Christian virtue of love. Marcel begins his reflection on availability (*disponibilité*) with the idea of making your presence felt. His first insight is that presence is a grace. But he does not mean it in the sense that wisdom is a grace. This is not presence infused by God; it is simply a gift that one does or does not possess. However, we do think that Marcel would agree that God inspires every person who makes their present felt in a gracious, life-giving, and uplifting manner.

Marcel observes what many others interested in intersubjectivity have also seen: the depth dimension in life emerges through communion. Communion is more profound than communication. In an important passage from the first volume of his book, *The Mystery of Being*, Marcel distinguishes these two forms of being present to another person. [5] He refers to the situation where a person is sitting in a room with someone else, but somehow the other fails to make their presence felt. While you can communicate with this other person, there is no communion. It is a beautiful and joyous engagement, however, when the opposite takes place. A person really does make their presence felt, and it is stimulating and revelatory. I discover something in myself that I had not seen before.

Marcel tells us that it is not possible to teach someone how to make their presence felt. It would be like attempting to teach a person to be charming. We should not regard charm and presence as simply identical.[6] Charm, nonetheless, is one of the ways in which a person makes their presence felt. Marcel reflects systematically on the nature of charm in his *Metaphysical Journal*.[7] It is a grace; it "appears to decline with the decline of the gratuitous element in behaviour, or when a person's attention is more and more taken up with precise and specifiable ends."[8] If we try to will charm, the result is a tension that militates against our attempt

5. Marcel, *Mystery of Being* I, 205.

6. Marcel, *Mystery of Being* I, 207.

7. See Marcel, *Metaphysical Journal*, 300–301.

8. *Metaphysical Journal*, 300.

to be charming. It cannot be forced or manufactured; it is "the presence of the person round what he does and what he says."[9] It is not possible to isolate the quality or qualities that constitute a charming person. Charm is beyond conceptualization; it is that elusive factor that makes for what Marcel elsewhere refers to as a *lively* person.[10] This latter term probably captures Marcel's intention better for contemporary readers; we tend to think of a "charming" person as somewhat false and confected in their interpersonal style. What he means by the term "lively" is not that such a person is "the life of the party." A person who is quiet and introverted may be an exceedingly "lively" person. Individuals who are really alive have a "taste for life" and shower it around. The result is that their way-of-being-present is life-giving and creative.

For Marcel, charm cannot be considered as merely incidental to human existence. He makes the bold claim that charm can be linked "with all that is most metaphysical in the personality, with the quality which is irreducible and incapable of being objectivised—the quality which is doubtless only another facet of what we call existence."[11] What he is getting at here is that charm is not primarily about talent, or achievement, or intelligence, or wittiness. It is the stamp of your personality in an interpersonal situation. It is *who* you are (rather than *what* you are) making its presence felt. When the person that you are is filled with love for God and for others, imbued with grace and generosity, and marked by integrity and respectfulness, other people are enlivened, renewed, and uplifted by your presence.

Availability has close links with *agape*. Marcel was converted to the Catholic Christian faith in mid-life. He did not hesitate to say that availability is just another name for *caritas* or Christian charity. Marcel approaches giving of self from an interesting perspective. He asks questions such as these: What does it mean to promise to be there for the other ("fidelity")? What does it mean to say to the other, "I belong to you"? Fidelity and belonging are grounded in openness, being permeable, to the call of the other.

Marcel develops the link between openness to the other (receptivity) and disposability in an essay in *Creative Fidelity* entitled

---

9. *Metaphysical Journal*, 301.

10. See Marcel, *The Mystery of Being* I, 139.

11. Marcel, *Metaphysical Journal*, 301.

"Phenomenological Notes on Being in a Situation."[12] To exist with others, he observes, is to be exposed to influences. It is not possible to be human without to some extent being permeable to those influences. Permeability, in its broadest sense, is associated with a certain lack of cohesion or density. Thus, the fact of being exposed to external influences is linked with a kind of *in-cohesion*. I am "porous," open to a reality which seeks to communicate with me. "I must somehow make room," writes Marcel, "for the other in myself; if I am completely absorbed in myself, concentrated on my sensations, feelings, anxieties, it will obviously be impossible for me to receive, to incorporate in myself, the message of the other. What I called incohesion a moment ago here assumes the form of disposability . . . "[13]

Disposability or availability, then, is closely associated with receptivity. Receptivity involves a readiness to make available your personal center, your ownmost domain. We receive others in a room, in a house, or in a garden, but not on unknown ground or in the woods. Receptivity means that I invite the other to "be at home" with me. A home receives the imprint of one's personality; something of myself is infused into the way my home-space is constructed. Contrast this with "the nameless sadness" associated with a hotel room; this is no-one's home. To share one's home-space is disposability or availability because "[t]o provide hospitality is truly to communicate something of oneself to the other."[14]

The meaning of hospitality can also be broadened to include receiving into yourself the appeal of another for understanding and compassion. When I open myself to the call of the other to be with them in their personal journey, I spontaneously connect with them. The intonation of my words, my facial expressions, perhaps my tears, say to the other person, "I am with you." Contrasted to this responsiveness, however, there is an indisposability which Marcel refers to as an "inner inertia" or "spiritual asthenia."[15] The story of the other is experienced as something alien; I simply cannot receive it into my ownmost sphere.

In taking this line of investigation further, Marcel wonders: Why am I non-responsive to the experiences and feelings of the other? Why do

---

12. See Marcel, "Phenomenological Notes," 87–89.

13. Marcel, "Phenomenological Notes," 88.

14. Marcel, "Phenomenological Notes," 91.

15. See Marcel, "Belonging and Disposability," 50.

I feel opaque, non-permeable?[16] Marcel believes that non-availability is associated with the tendency to see one's existence in terms of possession. I will treat myself as indisposable "just so far as I construe my life or being as a having which is somehow quantifiable, hence as something capable of being wasted, exhausted or dissipated."[17] In this attitude, I become like a person who knows that his small sum of money must last a very long time. I become afflicted with an anxiety and a concern which discourage self-giving. These negative emotional states are "reabsorbed into a state of inner inertia."[18]

Building on these insights, we add that what is required of pastoral agents seeking to deepen capacity for presence is a persistent and faithful attitude of prayer that opens them to the grace of God in Christ, through the power of the Holy Spirit. The central orientation in the inner and missional life of the triune God is toward-the-other. The divine persons participate perichoretically in the infinite love that is the source of their missions. The Son and the Spirit are involved in a mission of outgoing, outpouring love in the world. As we open ourselves to this agapic drive in prayer, the miracle of conversion to disposability is accomplished over time. A personal sphere defined and limited by fear of being wasted, drained, and depleted is broken open by a divine power that infuses generosity, openness, and self-giving. That said, it is not that God creates in us an "always the other-never me" orientation. God is love and love does not lead individuals down a path of burnout, joylessness, and depression. Rather, the modality the Spirit empowers is giving fully in those times when it is right, reasonable and necessary, all things considered, to be available to others for ministry. At other times, relax, enjoy, and re-create!

Integrity

There is of course so much to be said on virtues for ministry; we are limiting ourselves to just three important ones. The final virtue selected for comment is integrity. "To possess integrity is to be incapable of compromising that which we believe to be true . . . To possess integrity is to have a kind of inner strength which prevents us from bending to the influence of what is thought expedient, or fashionable or calculated to win praise;

16. Marcel, "Belonging and Disposability," 51.

17. Marcel, "Belonging and Disposability," 54.

18. Marcel, "Belonging and Disposability," 54.

it is to be consistent and utterly trustworthy because of a constancy of purpose."[19] A person of integrity chooses convictions and personal consistency over satisfying the craving for popularity and conflict-free relations.

It goes without saying that integrity is right at the heart of the religious life. It is celebrated in the Wisdom literature. In the Psalms we read: "By this I know that you are pleased with me; because my enemy has not triumphed over me. But you uphold me because of my integrity, and set me in your presence forever" (Ps 41:11–12). In the Book of Proverbs, the blessing that parents with the virtue of integrity bring to their offspring is recognized: "The righteous walk in integrity—happy are the children who follow them!" (Prov 20:7). A hallmark of the life and ministry of Jesus is absolute consistency. The most powerful Gospel statements on spiritual integrity are Jesus' threefold resistance to Satan's temptations in the desert, standing firm to his fundamental spiritual convictions (Matt 4:1–11; Lk 4:1–13), his refusal to bow to the unrelenting pressure exerted by the Pharisees and the scribes, and his willingness to live faithful to his calling, even as it sealed his fate at Golgotha.

It is important to note that it is not always clear what acting with integrity means. In Galatians 2:11–14, we read that Paul considers that Peter buckled under pressure and turned away from his practice of sharing in table fellowship with Gentiles. Is this really a failure to act with integrity? Here is what Paul tells us:

> When Cephas came to Antioch, however, I opposed him to his face, since he was manifestly in the wrong. His custom had been to eat with pagans, but after certain friends of James arrived he stopped doing this and kept away from them altogether for fear of the group that insisted on circumcision. The other Jews joined him in this pretence, and even Barnabas felt himself obliged to copy his behavior.
>
> When I saw they were not respecting the true meaning of the Good News, I said to Cephas in front of everyone, "In spite of being a Jew, you live like the pagans and not like the Jews, so you have no right to make the pagans copy Jewish ways."

Given this account, it might seem that Paul had every right to challenge Peter. The latter capitulated because he was afraid of the circumcision party. But we do only have one version of the incident. How would Peter have defended himself? "He would have claimed," suggests F.F.

19. Campbell, *Rediscovering Pastoral Care*, 12.

Bruce, "that he acted out of consideration for the weaker brethren—the weaker brethren on this occasion being those back home in Jerusalem."[20] This points to the fact that it is not always clear what it means to act with integrity. It may indeed have been that Peter was not so much acting out of fear, but rather out of a concern for those Jewish Christians who were vulnerable, who were not yet secure enough in their faith to cope with such a momentous challenge.

A number of psychologists refer to the true or authentic self, on the one hand, and the false or conforming self, on the other. They contend that values are the primary factor in establishing a coherent sense of self-hood.[21] The suggestion is that when a person acts in accordance with their value structure, they feel in touch with their core self. Living true to our deepest values leads to a sense of authenticity. A person whose words and actions are congruent with their value structure feels as though they are living out of their true self. It goes without saying that such authentic living is difficult to enact.

Because there are large benefits that accrue from conforming to the wishes and desires of others, especially popularity and praise, many of us find that over time we lose touch to an extent with our real selves. We have become so used to responding to the question, "What does she or he want me to say?" that we too often fail to ask, "What do I really think?", and "What needs to be said here?" Another way of talking about the virtue of integrity is to say that it belongs to those who live out of their real selves. The following stances are what matter most to persons of integrity. First, they value getting in touch with their own deepest ideas, values, and convictions. And secondly, they put a high priority on putting those ideas and values before others. It is possible to fail at either point. Some of us, for instance, have become so habituated to an inner dialogue dominated by external demands that we no longer have access to our deepest beliefs. In a moment of scary self-discovery, we are hit with the awareness of a loss of self-contact. We realize that we have no immediate contact with a personal center.

It may be, on the other hand, that a person is able to access his personal beliefs quite readily but is too afraid to speak the truth. In his book *Who is Worthy?* Father Ted Kennedy opens his deeply challenging reflections on his Church's relationship to gay people and to Australia's First

20. Bruce, *Galatians*, 133.

21. See Hitlin, "Values as the Core."

Peoples with this comment: "Some time ago I suffered a stroke which triggered in me a decision to live the rest of my life as if I were already dead. I am now more inclined to state things as they are, or as I see them, without fear or compromise."[22] The problem for many of us is that we can't achieve this illusion. We are very aware of being alive, and we are even more aware of the living hell others may choose to create for us!

In the context of pastoral conversation, this discussion reminds us of how crucially important it is to relate honestly and genuinely. There are times when we need to speak "an inconvenient truth" to a parishioner. Folk love us when we are understanding, affirming, and supportive; they are usually not so appreciative when we invite them to face an issue they are avoiding, or challenge an aspect of their comfortable, limited, or distorted view of God and the vocation of following Christ. It requires integrity to speak an uncomfortable truth when one is required to.

Integrity in a pastoral relationship also refers to a capacity to be "dependably real," as Carl Rogers so nicely put it. Assuming the persona of the all-knowing and wise one, projecting a saintly persona, mimicking the style of another (admired) pastor, refusing to acknowledge their own laughable humanity, hiding the true self, and failing to be honest are just some of the ways a pastor fails the realness test.

As has already been indicated, so much more should be said on virtue in pastoral ministry. Unfortunately, lack of space prevents a deeper and wider investigation. It is to a reflection on pastoral capacities that we now turn.

THE CAPACITIES

Embrace of Weakness

Our focus here is accepting our laughable humanity and using it as a strength in companioning others on their spiritual journey. In our teaching and pastoral ministries, we have observed that many pastors—and we put ourselves in this category—struggle to come to grips with their fears, sense of inadequacy, and personal short-comings. The wish is often that this reality could simply be thrown off, to allow the emergence— like a butterfly out of a chrysalis— of a strong, confident, fully capable, and in-control pastoral leader. To all of us suffering under the burden

---

22. Kennedy, *Who is Worthy?* 27.

of unrealistic, destructive, and futile expectations we offer this outlook on ministry: accepting our weaknesses and limitations, embracing our farcical humanity, is actually a positive. Such an attitude is an asset for those engaged in pastoral work. Jeanne Ellin gives sound counsel when she says this:

> Acknowledge your weakness and make it work for you; it can be a source of strength, a resource for you, whether it makes you aware of your humanness or is a source of increased sensitivity to the varied ways in which people respond to painful or stressful situations.[23]

Henri Nouwen tells the story of taking a group of final-year seminarians on retreat in preparation for their ordination. One of the students, feeling anxious about his future ministry, said, "I just hope that I'll be strong enough to be a good priest." To which Nouwen responded, "I don't think your strength is really the issue. The question is whether or not you are weak enough for priesthood."

So what did Nouwen mean by this paradoxical reference to weakness as a strength in ministry? Well, for a start, it is evident that he is *not* alluding to the Pauline approach to the value of weakness. Recall what Paul says in Second Corinthians chapter 12:

> About this thing, I have pleaded with the Lord three times for it to leave me, but he has said, "My grace is enough for you: my power is at its best in weakness." So shall I be very happy to make my weaknesses my special boast so that the power of Christ may stay over me, and that is why I am quite content with my weaknesses, and with insults, hardships, persecutions, and the agonies I go through for Christ's sake. For it is when I am weak that I am strong (vv. 8–10).

Paul is here extolling the virtue of embracing weakness in order to manifest the greatness of God. That God can change lives via the vehicle of "damaged goods" shows just how majestic God is. In this text, Paul is presenting an important gospel truth, but it is not what Nouwen has in mind. Rather, what we have is a theme that comes through quite often in Nouwen's writings, and especially in his classic book, *The Wounded Healer*.[24] That theme is that an inflated, unrealistic sense of one's personal strength keeps us apart from others. An unavoidable part of being human

23. Ellin, *Listening Helpfully*, 32.

24. See Nouwen, *Wounded Healer*.

is to live in confusion, fear, destructive urges, deceit, failure, shame, and guilt. To pretend to ourselves and to others that we are always strong emotionally, intellectually, spiritually, and morally is futile, silly, dishonest, and destructive. Our weakness is part of our common humanity. It is only when it is acknowledged and accepted that we can relate to others in an honest and real way. Moreover, it is through being in touch with our weakness that we release within ourselves a flow of compassion and understanding. It is not that a pastor must have experienced precisely the same kind of confusion, disorientation, or suffering as the other person. Rather, it is that through their own difficult and challenging experiences, whatever they may be, they entered for a time into that place of shadows in which the parishioner now finds themselves. In the pastoral conversation, we find two fellow travellers who have passed the same way and feel a bond of communion. Alastair Campbell puts it well when he says that "[t]he wounded healer heals, because he or she is able to convey, as much by presence as by the words used, both an awareness and a transcendence of loss."[25]

It is when we feel a bond of solidarity with another, borne out of a common journey into the shadowlands of human existence, that there is confidence, trust, and openness, and beyond that, hope. An important gift that a minister can offer a person feeling lost, confused, despairing, or inadequate as a Christ follower is hope. A person sitting in this place suffers under the awful burden of the thought, so powerful and all-pervasive, that they will always be there. The presence of the pastor, usually without them needing or wanting to make a specific reference to transcendence of similar experiences, becomes a sign of hope. It is not that the pastor says straight out, "I've been there and I came through it. You can too. Just hang in there." Rather, the very fact that the minister so clearly understands and is prepared to enter into the difficult experience of the other, witnesses to the fact that they are not a stranger to the struggles of faith and life. To quote Campbell once more:

> Wounded healers heal because they, to some degree at least, have entered the depths of their own experiences of loss and in those depths found hope again. The wounded healer has learned that it is useless to base security on material possessions, on popularity and worldly success, even on the closest and most important of personal relationships. The wounded healer has learned (a little at least) from the Son of Man, who had nowhere to lay his

25. Campbell, *Rediscovering Pastoral Care*, 42.

head . . . and has understood the wisdom of Job's words: "Naked I came from my mother's womb, naked I shall return . . . "[26]

Attentiveness

The simple fact of embracing one's woundedness and human frailty—as crucial as that is—is not enough to connect with the story a person is sharing. You have to actually listen well and hear it. Those who have never done any pastoral ministry or similar helping work such as counseling and social work usually underestimate how difficult and demanding listening is. Jeanne Ellin has it just right when she says this: "This is a simple-sounding task—many of us like to think we are good listeners. Just sitting and listening sounds like one of those dream jobs like mattress tester or taster in a brewery."[27] It is true that listening comes more naturally to some than to others, but the view that it is a simple task is very far wide of the mark.

Attentive listening involves hearing personal stories "in all their experiential richness and complexity."[28] The question that immediately arises is this: How do you become attuned in this deep way to the person and their story? There have been many helpful treatments of this issue; we don't want to walk over ground that others have already been on. In the search for fresh and challenging insights, we ended up with Simone Weil's (1909–1943) concept of "attention." In order to give you a sense of why we chose Weil as a guide in unpacking attentive listening, we submit this quote: "Those who are unhappy have no need for anything in the world but people capable of giving them their attention. The capacity to give one's attention . . . is a very rare and difficult thing; it is almost a miracle; it *is* a miracle. Nearly all those who think they have this capacity do not possess it."[29] Already we have learnt something that is vitally important: do not underestimate how difficult it is to pay attention to another person.

Weil has been described as "a mystic without a church, a political activist without a party, a wandering Jew with a Christian faith."[30] She is a

26. Campbell, *Rediscovering Pastoral Care*, 43.

27. Ellin, *Listening Helpfully*, 40.

28. Capps, *Living Stories*, 14.

29. Weil, *Waiting on God*, 58.

30. Delaruelle, "Attention as Prayer," 19.

challenging and unconventional thinker. The ideas she generates are un-settling, provocative, and most often cryptically expressed. Many readers of Weil's work report that they find it difficult to pin her conceptualizations down; the meaning is not immediately clear. But the wrestling is thoroughly worth it. She produces perspectives that are sparkling lights and deeply transformative.

Weil's work on attention[31] is relatively straightforward by her standards, but there are definitely some tricky bits. Attention involves fully opening yourself to that which is before you. In order to attend in this way, it is necessary to exert negative effort (to be passively active) and to wait and be receptive. In what follows, these two facets of attention are addressed to help us in understanding the nature of attentive listening. The first port of call is reflection on attention as passive activity.

Attention as Negative Effort

One of the team members (Neil Pembroke) offered the following story to illustrate what Weil is getting at here:

> My first degree was in engineering. When I came to the study of theology and the humanities, I was very aware of my deficits. I had devoted most of my secondary education to the study of maths, physics, chemistry, and biology. At university I progressed to algebra, calculus, computer science, materials science, and soil and water engineering (I trained in agricultural engineering). There was virtually no place in my education for the great historical works, the literary masterpieces, and the brilliant works of philosophy. (I say "virtually no place" rather than "no place" because engineering students at my institution were required to take two elective courses in the humanities.)
>
> At the beginning of my new direction in tertiary education I had a strong sense of needing to fill in the gaps. I remember buying a copy of Tolstoy's Anna Karenina. I was motivated not so much by the thought that I would have the wonderful privilege and joy of engaging with a masterfully told story. I didn't really expect to become absorbed in the plot, to get caught up in the sexual tension, or gain fresh insight into human frailty or Russian cultural mores in the latter part of the 19th century. In fact, at the time of making the purchase I didn't actually know what the book was

31. Weil's thoughts on attention can be found in *Waiting on God*, in *Gravity and Grace*, and scattered throughout her notebooks.

about. I decided to buy and read the book because it had the reputation of being a great work of literature. It presented as the sort of book that a young man embarking on the study of theology and the humanities really should read.

Almost from the start, it was clear to me that this was not my kind of novel; it simply wasn't engaging me. But I manfully ploughed on, determined that I would read this novel that was essential reading for any truly cultured person. I almost made it to the end. After many months of going to it on and off, I had about eighty pages to go and I stopped. I just couldn't bring myself to read one more page. My wife, intrigued that I was reading Anna Karenina, *asked me about the story. Though I had read most of it, I could barely remember anything about it.*

What would Simone Weil say about this failed foray into the world of great literature? She would no doubt remark that Neil had confused attention with "muscular effort."[32] In her essay on attention in school studies, she has this to say:

If one says to one's pupils: "Now you must pay attention," one sees them contracting their brows, holding their breath, stiffening their muscles. If after two minutes they are asked what they have been paying attention to, they cannot reply. They have been concentrating on nothing. They have not been paying attention. They have been contracting their muscles.[33]

She goes on to say that this kind of muscular effort is "entirely barren."[34] When we muscle up on a task, so to speak, the result is that we get tired. This creates the false impression of actually having done some work. But "[t]iredness has nothing to do with work."[35]

According to Simone, will power helps the person doing intellectual work only a little. The learning process is led by desire, and by pleasure and joy in the work. "The joy of learning is as indispensable in study as breathing is in running. Where it is lacking there are no real students, but only poor caricatures of apprentices who, at the end of their apprenticeship, will not even have a trade."[36]

---

32. Weil, *Waiting on God*, 54.

33. Weil, *Waiting on God*, 54.

34. Weil, *Waiting on God*, 55.

35. Weil, *Waiting on God*, 55.

36. Weil, *Waiting on God*, 55.

It may seem that Simone is arguing here for something that experience tells us simply is not true. Students by the tens of thousands muscle their way through courses and programs. Desire for learning is not what drives them; they get almost no pleasure and joy out of their studies. Simone is of course aware of this. She distinguishes between learning and passing examinations: "Studies conducted in such a way [through muscular effort] can sometimes succeed academically from the point of view of gaining marks and passing examinations, but that is in spite of the effort and thanks to natural gifts; moreover such studies are never of any use."[37]

Our contention is that there is a direct correlation between Weil's concept of attention led by desire and really hearing a person. The pastors who engage in highly attentive listening on the whole love to do what they do. Though inevitably there are times when intense listening is a struggle, most often they find deep satisfaction in hearing and responding to the stories others tell them. For them, engaging with the subtleties and complexity of another's life-world and making sense of it is a privilege and an interesting challenge.

Listening intently to another person is demanding, challenging, and draining. Sometimes the stories are not especially engaging and the task unrewarding. This ministry is difficult; that goes without saying. It is also true that there are days when virtually every pastor feels like they're not up for the task. But the salient fact is that, for the most part, the act of listening carefully to a person who is opening up about their personal and spiritual questions, struggles, fears, and hopes is something that a faithful and loving pastor wants to do. They count it as a privilege that they are trusted enough by a parishioner to share a personal story and pilgrimage. Being led by desire and experiencing joy in pastoral work are the necessary conditions of attentive listening. Attention is counterfeit if it is driven by muscular effort.

We do not mean to create the impression that a pastor must float at every moment on a cloud of joy and passion. Pastors are flesh and blood beings; they are not divine spirits who never fall from the perfection of loving attention. Sometimes they feel a little grumpy and off their game because last night they had a bad sleep, or their favorite team received a thrashing in the Grand Final, or they are feeling overrun by the demands and annoyances in the home (or in a bad week, all of these!). Sometimes

37. Weil, *Waiting on God*, 55.

they lose interest for a moment (or many moments), or find the intensity of the conversation a bit much, and they think about their favorite leisure pastime. Putting it another way, pastoral ministry is not all "beer and skittles." It requires effort. One human being aims to be fully present to another; it is a process that needs to be energized in some way.

People of faith seek to live their lives constantly open to the power of the Spirit of Christ. Simone refers only to human effort. But for followers of Christ, the truth is that we expend fully our human energy—the Christian vocation is not an armchair occupation—confident that the Holy Spirit brings all the resources of heaven to bear on our earthly efforts. For her part, Weil identifies the need for effort, but it must not be of the "muscular" variety. That helps not a bit in paying attention. But she also says that "attention is an effort, the greatest of all efforts."[38]

Intriguingly and a little cryptically, the exertion of which she speaks is a negative one. Whatever can Weil mean by her term, "negative effort"? Her only elaboration on the term is that "it does not involve tiredness."[39] This tells us something—namely, that attending through negative effort is energizing in some way. But we are still none the wiser about the exact nature of negative effort. Angelo Caranfa associates the term with "passive activity."[40] What might this equally paradoxical term mean? Well, let us offer an illustration that may help. Everyone who has done some creative writing is aware of the negative impact of writing under the influence of an extrinsic factor. It may be a deadline that has been imposed. It may be the fact that you are bored with the project and with writing in general and just want to get it done. The result is that instead of waiting for the gift of a fresh and interesting idea to come, you try to muscle it out of yourself. What is required is a patient, passive stance in which one simply lingers until the great idea arrives. In a similar fashion, attention in an interpersonal engagement requires passively waiting for the other to show themselves. We must not force our assumptions, preconceptions, and frame of reference onto them. In attending to a person, we need to be active through passivity. We cannot wrench meaning out of that which is in front of us; we must wait for the meaning to emerge. The other person needs to reveal themselves. Mary Dietz captures this very nicely when she comments: "For Weil, attention is a quality of openness to the world,

38. Weil, *Waiting on God*, 55.

39. Weil, *Waiting on God*, 55.

40. See Caranfa, "Aesthetic and Spiritual Attitude," 67.

a quiescent readiness toward the 'out there,' without any solid expectation of what one will find."[41] Attention requires us to wait upon the parishioner to show themselves.

Waiting and Receptive

Prayer is first and foremost about waiting on God. According to Simone, "[i]t is the orientation of all the attention of which the soul is capable towards God."[42] The most important question is not, what must I say to God? But rather, what does God want to say to me?

Attention is like prayer; it is a contemplative act. In contemplation, one maintains a state of suspension. The French words *attente* (wait) and *attention* (attention) have the same etymology. They both refer to being in a state of tension in relation to an object that has yet to show itself.[43] Weil puts it this way: "Attention consists of suspending our thought, leaving it detached, empty and ready to be penetrated by the object, it means holding in our minds . . . "[44]

Weil's insight that if we really want to know an object, a phenomenon, or a person we need to be open and receptive to it is shared by Bernard Meland (though he does not refer to her work). Meland offers us the concept of "appreciative awareness." In order to understand the phenomenon under investigation as fully and deeply as possible, he contends that a person must wait upon it in an attitude of expectancy. "In an act of reflection," he writes, "there is not simply a direct act of observation, but, as it were, a waiting and an expectancy that what is so envisaged will disclose its fuller pattern of meaning."[45]

It is interesting to note in this context that for the Early Church Fathers prayer is essentially being attentive to God and to God's subtle presence in the world. Gregory of Nazianzus wrote a beautiful prayer with this theme:

> All things proclaim you—
> things that can speak and things that cannot . . .

41. Dietz, *Between Human and Divine*, 97.

42. Weil, *Waiting on God*, 51.

43. We are indebted to Jacques Delaruelle for this insight. See his "Attention as Prayer," 20.

44. Weil, *Waiting on God*, 56.

45. Meland, "Can Empirical Theology Learn Something," 301.

All things breathe you a prayer,
a silent hymn of your own composing . . .
What mind's affinities with heaven
can pierce the veils above the clouds?
Mercy, all transcendent God
(what other name describes you?)[46]

"Appreciative awareness" is an essential modality for pastors. They need to consistently adopt this stance in tracing God's presence and activity in their personal sphere of experience and in the world around them. This is prayer-as-attending. It is also the case that in order to really hear another person, a pastor needs a waiting stance. It takes time for the patterns in the life-world of a parishioner to manifest; this process cannot be rushed. It is uncomfortable living with confusion and messiness. There is a natural urge to bring order out of the chaos. What is crucial here is to take a receptive rather than an active stance in the listening process. The deep meaning in what the parishioner is saying about themselves—their view of the world and of God, their pain perhaps, their confusion, their struggles and fears, hopes and joys—needs to be allowed to unfold. The patterns need to show themselves; they cannot be forced through the grid of a minister's own particular way of seeing the world.

We are very aware that this discussion on the virtues and personal attributes of the pastor is incomplete and inadequate. This vitally important topic deserves a much fuller treatment. At least some crucially important dimensions have been covered.

The decision to reflect at depth on the character of faithful and loving pastoral work, rather than simply offering some helpful tips and strategies, flows from our strong conviction that what we bring as persons contributes at least as much to the quality and effectiveness of our pastoral work as does our skilful technique. The conscientious and faithful pastor constantly works on enhancing knowledge of, and skill in, the pastoral arts. But just as importantly, and probably more so, they continually open themselves to the Spirit of God in the journey into deeper faith, greater availability, and firmer character.

---

46. Gregory Nazianzen, *Poemata Dogmatica* (PG 37:507); cited in Harrison, *The Art of Listening*, 186.

5

SPIRITUAL PERSPECTIVES ON FORMATION

IDENTIFYING AND CLAIMING MEANINGFUL and beneficial spiritual perspectives is not a simple, straightforward enterprise. For some of us our spiritual lives may have become static and stale, perhaps no longer connected to their living source. Perhaps our practices have become too removed from their original inspiration. They no longer touch the hungers of our hearts; perhaps they linger as an artifact from another time when we were living the challenges and resolutions of that moment.

Others of us may resist broadening our spiritual horizon and the perspectives and practices that support it, especially if it becomes just another "to do list," or "one more thing to try." Approaching spiritual practices "cafeteria style" runs the risk of over-emphasizing the *doing* of our spiritual practices at the expense of *being*; in the spiritual life we need to first address *who we are*. What we seek ultimately is a spiritual pattern of life that unifies who we are by bringing head, heart, and hands into a pattern of life that unifies and integrates us.

We can illustrate this dilemma by using the analogy of the difference between a map and the territory. Planning a trip, for instance, can be very engaging and inviting, as we scour travel guides and maps, and begin to imagine ourselves there. But this is a far cry from actually going, from full immersion in the sights and sounds and the immediacy of "being there." Spiritual perspectives and practices, to be efficacious and meaningful, need to be grounded in our actual lived experience. Said another way, authentic spiritual practices will *find us,* since they will most likely emerge out of the heart and soul struggles of our own spiritual formation.

In seeking to embark on a journey of spiritual growth and maturation we need to consider the hopes, desires, and objectives we would seek to achieve. What might we seek to gain from such a quest, and what perspectives and attitudes might be needed to help guide us on our way? The insights from the classic spiritual writer Evelyn Underhill give us valuable first clues when she suggests that our spiritual growth must be in two directions: an "expansion in depth" and an "expansion in love."[1] Underhill affirms that an ever-deepening relationship with God must be directly linked to a consistently widening and generously loving movement toward our fellow human beings.

Yet, this commitment is not so simple or self-evident that we can assume the methods or means by which we might advance spiritual maturation. Underhill reminds us that we are all unique in our spiritual development, both in our perspectives/attitudes and in our modes of engagement with God. There is an infinite variety to our souls, she says, whether in our temperaments, our capacities, or the developmental stages in which we find ourselves. We must, she insists, find out what kinds of commitments "suit *our* souls" so that we do not simply end up borrowing or mimicking someone else. In short, self-awareness and self-ownership are essential for spiritual growth.

Underhill's challenge to us does not end here. Our spiritual commitments, she says, must invite us in and should not "overstrain" us, since we need to remain "supple before God." What she means here is that practices that refresh us, brace us, and expand us, are better able to sustain us through the inevitable spiritual challenges we will encounter along the way. Furthermore, we should seek the methods that most deeply attract us so that the spiritual food our souls need can be digested. Underhill insists that we must retain a wide receptivity to the spiritual practices of others who may require a different diet, and we must encourage and support such practices.

Underhill does not stop here either; she insists that for the sake of others we should learn all we can about others' spiritual inclinations beyond our own. For Underhill, all the various methods and spiritual practices that might benefit our lives and the lives of others will only find their validation as they strengthen our "bond with the Sacred." The

1. Underhill, *Concerning Inner Life,* 109.

overarching mission of Christian growth, as Underhill sees it, is not attaining quiet serenity, but a "whole life" engagement of action and service in the spirit of contemplation. She adds a special note of caution to those pastors who may become so specialized that they lose sight of the objectives of their work—namely, to seek to improve their own and others' "communion of the soul with God."[2]

This broad commitment to our work as Christians matches the classic pattern of Jesus, in which his unity of personhood is revealed in his interior intentions (head), his affective congruence (heart), and his committed service (hands). We are called to do what Jesus does, seeking to "imitate Christ," just as the Apostle John notes: Jesus does "what he sees the Father doing" (John 5:19). Our spiritual lives should reflect this constant interplay of our heads, hearts, and hands, as echoed in the work of Jesuit Joseph Tetlow on discernment.[3] This triad of Head, Heart, and Hands is a simple way of describing the necessary interplay or integration of Faith, Belief, and Action which informs and shapes our spiritual growth and maturation. The lines of triadic connection are these:

HEAD/HEART/HANDS
FAITH/BELIEF/ACTION
THINKING/FEELING/DOING

Each of these components flows into the others and is affected by them. Yet, we inevitably come into periods of erosion or challenge, a crisis of purpose or praxis, where personal integration fails us. We can become disjointed and lose our way. Just as our personal lives are not static, our life contexts and our faith communities are all subject to change at every level. Every age will place demands on us as persons and practitioners as we seek to be faithful stewards of the gifts and resources given to us. Yet to do so with integrity and congruence, we need a working compass that orients, guides, and mediates our changing realities from God's point of view.

Cultivating a spiritual vision thus requires the capacity to see more deeply the truth(s) of our own lives, but also the realities of the situations in which we find ourselves. Our spiritual work may need to be concentrated in one or more of these spiritual domains. Our intentional spiritual growth work should reflect this. Sometimes our lives are flooded with affect, and our hearts are deeply bruised and overwhelmed. This

2. Underhill, *Concerning Inner Life*, 111.

3. Tetlow, *Always Discerning*, 5.

situation calls for particular practices of loving. Our practices need to be intentionally directed toward the specific disciplines that might meet the dilemmas.

At other times we lose faith, when the whole structure of meaning and purpose doesn't seem to hang together, and things no longer make sense. Our propositions of faith and the symbols that support them become hollowed out and lose their power. Having a crisis of meaning should not particularly surprise us. Our minds are not so pre-programmed, so well-informed, or so enlightened, that we can easily make sense of our complex, ever-changing world. Accelerated change in the lives of our communities, our families, our children, or in ourselves, generally arrives with ambiguity and confusion. We need to learn to spiritually lean into the challenges that come at us. Scripture reminds us that we must be "transformed by the renewing of our minds" (Rom 12:2), and that our relationship to the power centers of this world requires the discernment of a renewed mind.

For others of us the challenge to spiritual integrity might be focused on our hands. Our commitment to doing, to serving and giving, may be unfocused and scattered. Conversely, we may be overwhelmed by doing and become "spent." We are worn out and depleted. Our exhaustion may come with a sense of futility. Were our efforts truly worth it? In a data-driven world we may struggle with the fact that our so-called successes are largely intangible. In a strict evidence-based world, there is little time allowed for incubation, for ripening, so our outcomes become over-scrutinized and found wanting.

The need for continuous reflection, reaffirmation, and discernment never ceases, yet our heavily structured daily lives don't easily allow for intentional reflection, praxis, and spiritual development. We can stay on "spiritual autopilot" for quite some time, perhaps drawing upon our reservoir of faith built up along the way. But at some point, for most of us, the well runs dry and our spirit will send out a distress call from deep within for renewal and reanimation. Reaching only for our familiar spiritual habits may not fill the hole, and this moment of restlessness and searching may be the critical tipping point, embarking us on a quest for new ways of engaging our spiritual growth.

PRAYER AS PATH TO SPIRITUAL GROWTH
AND RENEWAL

We could consider spiritual disciplines as "variations on a theme" of deepening our relationship with God. The superhighway for this deepening relationship is prayer. If we use Jesus as our template for this relating with God, we come to see that Jesus' entire life with God was a form of enacted prayer, prayer-in-action. Everything Jesus did was grounded in that relationship. Like any relationship it was not static. Jesus, in his full humanity, experienced the full gamut: temptation, growth, intimacy, wilderness, puzzlement, separateness, joy, and oneness. Yet, in all these life phases, he sought to remain in the orbit of God's intentions.

St Paul deepens this theme of prayer as relationship with God in his guidance for us to "pray without ceasing"; he exhorts us to continuously seek to be grounded in our relationship with the Holy (I Thess 5:16–18). What then are the potential core perspectives and practices that could be considered foundational disciplines for spiritual life? There are reliable, proven-over-time core practices that Christians have utilized that have helped us grow in our relationship with God, with our wider world, and of course with ourselves. We could call these the prayer pathways to God, and in varying degrees and perhaps with different emphases, we would do well to engage the gifts and disciplines we find there.

The Jewish theologian Abraham Joshua Heschel also sees our entire lives being framed by prayer, what he calls the "secret stillness that precedes our birth and succeeds our death."[4] The stillness of God is the ever-present reality of God within us. Listening to that silence, that mystery, is our lifelong task, yet according to Heschel, we so easily seem to stay at the edges of that mystery and ignore it. To be living outside that mystery describes our lostness, our restlessness, our longing. Prayer, then, is the gift, and becomes the means that opens us up to that Presence. For Heschel, "to pray is to take notice of the wonder, to regain a sense of the mystery that animates all being."[5] Thus understood, prayer in this mode reveals itself more as a way of being, rather than a set of precepts or prescriptions. The spiritual director Tilden Edwards echoes these assumptions and believes that cultivating prayer as "presence with the Sacred" touches our deepest problem, namely, our tendency to forget our connection with God. Yet, the good news is that our deepest problem

4. Heschel, "The Sigh," 9.
5. Heschel, "The Sigh," 10.

is matched by our deepest hope, that we can always find a way to that innermost center of our being in God. Prayer, then, in all its manifold forms is that "bridge to Home."[6]

To sharpen our understandings of prayer as linked to the ground of our being, we can identify four distinct pathways for spiritual development. These paths involve the spiritual disciplines of: (1) Contemplation (listening), (2) Seeing, (3) Relating, and (4) Discerning. As distinct as these pathways are, what they have in common provides a template for grounding us in God's life with us.

Prayer as Contemplation/Listening

Prayer with words. Most of us were formed in a prayer environment where public verbal prayer was taught and practiced. Perhaps many of us learned familiar prayers as a child (most likely before meals or at bedtime). Learning these familiar prayers was encouraged, and once memorized remained a reservoir of comfort and meaning. The 23rd Psalm or the Lord's Prayer, for example, have retained their familiarity and constitute a central liturgical structure for all Christians, as well as a resource for personal praxis.

Monastic traditions have also had prayer as a core element in which structured verbal prayers are offered in the form of the Daily Office; a central element is praying the Psalms, for example. Over the centuries many variations of verbal prayer have emerged, some falling into disuse, only to be picked up in subsequent generations. In 2015 a rare medieval manuscript was discovered at the Liesborn Abbey in Germany, which included the practice of the prayer wheel; this is an extensive handbook which utilizes a seven-day structure of prayer arranged in a circle with God at the center. The Lord's Prayer and the Beatitudes serve as the spokes of the wheel, and these interwoven elements provide a step-by-step, seven-day structure as a "prayer of homecoming," again suggesting one continuous round of "prayer without ceasing."[7] This prayer wheel is a labyrinth with words, and points to the rich variations our medieval Christian ancestors were using to unlock the mysteries of these varied paths to prayer.

---

6. Edwards, *Living in Presence*, 11.

7. Dodd et al., *Prayer Wheel*.

There are many other verbal paths to prayer we could name, such as prayers of intercession, petition, thanksgiving, and praise. Our voices raised in song or chant all give utterance to the sense of the Holy in praise and devotion. When we sing "Bless the Lord, O my soul: and all that is within me bless his Holy name," we praise the Source of our very being. Our joy and praise almost demand vocalization: "Yes, this is who we know you to be" (Psalm 103:1)! These promptings, whether through communal worship or private affirmation could be considered a form of "active prayer" where we find articulation through asking, seeking, thanking, and praising.[8] Yet many of us experience a limitation when we rely too heavily, or even exclusively, on words or verbalization as our primary, or even singular mode of communication with God.

The spiritual writer Cynthia Bourgeault puts her finger on this limitation as she describes this common approach to God as prayer in which *we* do all the talking. Her early life experience in a Quaker school alerted her to the possibility that prayer might ultimately need to be more a matter of *listening to* rather than *talking to* God. [9]

Prayer as Listening through Contemplation

In shifting our focus to prayer in the form of contemplative listening, we are beginning to attend to the inner chambers of our hearts. In listening through contemplation we seek to create space for God in the deeper inner workings of our souls. In so doing we follow the precept of the Psalmist: "Be still and know that I am God" (Psalm 46:10). The ever-increasing intensity of modern life can generate drivenness in our life-agendas; we are pushed along by our planning, calculating, and thinking. Listening for the presence of God can be easily crowded out. Always forging ahead to the next important thing can easily lead to loss of intimacy with God. Our connection to silence becomes lost, and perhaps more ominously, we may find it supremely difficult to stop the treadmill of our lives and the persistent noise in our heads.

To begin to enter into prayer in the form of silence requires that we have an awareness of its forms. Cynthia Bourgeault provides helpful clarity when she makes a distinction between "free silence" and "intentional

8. Faricy, *Prayer*, 5.

9. Bourgeault, *Centering Prayer*, 4.

silence."[10] Free silence involves a quiet attending to the flow of our inner life in the form of non-clinging observation. In free silence we attend to what appears in our awareness, including our thoughts and feelings. But we must do so non-judgmentally. Our ordinary awareness is full of the chatter in our heads—what Buddhists call the "monkey mind"—but this is not what true listening entails. A grounded "free silence" is a form of listening in which we learn to simply observe, without grasping, clinging, or manipulating any thought or feeling. In contemporary terms it could be called mindfulness, and through this discipline of non-clinging or fixing, a first form of stillness emerges.

Intentional silence, however, is another deeper layer of silence, in which we deliberately attempt to quiet the mind. A classic form of this discipline from a Christian perspective is found in centering prayer, reintroduced to the Christian community by Thomas Keating.[11] This mode of prayer as centering is an active process of seeking distance from one's attachments to the "small self," or ego-based "false self," in contrast to the deeper and more authentic essential self or "real" self, to use Keating's terms. This deeper layer provides impetus to our journey to the center of our being, what Keating calls our divine awareness, or divine indwelling. This process is wonderfully biblically described through the scriptural analogy of the "vine and the branches" (John 15:5). Divine indwelling is not a static, frozen state. It is a form of mutual engagement. If we understand God to be our gardener in the vineyard, this includes the pruning action of God, which deepens our capacity for love. To affirm mutual indwelling does not mean that we are divine, but as we grow, we are called more and more into the life pattern of Christ-likeness.

The Gospel story of Mary and Martha illustrates these two different ways of cultivating presence with the Sacred. As we recall from the story, Martha is fully engaged in the work of preparation for dinner, while Mary is already sitting in direct presence with Jesus in full attunement with him (Luke 10:38–41). Mary is fussing about, doing something vital and important, but she feels left out and insignificant. She feels unappreciated and empty in comparison with the closeness that Mary and Jesus are enjoying.

At first glance we might be tempted to jump to the conclusion that Mary takes the "good" path and Martha the "bad." We should resist

10. Bourgeault, *Centering Prayer*, 10.

11. Keating, *Invitation to Love*, 1–4, 144–148; and Keating, *Open Mind, Open Heart.*

that interpretation and not assume that spiritual vitality is only found in Mary's quiet contemplation, and that Martha's "doing" is inherently second-rate. We all have both an inner Mary and an outer Martha, and our spiritual challenge emerges when we are out of alignment, with these two selves operating at cross purposes. Reconciling and harmonizing the inner and outer facets of our lives should be one of our key spiritual objectives. Reconciling our outer Martha with our inner Mary allows for a vital cohesion between our head, heart, and hands.

Prayer as Pondering

The Mary and Martha relationship offers us a useful analogy to our potential splits between head and heart (Mary) and hands (Martha). It also lets us consider a third mode of listening which we could call "pondering." This model of contemplation as pondering is embodied most dramatically in Jesus's mother, Mary. Mary "pondered all these things in her heart" (Luke 2:19). Mary's pondering began with her pregnancy, and surely continued throughout her life. First there was the experience of puzzlement and devotion around Jesus' birth. The contemplation extended through her encounters with the adolescent Jesus in the Temple, to the wedding at Cana, and the overwhelming experience at the foot of the Cross, as she watches her son die.

This model of pondering represents a deep commitment to holding the tension(s) of life. Ron Rohlheiser, in his book *Sacred Fire*, helps unpack the deep wisdom embedded in pondering. He notes that pondering must not be understood in the Greek philosophical sense of intellectual analysis and disputation, but in the Hebraic sense of being able to hold, carry, and transform tension "so as not to give it back in kind, knowing that whatever energies we do not transform, we will transmit." [12]

The cross represents the rawest of alienations, a splitting open of the world at its heart. Mary, standing at the foot of the cross, can be considered an exemplar of faith that points to pondering as a deep form of participation. Mary can model for us a call to faithfulness to the inevitable tensions of our existence. Our world is full of alienations and the absence of harmony in ourselves and in the world around us. Jesus' death on the cross, and the pondering it elicits in Mary, invites us to our own immersion in alienation and rupture. Rohlheiser helpfully offers a theological

---

12. Rohlheiser, *Sacred Fire*, 147.

grounding for this awareness with Jesus as the sacrificial lamb that "takes away the sin of the world" (John 1: 29). This does not turn Jesus into some sort of divine magic-maker; there is a deep spiritual truth in the lamb metaphor. Jesus as the Lamb is one that is willing to take in the hatred, tension, and sin of the community by absorbing it, transforming it, and detoxifying it, and thereby giving the pain back with love.[13]

Mary, and those present with her at the cross, are the first witnesses of that power through silent pondering. We too are now called into that mode of being. In our modern lives we don't use sacrificial lambs or scapegoats in a physical sense, but we are all familiar with the patterns of displacement when we and our communities want to unload our pain, distress, anger and rage at another. The silent listening of pondering can give us the power to linger a bit longer in the tension, where the Spirit joins us in solidarity with truth, thus drawing us ever closer to the wounded, yet strength-bringing heart of God.

To be able to stand in the tension a little longer is the spiritual resource that silent pondering provides. There is nothing passive about such silent pondering; rather, it provides a state of engagement with the raw existential question(s) of our own personal lives, and the environments we inhabit. The purpose of pondering, therefore, is not an escape or a resolution, but a commitment to spiritual deepening and steadfastness.

Prayer as Seeing

In his book, *The Naked Now: Learning to See as the Mystics See*, Richard Rohr describes three ways of seeing a sunset.[14] His sunset metaphor describes three persons in their different modes of seeing. The first person enjoys the scene through their senses; they have little regard for anything beyond what they see with their physical eyes. The second person enjoys all that the first person sees, and appreciates the beauty also, but is drawn to explain the science behind what they see. Their powers of reason and analysis make their viewing even better. A third person also sees the sunset, and enjoys all that the first and second persons do, but in addition to seeing and explaining, this third person enters into savoring and awe. In seeing with this third eye, they see the underlying mystery and coherence that connects them with all that is. This third eye is seeing the unity in all

---

13. Rohlheiser, *Sacred Fire*, 156.
14. Rohr, *Naked Now*, 27.

things. We could represent these three modes of seeing as: (1) Eye of flesh (seeing with the senses); (2) Eye of reason (analysis, reflection, meditation), and (3) Eye of understanding (contemplation).[15]

Shifting to a deeper, richer mode of seeing requires a different set of perceptions and attitudes than we normally work with. Beyond simply needing to relinquish some limiting inherited habits or assumptions, it may call for a transformation of consciousness. It may require a de-centering of sorts, not a rejection of any of the three eyes of seeing just described, but more a shift into imitating God's mode of being. This is seeing through God's eyes; seeing "God in all things." One of its hall-marks is humility, which includes an attitude of nonattachment to one's own rightness or treasured presuppositions. Richard Rohr's word for this mode of prayer is "resonance."[16] Prayer is the tuning fork that invites you to vibrate on a different frequency. Here, our own agendas recede, and we await guidance from another. From Rohr's point of view, it is not so much something we are doing, but something that begins to happen to us. We have now moved beyond supplication, beyond prayer that seeks to change God's mind. Through contemplative listening we find *the self we are* being changed.

Seeing Beyond Spiritual Blind Spots

Yet, our capacity for seeing with our spiritual lenses seems to have a flaw in it, according to many respected spiritual guides. These spiritual wisdom voices, including luminaries such as Thomas Merton, Tilden Edwards, Henri Nouwen, Margaret Silf, Carl McColman, and Martin Laird, speak of the veil of separation between ourselves and God. In different ways they speak of this factor in our human nature as a "house divided," a stubborn alienation at the heart of our identities. Our Christian theological inheritance has heavily reinforced this perspective through notions of the fall, sin and alienation, and rebellion. Most contemporary spiritual writers understand this tension between our true self/false self as a duality, and as a structural challenge to unified selfhood. It's interesting that modern psychology has reinforced this picture of humanity as a house divided through its own reliance on the false self /true self duality; we see

15. Rohr, *Naked Now*, 28.
16. Rohr, *Naked Now*, 101.

this in the work of depth psychologists such as D.W. Winnicott and Carl Jung (his idea of the Shadow), for example.

The challenge this poses for spiritual life and our growth in wholeness is that we tend to reenact the split of head/heart/hands, where the seemingly forever messy self never completely arrives at home. We can appreciate the work of Richard Rohr, and many others, in their efforts to transcend such fractured thinking.[17] This is not to say that we ever permanently move beyond the risk of falling into unhappy selfhood and a less centered, less loving version of ourselves. Richard Rohr offers another set of terms to consider beyond true self/false self; he suggests the idea of "big self" vs. "small self" as an alternative.[18] Rohr's alternative suggestion with this shift is not simply an adjustment in tone, but a recognition that we operate along a continuum of seeing and not seeing, listening and not listening, knowing and not knowing, belief and unbelief. This shift in perspective brings a necessary humility into our quest for spiritual growth. Our growth, however well it develops, will retain its limitations, inevitable imperfections, perhaps dark nights of the soul, even as we grow in increments toward wholeness.

By way of analogy, even when seeing with our physical eyes we may not automatically see with 20/20 vision. The shimmering desert sun generates mirages, and twilight darkness mimics ominous figures among the trees; our physical eyes cannot be automatically assumed to bring clear and reliable data to our brains. Surely seeing with our inner eyes requires similar discernment, given our potential for distortion. Seeing with our inner eyes means seeing as Jesus sees, who sees the divine light in everyone, and perhaps most noteworthy, truly sees those who live on the margins of society: the sinners, the lepers, the lame, the outcasts. Moreover, their marginalization, their woundedness, may grant them an extra increment of spiritual seeing.

Richard Rohr goes so far as to say that if we want to see the Divine, we should look more for what we would rather *not see*. There, where we resist seeing, holds the key to how the Divine image is seeking to operate in us. That which we avoid or deflect may reveal not only our potential blind spots, but the place where our growth resides.[19] This is not intended to be an indictment of us, but an invitation to decentering our

17. Rohr, *Divine Dance*.

18. Rohr, *Naked Now*, 102.

19. Rohr, *Divine Dance*, 66.

ego-based "small self" and its limiting vantage point. This shift in seeing takes us beyond the mirror and only seeing ourselves to a window onto the Sacred. This is the center of Jesus' prayer life: a consistent orientation of his life compass toward God's heart.

Centering Prayer as Support for Inner Seeing

Among the perspectives that can support prayer as "seeing," our spiritual growth can be enhanced by developing an "inner observer." An inner observer is certainly not an inner critic; this is not about obsessive, ego-based analyzing of our thoughts, feelings, and affects. Cynthia Bourgeault captures this alternative way of seeing beautifully when she names a shift in our center of gravity from our limited ego-based preoccupations to a deeper place where *we* are seen from the perspective of God's own self.[20]

The distinctive element which supports this shift in "inner observer" prayer is its non-clinging character. It does not grab what it sees, feels, or hears, but maintains a neutrality to what it sees. From this place we are not simply "observing the observer," as in standard meditation practices, but engaging the "attention of the heart," in which the Spirit "watches through us."[21] Beyond simply not doing anything in this mode of prayer, we open ourselves up to the Spirit-center of our being. In so doing we are being witnessed by the Spirit. Being watched by the Spirit is a form of being carried by the Spirit, in all times and places, and even when we sleep; we live always in Presence.

So what is the point to prayer as "being seen" with God's eyes? Its core spiritual objective is to live more freely and fully in the complex intersections of our lives, where our inner and outer selves, our so-called lower and higher selves intersect, and from that place sacred presence grounds and guides us. Its greatest gift is inner freedom, an "entry into the joy of your master" (Matt 25:21). It lets us live without a why, in abandonment to Providence. In Cynthia Bourgeault's words:

> Seeing creates a new relationship with yourself, and eventually that new relationship will bear fruit in the power to do. But doing is never the point. Every seeing, no matter how calamitous

20. Bourgeault, *Centering Prayer*, 127.

21. Bourgeault, *Centering Prayer*, 130.

to the ego, is an enhancement of being, a strengthening of the connection of the worlds within you.[22]

Prayer as Relating

Our lives are forged in relationship. Being "in relationship" suggests we are forever invited to be truly connected to ourselves, to one another, and to God. The simplest way to track these spiritual growth movements of self, other, and God, is to ask ourselves the question: "What do I love?" The spiritual author, Brian McLaren, in his book on spiritual formation, describes our aliveness as a moving of the Spirit of God in and toward love.[23] Since we are created in the image and likeness of God, this pattern of love animates all our love yearnings toward self, other, and God.

Richard Rohr echoes this awareness: we all have this inherent inner aliveness that draws us forward in our yearnings and desires, whether fulfilled or not. We live in that "flow of love" which includes all that is, whether we want to call it God, ground of being, consciousness, or love. According to Rohr, this dynamism is the creative force of the universe, a flowing river in which we swim whether we are enjoying it or not[24] (see also James 1:17). It represents our life force, and through our spiritual awareness it gives us the capacity to recognize and to see how our "flow" is moving in us right now. It can appear perhaps as a negative, defensive flow that closes us up, or on the other hand as a life-enhancing energy that animates and confirms our journey. Discerning these different life energies is a key spiritual capacity, and our prayer life can serve as a guide to that awareness. Our everyday experiences thus become the necessary raw material for teaching and guiding us how to pray, to love, and to serve.

Being forged by relationships also means we are never self-contained or sustained only within our own skin. Our spiritual health needs authentic spiritual mirroring that reflects who we truly are back to us, truthfully, honestly, as we really are. Our personhood is a forever construct, through the process of truth-seeking and authentic mirroring. This process never ceases, and our life in the form of relatedness is a central vehicle for consistently needing the image of God reflected back

22. Bourgeault, *Centering Prayer*, 132.
23. McLaren, *We Make the Road*, 202.
24. Rohr, *Divine Dance*, 87.

to us, as St Paul so clearly articulates: "And we, with our unveiled faces reflecting like mirrors the brightness of the Lord, all grow brighter as we are turned into the image that we reflect; this is the work of the Lord who is Spirit" (2 Cor 3:18).

Evelyn Underhill specifically sees this ongoing work of spiritual transformation in us working through our personalities. Through prayer, she says, we abide in "God's atmosphere," which draws us into ever greater alignment with God's creative will for us.[25] Such growth is visible through growing harmony between the inner and the outer orbits of our lives where external actions and inner reflection align. Head, heart, and hands inform and ground both attitude and action.

Spiritual writer and psychologist David Benner adds the additional element that our personalities shape our identities, which are thus revealed in our attachments. Just as our history of loving reveals where our hearts reside, our identities are forged by what we most identify with.[26] Here again, the theme of small self/large self resurfaces as a vital growth measure through the discipline of honest self-reflection. This requires a conscious willingness to name and claim our potential for distortion and self-deception. Being willing to see the truth of ourselves toward oneself, others, and God, takes courage, humility, and often hard-to-achieve honesty. Honest transparency toward self, other, and God needs these distinct commitments.

Brian McLaren adds his voice to this affirmation; he contends that whenever God's Spirit is at work in the world it draws persons more deeply into love: loving self, loving neighbor, and loving God.[27] Our capacity for love is measured by our relationships and the Spirit of God is at our disposal to assist us in our potential for authentic loving. Yet our capacity for loving is not so automatic or straightforward. Every one of our "love domains"—self, other, and God—has its own particular challenges and growth requirements. If we were asked to choose among loving God, loving others, and loving ourselves, many would likely think that loving ourselves would be the easiest of the three. Since we inhabit our own interiority, and live in our own skin, we should be able to be at home with ourselves. Yet it seems quite difficult to be one with oneself, to live graciously and lovingly toward ourselves. We find a clue to this difficulty

25. Underhill, *Concerning Inner Life*, 137.

26. Benner, *Spirituality and Awakening Self*, 60.

27. McClaren, *We Make the Road*, 211.

in the nature of our development, which reveals that we are not built up by ourselves, but by the presence and participation of others who mirror us and reflect ourselves back to us, for better or worse.

The challenge of being in relationship with ourselves and of our formation as persons and as spiritual beings is well illustrated in the work of Henri Nouwen. Here is a man of great spiritual depth and, even more important, someone who is a supremely honest reporter of his inner life, including his struggle with himself, his interpersonal world, and with God. His work as a prolific writer and spiritual guide—work revered long after his death—reveals a person who bares his soul for our benefit. His transparency can serve as a model for us of self-honesty in the journey toward greater loving.

Nouwen struggled all his life with clinical depression, struggled with his sexuality, struggled with clericalism, and struggled with God.[28] Nouwen's yearning for intimacy was the common thread through all these challenges, but his persistence in facing them and the spiritual depth it awakened in him gives us a clue to our own spiritual growth invitations.[29] Nouwen's relationship to his woundedness was the fuel for his spiritual growth. Seeking to understand and accept his own brokenness became his gift to the world, and this path to wholeness suggests that our paths might need their own equivalent version of truth-seeking.

The necessary ingredients for this path are the raw materials of our life. Coming to own our relational and spiritual autobiographies is the fuel for our growth, especially the tensions, contradictions, and yearnings that we all encounter. These narratives of ours, fully owned, become the authentic spiritual ground under our feet. What Nouwen discovered is that God participates in our lives at this deeper level, by helping us to de-center the narrow, petty, self-justified, self-righteous "small self" versions of ourselves, and embrace the expansive "large self" sacred core of our being:

> Because when we do not stay in touch with that center of our spiritual life called prayer, we lose touch with all that grows from it. We do not enter into the inner field of tension where the movement from illusion to prayer takes place, our solitude and our hospitality easily lose their depth.[30]

28. Higgins & Burns, *Genius Born of Anguish*, 42.

29. See Higgins & Burns, *Genius Born of Anguish*, 50. See also, Nouwen, *Reaching Out;* Nouwen, *Way of the Heart.*

30. Nouwen, *Reaching Out*, 115.

We should note that any of our "big three" relational environments—self, other, and God—are equally capable of experiencing disintegration, or on the other hand, being directed toward our wholeness. For most of us there is likely a flashpoint in which one or the other relational gap and its distress first gets our attention. Again, our restlessness, our discontentedness, our stressors will likely be a first signal that something is not aligned. Trusting that signal is vital for our subsequent growth. Since our personhood is interconnected, distress in one dimension will carry into another, whether self, other, or God-alienation. Here too the presence of the Sacred can nudge and guide. God eternally remains our potential partner. In this partnership, perhaps God is experienced as lure, or as a great void, sometimes in persistent restlessness, or perhaps an overwhelming cry from the heart.

Prayer as Discernment

In coming to understand prayer as a core expression of our seeking and maintaining a relationship with God we have arrived at discernment as a "capstone discipline," that builds on all the others and integrates them, especially around the guidance that our lives need. Joseph Tetlow SJ, in his book *Always Discerning*, has a chapter called, "Every Mature Disciple Discerns All Day Long"; in this way he underscores the centrality of seeking discernment in all things and at all times.[31] Discernment is also a key gospel commitment addressing our need to be guided: "When the Spirit of truth comes, he will guide you into the truth" (John 16:13); or "Test the spirits to see whether they are from God," (John 4:1); or "For all who are being led by the Spirit of God, are children of God" (Rom 8:14).

This suggests that discernment is not a secondary, situational moment of crisis where a difficult choice is pressing in on us, although it could certainly come in that form; more significantly, it speaks of a life-orientation where our path(s) are affirmed and confirmed. The work of John Neafsey on personal vocation can be very helpful here. He describes discernment as "the inner compass of the heart."[32] His insight takes us beyond the traditional understanding of discernment as decision-making in various life situations. What he refers to is more about the process

---

31. Tetlow, *Always Discerning*, 17–20.
32. Neafsey, *Sacred Voice*, 36.

of differentiation, of finding our spiritual center among the clamor of all the competing voices that echo in our minds.

Discernment looks deeper; it attunes to the "still small voice" of God in us, to the voice that Elijah came to discern, in contrast to the loud and flashy confirmations we often seek (I Kings 19:11). What discernment is really about is cultivation of a spiritual vision, of a spiritual consciousness. It is a way of finding God more fully in ourselves and in the world.

We can begin to make useful distinctions among types of discernment. Joseph Tetlow uses the term "ordinary discernment," or "moral discernment," as a first layer of discernment in which our moral compass is utilized for keeping the precepts and commandments of a good life, but often with little personal ownership.[33] Generally, this layer of discernment does not go very deep and is more akin to compliance with social and religious norms.

This first form of discernment nevertheless allows us to choose, shape, and claim who we might be. It is discernment that helps us move along the many pathways of growth, and this movement is grounded in God as our Creator. The creator God permeates all things. We are made in the image of God, however faintly it might register in us. God delights in us all the time, and lovingly holds us in God's image, whether we can perceive it or not.[34] This image is acting on us all the time, just as gravity always holds us in place. Recognizing God as a "force" holding us up, is a foundational assumption to be sure, but it is more than simply some impersonal factor like fate or destiny; it is more like the gift of God's freedom for us "to be," allowing us to choose and shape who we might be. It is discernment that helps us grow, to say yes or no, and is the basis for our freedom.

Discernment as Inner Compass

To name discernment as the core task for developing our inner compass, directs our attention to the necessary process of getting oriented to who and what we are, and thus finding direction. It requires a commitment to listen to the inner stirrings of our hearts, rather than to our superficial "likes and dislikes"; we need to attend to the deeper tugs and emotional currents that move us. It includes all the attractions and repulsions, and

33. Tetlow, *Always Discerning*, 36.
34. Tetlow, *Always Discerning*, 63.

all the desires and resistances, that are present in the affective dimension of our lives. For many of us, our socialization has made us suspicious of feelings, and we tend to believe that our rational minds are superior to affect, and perhaps even that our feelings cannot be trusted.

We might be surprised to discover that a model developed 500 years ago by St Ignatius of Loyola can provide us a valuable corrective on this perspective. The insights of St Ignatius have as their very purpose a sharpening of our awareness within the processes of discernment. His model, called *The Examen* (examination of conscience/consciousness), is a resource for prayer that focuses on our inner experiences of *Consolation* and *Desolation* as guideposts of God's presence and guidance in our lives.[35]

St Ignatius understood that we as human beings move along the continuum of closeness or distance from God, and that movement can be experienced and "discerned" through all our inner currents of awareness, including our feelings, as well as our experiences of despair or delight. Our feelings of consolation, of peace and harmony, surface when we are aligned and in congruence with God's intentions. We experience these states of mind in the form of a "felt rightness." Our feelings of desolation, of inner distress and darkness, can register through our discontents and restless agitation. The basis for trusting these movements is our fundamental interconnectedness of mind, body, and spirit in ourselves and our personal interconnectedness and social orbits.

At this our deepest level, God's presence touches our core selves and can be discerned there. This movement toward the center of our being or away from our center, can be sensed and perceived, including our feelings, moods, desires, and resistances. They reveal how we are in relationship at the deeper hidden layers of ourselves. These stirrings are not provided for the purpose of judgment, but for the purpose of awareness, which is the true intention of all discernment.

Discernment of Spirits

Our modern psychological understandings do not consider the presence of "good" or "evil" spirits as determinative for our lives. We generally don't imagine ourselves to be invaded by invisible spirits that are directed

---

35. Manney, *Simple Life-Changing Prayer*, 1–3, 71–81. See also Thibodeaux, *Reimagining Ignatian Examen*.

or controlled by a dark spiritual force. We can, however, understand repetitive patterns in our lives that take us either in healthy or unhealthy directions, even self-destructive ones, with obvious significant implications for our emotional and spiritual health.

John Neafsey offers helpful contemporary language for such spirit orientations—namely, the difference between "ego-centered" and "God-centered" inclinations.[36] Our lopsided, driven, ego-bound inclinations can be self-serving and self-protective in ways that close us off from wholeness and our authentic selves. These patterns of self-gratification and the power moves that accompany them, over time, close off healthy paths of authentic loving. Discernment sheds light on these desires and reveals their true intentions, thus empowering us to do the loving things that God-centeredness awakens and prompts in us.

A good spirit awakens "love, joy, peace, patience, kindness, goodness, faithfulness, gentleness, and self-control" (Gal 5:22). We can have confidence in these states of being, especially when things get tough, because the consolations of Spirit are not manufactured or artificially given through expediency or "good luck." In contrast, desolation is the experience of being stuck in dread, hopelessness, and futility. A "good" spirit is open, transparent, and inviting. An "oppressive" spirit fosters animosity and looks to power-over to solve its problems.

Social Discernment

It is critical to note that discernment is not simply a matter of personal self-ownership or personal equanimity. Our social world in all its complexity is also in great need of discernment. To develop an eye toward the critical cultural questions of the day invites us to discern and critique our social world and our responsibilities toward it. Discernment looks to the social structures and oppression that any society contains: gross injustices and deeply embedded alienations that are clustered around cultural "-isms" such as racism, sexism, and classism.

It seems every society contains patterns of alienation in which those that are labeled "different," whether because of their ethnicity, gender, social class, or relational or neurological diversity, are marginalized. These "otherings" impose suffering through the enforced limitations of "difference" upon its members, and its attendant discriminations and

36. Neafsey, *Sacred Voice is Calling*, 41.

alienations. Ecological degradation could be added to this sad litany and surely should disturb any conscious Christian, as God's earth is despoiled and even destroyed, and exists as a further source of communal wounding. Economic exploitation of the poor, the immigrant rejected as "the other," all cry out for justice and the need to see the structural sin that keep it so.

John Neafsey offers us a three-step methodology for awakening in our social/communal discernment: (1) observe, (2) judge, (3) act.[37] These steps involve careful looking and listening along the lines of prayer awareness we have already considered, but now we must add the ingredient of perceiving the particular situation we are seeing. It involves being able to recognize that "something is wrong." This means not only sharpening the focus, but also *acting* upon the awareness, in light of our awakened consciousness.

Where discernment becomes especially challenging is when we become aware of our own social location in our world and the burden that this may place upon us.[38] We may have been unwittingly participating and benefiting from the privileges of our position in the society, and this may hold us back from solidarity. It takes discernment to accept a "greater burden" of social responsibility if our social position has granted us these automatic privileges. This is the prophetic invitation growing from discernment; it takes us toward a fuller vocational discernment as a form of Spirit-groundedness in which love of God moves us toward love of neighbor.

SUMMARY

Our spiritual lives flourish when centered in prayer. Our ever-changing lives need living water, and intentional spiritual practices can give access to that water. The spiritual disciplines of contemplation/listening, seeing, relating, and discernment together form a conduit for that water, perhaps not in equal measure all the time, but taken together they make for a reliable pathway to deepen the immersion of our lives in God. When we avail ourselves of these resources our engagement with life becomes centered and unified. Our head, heart, and hands when unified in this way find the nourishment needed for sustained loving in our complex worlds.

37. Neafsey, *Sacred Voice is Calling*, 47.
38. Neafsey, *Sacred Voice is Calling*, 49

6

Spiritual Practices
Supporting Formation

In using just ten prompt cards, we could not possibly cover all the important spiritual practices in our Christian heritage. Here we extend the conversation around practices that support spiritual formation. We contend that practicing Presence is the key. Prayer is our conduit to the Sacred. All the many modes of prayer can be considered as potential doorways to our engagement with the divine. Given the uniqueness of our personhood and God's willingness to say "yes" to the particular form(s) we embody, it follows that God's imprint upon us is present in a wide range of possibilities. Most of us live with a mixture of consciousness and unconsciousness about God's presence around us. Our innate personalities, our histories and our life contexts, our trials and tribulations, joys and overcomings all impinge upon our capacity and receptivity for the sacred signals that the Holy provides.

Given all this variability and our life contingencies, we may well be thrown into life situations where sacred signals get drowned out, are unrecognized, or neglected. But when the sacred invitation comes, it must be welcomed in, appropriated and worked with, to receive its full effects. Among the assumptions that skew our expectations of Sacred Presence are our own norms concerning what such Presence means. Some of us want effects that are immediate and tangible, no questions asked. We may want "signs and wonders," or we might want things working out for our benefit as confirmations of God's blessings.

Most of us likely don't think of God as our own private heavenly vending machine, dispensing quick resolutions or advice. God does not violate our freedom even if we might want to influence God in our favor. Regardless of where we might stand with regard to God's direct involvement, we would do well to adhere to St Paul's reminder that we inevitably "see through a glass darkly" (I Cor 13:12). Of course, there are life moments, often crisis-driven, that we perceive as direct signals from God for this or that change of path. St Paul's Damascus Road conversion would be of that type.

Most of the time, however, our capacity for presence of the Sacred is faint and subtle, yet discernible. Jesus' prayer "not my will but your will be done" is instructive here (Luke 22:42). Of all the possible ways we might approach God, perhaps the most important stance is one of openness and receptivity. We also need a desire to cultivate our trust toward God without additional requirements of validation or reinforcement.

Perhaps the most important insight that we might gain from a trust trajectory is living "without a why." Our lives inevitably move along the continuum of felt Presence and Absence. Growth in trust lets us hold that tension in God's mercy and grace, not dependent on immediate signals or confirmations. Yet, at the same time, there are spiritual commitments that strengthen our pathways and access to the Sacred—namely, the well-trod disciplines that support our trust capacity. There are practices that support Presence. In our practices, we need to eschew any demand on God or need for overt confirmations. These practices, governed by faithfulness to the quest, are not dependent on its results; they are habits of the heart that cultivate trust.

EMBODIED PRAYER(S)

Our prayer practices should be understood as fully embodied activities. We are not compartmentalized entities, disembodied creatures, but unified beings where all aspects of our selves affect the others. Our lives in prayer should reflect this reality, and our bodies also are necessarily included in our practices. Everything from our body postures to our body movements can provide alignment with the Sacred. So much of the Presence we seek depends on our intentions, and what we do spiritually can also be reflected in our physical actions and behaviors. Postures that contribute to attentiveness without distraction or discomfort, such as sitting or kneeling, can allow for extended immersion in God's presence as mediated by our bodies.

Prayer and Breathing

But perhaps the most basic yet fundamental mode of embodied prayer is to focus on our breathing. Scripture declares that God breathed life into us through God's Holy Spirit (Gen 2:7). God's gift of breath in us is a symbolic declaration of God's Spirit as connected to our spirit. Every moment of breath reveals the eternal quality of this movement, in and out, always drawing us in to ourselves and returning outward, a "literal interdependence with life," as Tilden Edwards describes it.[1]

Our breath is intimately tied to our embodied selves and through attention to our breathing we are given reliable internal data on our state of being. The slowing down or speeding up of our breathing reveals either the tension or calmness of our minds. Our rapid shallow breathing suggests drivenness; it's a signal of anxiety that invites our attention. Deep slow breathing brings relief; it creates room for other states of mind in which we can become more present to ourselves as well as the Sacred within us. We can see this shift reductively, in purely mechanical terms, as "nothing more" than an apparatus doing its thing. Yet with awareness, even the sheer regularity of our breathing becomes an invitation to fuller awareness and thus a doorway into Presence.

Prayer as Movement

Next to breathing, walking is probably our second-most commonly embodied natural activity. Here again, we might dismiss it as a purely automatic activity, unworthy of consideration as a spiritual praxis. We can easily minimize walking as a spiritual activity and view it simply as having the purpose of getting from one place to another. We might do better, however, to recall St Paul's injunction when he suggests: "If we live by the Spirit, let us also 'walk' by the Spirit" (Gal 5:25). We should not understand this as simple literalism. We can extend Paul's meaning and embrace the notion that Grace accompanies our walking. When in prayer we invoke the kingdom of God to be realized "on earth as it is in heaven" (Matt 6:10), it requires step-by-step walking in the light of God.

1. Edwards, *Living in Presence*, 21.

Walking with God's intentions in mind draws our walking toward the reverence which should accompany all our paths, whether structured or unstructured, conscious or unconscious. The existentialist philosopher Søren Kierkegaard noted the following in a letter:

> Above all, do not lose your desire to walk; every day I walk myself into a state of well-being, and walk away from every illness; I have walked myself into my best thoughts, and I know of no thought so burdensome that one cannot walk away from it . . . If one just keeps on walking, everything will be all right.[2]

Beyond its wellness benefits, Kierkegaard notes that walking intentionally takes us into more centered, more "Spirit inspired" states of mind where clarity and discernment can flourish. Such a discipline and the consciousness that it awakens can become a conduit to hope.

The Buddhist scholar and teacher, Thich Nhat Hanh, formalizes such a commitment in the form of mindful walking as a way of deepening our connection with our body and to the earth.[3] The earth is our home and since God pronounced it as good, we too are called to respect the earth as sacred and to treat it with reverence. Intentional sacred walking lets us be here, now, with nature as God's canopy. Conscious walking makes room for pondering, even as we walk. But this is not simply an invitation to isolation—"me and Jesus in the garden alone"—although it may include such resonance; the more important factor is that it connects us to our common home on this earth as co-stewards who take responsibility to care for each other and the earth we share.

Any spiritually-aware and intentional walking can accentuate our spiritual alertness. Meditative walking brings renewal and restoration of mind, body, and spirit. Awareness of intention strengthens such praxis. With Kierkegaard's reminder in mind, God's Spirit not only grounds us in ourselves as we put one foot after the other; it contributes to our healing. Whether in joy or sorrow we can come home to ourselves in embodied, spiritually-aware walking. Our prayerful embodiment in walking with purpose could include many other modes of walking such as vigils, or peaceful marches for justice. Our immersion in nature through walking can have transformational potential in bringing body, mind, and spirit as well as head, heart, and hands into greater alignment.

2. From one of Kierkegaard's letters, 1847. Cited in Schmidt, *Walking with Stones*, 126.

3. Hanh, *Walking Meditation*.

Prayerful Embodiment in Sounds and Silence

Spiritual practices are surrounded by both sound and silence. We ascribe the "voice of God" to God's eternal desire to communicate with us in a vast array of vibrations that can have spiritual and sacred meanings. Throughout history religious persons have recognized that vibrations through sound have spiritual impact. Everything from drums to bells to musical instruments, to the sounds of nature, can assist in experiencing Presence. Chanting or singing adds another layer of vibration; a sound comes out of our own bodies (which may or may not be a word) with significant spiritual resonance. Such immersion through sound, and the sound waves that flow in and through us, are in continuity with the sounds of the universe, a universe that lifts its voice to its creator.

Our immersion in sacred sound through music has the capacity to transport us into the highest states of bliss and awe. Many of us likely have a favorite sacred song, hymn, or chorale that has the power to lift us into a spiritual synergy where the "veil" of separation melts, and we sense our continuity with the Sacred. Harmony, rhythm, and meaning merge into a joyful resonance that lifts us up and renews and heals.

Yet our lives are not only surrounded by blissful harmony; our world is also bombarded by sounds of dissonance that require our spiritual attention. The screams and shouts of violence and rage also land in our ears and require a spiritual reckoning. Closing our ears to the sounds of pain in our world is a spiritual bypass and a form of neglect. We do not have the power to bring harmony to all the dissonance we meet in our world, but we do have the presence of the Prince of Peace in our hearts, so that the sounds we admit can be sounds of peace.

Practicing presence through sound gives us the inner harmony that lets us absorb the dissonance. St Paul reminds us that "the whole creation groans in labor pains until now, and not only the creation . . . but we ourselves groan within ourselves . . . The Spirit also helps us in our weakness for we do not know how to pray as we should, but the Spirit intercedes for us with groanings too deep for words" (Rom 8:22–26). As St Paul affirms, even our unspoken groans invite us into the disciplines of prayer, into solidarity with the groans of our world. This mode of prayer is not a prayer of overt verbalized content, of fancy words, or even specific actions, but an openness to the Spirit that prays for the world "through" us. This solidarity through sound may include activity, but more importantly, it conveys an attitude, an attentiveness, that lets us set aside our personal agendas for a while, so that we can create a wider space to meet Presence.

A God-given ally we have in reaching such states of presence is silence. Among the qualities of silence is its stillness, calmness, and the hush that accompanies it. Silence is gentle and open and draws us in, yet we may be frightened of silence and fear that we might lose ourselves in it. Among the conditions that are required for silence is to set aside the insertion of our own agendas onto reality. Silence makes room for God even when our busy minds are clamoring for attention.

Tilden Edwards quite rightly reminds us that silence and sound are not separate realities; sound emerges out of silence as a "particular expression of the silence."[4] Sound and silence therefore inform one another. Silence is the space between the notes. Edwards goes on to suggest that all sound retains a quality of silence and that every sound has pure silence present at its center. To the extent that we emit "particular sustained sounds of God," we share that same spacious silent core.

A vital implication we can draw from these insights is that God can draw equally near to us through sound or silence. Our pathways to Presence therefore are equally available to us in our sounds and in our silences. This assumption does not require a metaphysical leap from us, but rather a recognition that God is the intimate subject of our lives, and the true core of our embodied selves.

Many persons find nature to be a helpful domain for practicing silence. Immersion events such as exploring fields, meadows, and woods facilitate the practice of silence since they offer a hush that invites the empty sacred space inside ourselves, ready to receive us. Forests and meadows also provide companions and sound partners such as birds and animals, with trees and rustling leaves also exuding their silent speech.[5] A critical step in receiving the sounds of the forest or natural environment is to receive the sounds with utter neutrality; we need to suppress the almost irresistible desire to jump into analysis or judgment. We are so wired for quick assessment and labeling that we lose our continuity with the sound in our desire to classify it. As an alternative, we need to practice remaining in the sound, not as a distraction, but as "an experience of expansive awareness."[6] For most of us, these disciplines of inviting si-

4. Edwards, *Living in Presence*, 35.

5. See also Chase, *Nature*; Sleeth, *Reinforcing Faith*.

6. Edwards, *Living in Presence*, 37.

lence must be practiced for them to become a reliable tool for practicing Presence.

Those immersed in the life of prayer have long known of the significant spiritual benefits associated with pilgrimage. It is to this practice that we now turn.

EMBODIED SPIRITUAL JOURNEYS

Pilgrimages

The metaphor of "journey" is a central theme in most any description of the spiritual life. This is so because it engages vital elements in our spiritual growth and formation. The image of "journeying" suggests that we are spiritual persons on the way, that our lives are active and changing, always moving, transforming, and seeking deepening. Such prayerful movement is not to be confused with mindless wandering. Spiritually grounded movement could be best described as any intentional movement toward our sacred center in God. Among the most ancient of spiritual practices that have been utilized over the ages for this purpose is the intentional journey we call pilgrimage.

The pastoral counselors and theologians, Jean and Wallace Clift, view pilgrimage as an archetypal journey with profound transformational potential.[7] The philosopher of religion, Charles Taylor, construes pilgrimage as a journey into a higher and deeper space, and a higher and deeper time.[8] What these thinkers suggest is that pilgrimage represents a specific spiritual practice that engages transcendence and immanence in more direct and immediate ways.

Intentional spiritual journeys can open us up to the eternal now, to timelessness, to transcendence, as an experiential and transformational event. Anthropologists and historians of religion have long recognized that all historical religions have incorporated pilgrimage into their practices.[9] The particular practices that pilgrims have utilized over the ages vary greatly, from devotional pilgrimages, to healing pilgrimages, to life-cycle ritualized pilgrimages, but what they all have in common are the

---

7. Clift & Clift, *Archetype of Pilgrimage*, 9.

8. Taylor, *Secular Age*, 96, 554.

9. Turner & Turner, *Image and Pilgrimage*, 1.

transformational yearnings of the participants.[10] As immersion events they incorporate mind, body, and soul, giving the sojourner more direct experiential access to the objects of spiritual desire, whether growth, healing, devotion, or renewal of purpose, or something else.

Pilgrimages are encompassing events for those who embark on them. They take planning, preparation, ritual, and physical preparation. For many pilgrims it is a once-in-a-lifetime event. Much of the spiritual power that pilgrimages provide is generated by the life questions that the pilgrim is living. The existential context of the pilgrim that awakens the desire to embark is often an experience of personal limit and boundary in the pilgrim's life. This can include a spiritual or physical crisis of some sort, perhaps some extended experience of suffering and loss.

For others, the prompting may be more about meaning-making. It may be that life has dried out, spiritual vitality has waned, and familiar sources of renewal seem inadequate. But whatever the prompting, the sheer fact of embracing the possibility for change invites the Spirit's partnership and participation. The quest itself includes this element of mystery and surprise, which is often why the journey itself is so effective. It shakes up the rigid and limiting patterns that have likely gummed up one's life. As seasoned pilgrims like to say: "You may not get the pilgrimage you want, but you will get the pilgrimage you need."

Labyrinths

Given the magnitude and rigors of most pilgrimages, they are not necessarily suitable for regular spiritual praxis. The earliest Christian pilgrimages had Jerusalem as their destination, which is not surprising, since the place where Jesus and the disciples walked, and most significantly the locale of Jesus' passion and death, had profound holy significance for pilgrims. Given the enormous difficulties pilgrims encountered when traveling from all over Christendom to reach Jerusalem, Rome also emerged as a popular alternative. The loss of Jerusalem as a pilgrimage destination contributed to the emergence of the labyrinth as a practical and easily accessible alternative.

Not unlike the earlier description of pilgrimages as archetypes, a symbolic enactment of sacred movement toward the center of our lives, labyrinths can serve as a reliable alternative with similar spiritual benefits.

---

10. Schmidt, "Transforming Pilgrimage," 65.

Labyrinths also have an ancient and seemingly universal utilization, beginning as early as 2000 BCE in Europe, and are found worldwide.[11] The most famous early Christian labyrinth is located at Chartres Cathedral in France. This labyrinth, laid out in the Nave of the Cathedral in the year 1200 CE, is organized in four quadrants, symbolic of the Cross, and reputably pilgrims originally took this as a metaphor for the journey to Jerusalem and as an analog to Christ's life and destiny.

Labyrinths are ideally suited for regular, even daily use, especially if a full-sized labyrinth is not available in one's immediate community. A more recent innovation is the "finger-walking" labyrinth; it can be found in all shapes and sizes. These portable labyrinths make use of either a finger or pen and produce many of the same effects as full-fledged labyrinth walks. Again, not unlike the healing potential of pilgrimages, labyrinths also have explicit renewing and centering possibilities. As regular practitioners have affirmed, walking a labyrinth in any mode can reduce innate judgmentalism, support growth in patience, deepen compassion, and offer the reflective space we need when discernment is sought.[12]

We turn now to a universal Christian spiritual practice. It is one that features, unsurprisingly, in our prompt cards.

PRAYING THE SCRIPTURES

The Scriptures contain the repository of sacred wisdom, mediated by the Holy Spirit, and give witness to the relationship God has forged with God's people. The Hebrew and Christian Scriptures are a collection of texts, written over 1200 years by multiple authors, utilizing three languages, and representing a wide array of cultural, tribal, and political contexts and realities. As David Gushee notes, the Bible is an extraordinarily diverse collection of texts including genre, context, authorship, and purposes.[13] Finding absolute coherence and uniform consistency is impossible. Further, many in the traditions we share in reject the positions of taking only the literal meaning in all instances and universal infallibility.

11. Curry, *Way of Labyrinth*, 18–33.

12. Artress, *Sacred Path Companion*, 11–19. See also West, *Exploring the Labyrinth*, 155–175.

13. Gushee, *After Evangelicalism*, 34.

While Biblical literacy and exegetical awareness are obvious assets and can help deepen our respect for the wisdom we find there, an analytic and scientific relationship to Scripture does not necessarily take us to the nurture available in the sacred text. St Paul's declaration to Timothy reminds us that "all Scripture is inspired by God" and guides our lives to become "equipped for any good work" (2 Tim 3:16–17). The invitation we are given through Scripture is toward guidance, not in a literalistic or mechanical way, but as an invitation to a relationship with God into and through the text. It is an invitation to intimacy with God: "I shall no longer call you servants, because a servant does not know his master's business; I call you friends because I have made known to you everything I have learned from my Father" (John 15:15).

Lectio Divina

In the passage from John 15 just cited, we are invited into intimacy with the Sacred in the form of friendship, and perhaps the most critical element in any friend relationship is listening. Without listening we have no friendship. In her work on intimacy with God, Mary Darling notes that for us to deepen our friendship with God we must be able to deeply listen, and one of the classic ways to cultivate such listening is through a particular kind of Scripture reading called *Lectio Divina*, or "holy or divine reading."[14]

Lectio Divina is a mode of sacred reading practiced as early as the 4th century. It is a practice that draws one into Sacred Presence and became one of the distinctive elements of Benedictine and Cistercian spirituality.[15] Corrine Ware notes that *Lectio Divina* is a practice that has an integrating effect in that it is simultaneously verbal, mental, affective, and contemplative. It appeals to many types of temperaments and personality types, thus giving room for our individual differences and deepest spiritual inclinations. It does not impose a cookie-cutter template on our ways of seeking the divine; consequently, it opens us up to being more directly met by God's response to us.

Step 1 Lectio *(Holy Reading)*. The method itself is quite simple. As a first step we are invited to select a short passage of Scripture, perhaps from the Psalms or the Gospels, and through reading the passage several

---

14. Darling & Campolo, *God of Intimacy and Action*, 115.

15. Ware, *Benedict on the Freeway*, 112.

times, we avoid trying to study or analyze it, but simply notice and pay attention to what is written. This can be enhanced by reading it out loud or reading it several times so that it penetrates more deeply.

Step 2 Meditatio *(Reflecting on the Reading).* In this second step we are called to meditate or reflect on the passage. Here we put ourselves into the story and whatever it might evoke for us. We take note of whatever meaning emerges. We enter into the text mindfully and with an "open heart" as we reflect and ponder on it.[16] This prayer stance is a receptive one, and this creates space for the Spirit to speak through the images, thoughts, and feelings that surface. Mary Darling adds the caution that *Lectio Divina* is not a "spectator sport," but requires our participation by using our God-given imaginative capacity to let the reading speak into our hearts and minds.

Step 3 Oratio *(Responding and Speaking).* In this third step we respond by selecting a word, phrase, or image from the text to carry with us through the day. This practice offers an anchoring point throughout the day. The image or phrase does not operate as a mantra, but as a vessel to receive Presence, not unlike the benefits arising from centering prayer. Pondering the image or word connects us to Presence; it reflects our intention to remain immersed in God's orbit. We must keep in mind, however, that the main purpose of such reflection is not acquiring more insight, but rather to grow in deeper trust and intimacy with God.

Step 4 Contemplatio *(Contemplation).* Mary Darling makes a strong case that the three prior steps we have discussed—*lectio, meditato,* and *oratio*—naturally draw us further into contemplation, compassion, and action.[17] Genuine contemplation through the work of the Holy Spirit awakens our compassion and care. If our contemplation does not activate our action in the service of others, it should prompt us to discern where the barriers and blockages are in our hearts. The centeredness in the Spirit that Lectio Divina generates, overcomes frenetic running about and desperately doing good; it awakens deliberate and thoughtful engagement with need(s) within the life challenges that present themselves.

---

16. Darling & Compolo, *God of Intimacy and Action,* 122.

17. Darling & Compolo, *God of Intimacy and Action,* 128.

PRAYER THROUGH SEEING (VISIO DIVINA)

Even as we claim Scripture as a prime mode of Sacred Presence and guidance through the written word, we recognize that God's desire to communicate with us is not limited to the written word alone. God's force field permeates all things; almost anything in God's domain is capable of revealing the divine presence. When the authorities in Jesus' day challenged his disciples to become silent when the multitude was praising Jesus, his reply was this: "If these become silent, the very stones will cry out" (Luke 19:39–40). The metaphor Jesus uses reminds us that even nature can reveal the glory of God. Certainly, the veneration of sacred objects such as statues, shrines, crosses, even Bibles, can be used in idolatrous fashion, by becoming their own objects of devotion, rather than a reminder of God's presence to whom they might point. The sheer fact of their representational capacity can become an invitation for discernment and deeper reflection on the place of the Sacred in our lives.

But what spiritual resonance should we give to objects and representations we find in our world? Christians over the centuries have drawn different conclusions about the degree of sacred meaning to be attributed to objects in the world. We carry legitimate fears about creating "golden calves" that serve only our own idolatrous purposes. Given these controversies we need discernment about the place of visible representations of sacred objects; we need to decide whether they are beneficial or potentially destructive. The critical issue seems to be how such objects are utilized. If they are held in reverence as reminders of sacred recollection, carrying authentic spiritual meanings, they can nourish and sustain. If they are held as magical, or invested with sacred power for the purposes of misuse or manipulation, they are clearly harmful.

The tension around this question for the Christian community surfaced most dramatically in the Byzantine period in which the hostility toward visual representation brought about the destruction of much precious art. A similar impulse surfaced during the Reformation where large amounts of religious objects and religious art were destroyed. The frenetic fear of idolatry drove these excesses. Beyond the tragedy of the loss of sacred art we must remember that in the early church iconography provided a viable prayer medium for the countless persons who had little or no access to written materials, or even the capacity to read them. Sacred images became the "text" through which the quest for God and dialogue with God could take place.

For most contemporary Christians in the "non-iconic" traditions, the use of image or representation does not carry the emotional charge of prior ages. Here again, the Ignatian commitment to "find God in all things" provides an additional affirmation for image-based prayerful practices. Their potential is to help guide our contemplation of visual arts, even where explicit religious or spiritual content is not immediately obvious. When we encounter representational objects or processes, we can ask God to open our eyes to God's presence in the work itself, the contents behind the work, its context, and its possible meanings. In short, God can become a prayer partner anywhere and everywhere, and this includes representational works of art.

Tilden Edwards adds his weight to the view that both images and words are helpful resources for spiritual formation. He suggests that we "do not need to choose between image and language in the emerging church of our time," and that both our images and written words are important means of formation, leaving us impoverished if we must choose between them.[18]

PRAYER WITH THE EXAMEN

There are tried and true spiritual gifts that enhance prayer arising out of long-established Christian practices. The use of texts, words, images, stories, and songs can provide a path for deepening our intimacy with God. What they all have in common are varying degrees of immersion in spiritual awareness in which we come into greater awareness of God's presence within us and around us. What Christians have discovered over the years is that these practices that connect with Presence are not random or haphazard; further, they can be supported by habits and disciplines that foster a deepening relationship with God.

Approximately 500 years ago St Ignatius of Loyola constructed a particularly effective prayer discipline in the form of the *Spiritual Exercises*. This method provided a reflective and comprehensive approach to life, a contemplative form of praying, that facilitates finding God on a daily basis.[19] Found within the *Exercises* is a special gem of supporting prayer called the *Examen*. Sometimes called the *Examen of Conscience*

---

18. Edwards, *Living in Presence*, 46.

19. Fleming, *What is Ignatian Spirituality?*

(or *Consciousness*), it is a method of reviewing one's day in the light of God's presence.[20]

Ignatius advocated spending a set amount of time, perhaps once or twice a day, reflecting on one's day to find traces of God's blessings in one's everyday life. Over the years there have been numerous adjustments made by practitioners of the method ranging from variations of daily frequency (once, twice, or more) to shifts in focus (thanksgiving, consciousness of God's gifts, recognition of shortcomings/failures, forgiveness, inviting God's presence for the day to come, and more).

Even with these adjustments over the years, the practice has maintained St Ignatius's original vision, which is to claim a prayer practice that would help us find God in our everyday lives. This focus puts the emphasis on being accompanied by God in all our daily challenges and blessings. Jim Manney, for instance, notes that it is a mode of prayer distinct from more common prayer practices such as devotional prayer, praying with the Scriptures, intercession, and centering prayer.[21]

The *Examen*'s theological foundation is the Incarnation, God-with-us, the Word becoming flesh and dwelling among us. This is a theology of God's involvement in the particulars, the minutia of life, and in all the ins and outs of everyday life. The *Examen* has a further theological basis in that it posits God as relational; there is the relational wholeness of God as Father, Son, and Holy Spirit, and we are drawn into a relationship of friendship with the triune God, as John 15:15 indicates.

Furthermore, the process is supremely practical. The *Examen* reveals a groundedness in experience, what's really going on, and addresses the daily rigors of our real life circumstances. The disciplines of discernment, decision-making, values clarification, and more are all supported and profoundly deepened by this reflective process. A scriptural passage from Psalm 139 is an example of how direct and intimate this process can be. Here, the Psalmist reveals his deep need for discernment, as he struggles with the hatred in his heart, and his deep desire for retribution (vv.19–22). Yet at the same time he cries out for God's guidance and intimate involvement with him in his distress and agitation: "Search me, O God, and know my heart; try me and know my anxious thoughts; and see if there be any hurtful way in me, and lead me in the way everlasting" (Psalm 139:23–24). This is such an honest reading of his nakedness

20. Manney, *Simple Life-changing Prayer*. See also Thibodeaux, *Reimagining Ignatian Examen*.

21. Manney, *Simple Life-changing Prayer*, 6.

before God; he recognizes that God is "intimately acquainted with all [his] ways" (v.3). He knows God's presence fills every fiber of his being, yet he knows he needs God's radiant light to penetrate his darkness and agitation (vv.7–10). The Psalmist's experience reveals the core of this spiritual praxis of prayer. We can enter meaningfully into our own raw experiences and find the Sacred waiting for us there. God engages us directly in and through our experiences, and the *Examen* is a practice that helps provide a viable path for that deepening.

The Examen as Method

The five-step method offered by St Ignatius is straightforward:

1. Give thanks for God's goodness.

2. Invite the Holy Spirit.

3. Review the day.

4. Repent from wrongdoing.

5. Resolve to live well tomorrow.[22]

As noted earlier, variations have been utilized over the years, and this flexibility has allowed the method to adjust to cultural and contextual variations, and the particular spiritual challenges that seekers are experiencing. One variation suggested by Jim Manney changes the order of the steps somewhat. He discovered that he needed to shift the order so that he could more directly address the particular spiritual and personal themes of his life. Again, the purpose of the adjustment was to more deeply align our embodied selves with God's presence, especially as we undergo life's challenges. Jim Manney insists he is in good company in rearranging the order, since St Ignatius himself suggested that the *Spiritual Exercises* should be adapted to the conditions of those who enter into them.[23] Manney's particular adjustment is to change the order slightly by beginning with the first step.[24]

Step 1 Praying for Light. This adjustment is subtle, yet important. In praying for light we invoke the Spirit of Truth (John 16:13); this is an acknowledgment that we need Spirit-informed awareness, not only relying

22. Thibodeaux, *Reimagining Ignatian Examen*, 3–4.

23. Manney, *Simple Life-changing Prayer*, 4.

24. Manney, *Simple Life-changing Prayer*, 230–231.

on our limited insight or narrow vantage points. This Spirit-infused light is not magic or some special dispensation of knowledge; rather, it is built upon an awareness that we need God's participation, particularly so that God's Spirit can flow through our thoughts, feelings, and memories. Inevitably, the shedding of the Spirit's light into our lives will direct us toward our relationships with others. That's often where our predominant joys and sorrows reside. As with any life dilemma, utilizing the *Examen* will stretch us into deeper paths of ownership and response capability. That stretching will likely not be immediately or gloriously life-changing, but more in the mode of fortifying us more deeply toward the existential matters at hand.

Step 2 Gratitude and Thankfulness. Regardless of where one places gratitude as a particular step in the panorama of spiritual disciplines, it surely touches all of them.[25] Gratitude marks our recognition of our very existence as derivative, as contingent on the graces that God bestows. Jesuit David Fleming goes so far as to suggest that sin is essentially a failure of gratitude.[26] He sees our alienations in life as occurring within the context of God's love, which we do not recognize when gratitude is absent. Thus, any "review of the day" should surely include gratitude as the awareness that the goodness of each day brings with it the gifts and graces God bestows—large and small—such as life and love, restful sleep, and so much more.

Yet our awareness through gratitude does not depend on nice things always happening for us, as if that were the basis for thankfulness. Our gratitude is often most meaningfully manifested in the negative things that occur. Because our life in prayer is comprehensive and encompassing, all things are subject to God's presence, including the messy or unpleasant aspects of our lives. The light of Grace that bathes us is often made more visible within our harsh realities. There, where our vulnerability and fragility are most visible, often becomes the place where Grace most clearly appears. The *Examen* cultivates "paying attention" to those daily, multiple movements of God. Our gratitude and thankfulness surge forth spontaneously when Grace appears, which suggests that gratitude is not hard work. It is the natural response of an awakened heart. Such awareness is also accompanied by humility. More and more we become

25. Steindl-Rast, *Gratefulness.*

26. Fleming, *What is Ignatian Spirituality?*, 26.

aware that our entire lives are a gift nourished and held in all the phases we pass through.

Step 3 Review the Day. Being grounded in the everydayness of things is the heart of the *Examen*, since it is a commitment to being "here" and "now." At this juncture the *Examen* reveals its deeper layer, what we could call the "reality beneath the reality."[27] This acknowledgment comes from the awareness that we are quite good at avoiding the here and now, often living in the past, or projecting ourselves into the future that is not here yet. Jim Manney's corrective stance is this: "God works with what is!" The *Examen* omits the "if onlys" of our lives by facing the real. It resists our speculations, analyses, or arguments; the invitation is movement toward "being one with the real."[28] The direction the *Examen* leads in is the opposite of escapism; it is genuine prayer that allows us to discern the deeper truths about ourselves and our situation in the light of God's Holy Spirit. We get to see our lives more through God's eyes than our own. It reveals how and where the voice of God is in this moment we are living.

As graced as this process can be a certain caution is also indicated, since we all carry personal inclinations or patterns of assessment and self-evaluation that can be lopsided or even extreme. St Ignatius himself had to wrestle with deeply embedded inclinations toward scrupulosity and excessive rumination. It is a testament to his perseverance and wrestling with his own interior harshness and intensity that today we benefit from the spiritual graces that he passed. His struggle with himself, under the grace of God and the tutelage of the Holy Spirit, allows us now to benefit from this transformational path.

Our own story might not include scrupulosity, but there is always something. For us it might be an innate judgmentalism—things never being good enough for us—which becomes the source of our despair. Others of us struggle with self-esteem, either in deflated form with chronic negativity and self-negation, or in its inflated version as narcissism, seeing ourselves as having to be at the center of everything and lost in a relentless grasping for worth and significance. Whatever our pattern might be, the discipline of the *Examen* will reveal it, and provide a secret partner in the Holy Spirit to reveal, heal, and renew and guide us persistently toward "being at home spiritually."

27. Manney, *Simple Life-changing Prayer*, 40.
28. Manney, *Simple Life-changing Prayer*, 41.

Step 4 Facing What's Wrong (Or Missing). As we grow in self-ownership, we don't get a free pass to perfection for our troubles. What the *Examen* does offer is better goggles and a capacity to see more; in particular, we notice our messiness. Jim Manney frames it well when he suggests we all fall short of our own ideals.[29] He reminds us that any athlete, however successful they may be, will "fail" every bit as much as they win. Our so-called failures are a permanent feature of our life condition. The gift of the *Examen* is to change the conditions of our self-scrutiny from the blame-game toward the ownership-claim. Facing up to our vulnerabilities and shortcomings is a significant step in spiritual growth, and it reflects a distinct shift in our relationship to God, from condemning judge to truth-seeking partner. God's loving action toward us is for the very purpose of being loved in our shortcomings; God does not love us only when we overcome them.

The very point of introspection in the *Examen* is to strengthen our capacity to see ourselves as we really are, not simply who we have been or yet want to be. Seeing what's real removes the ever-present temptation to gloss over, self-justify, and wiggle out from under the truths about ourselves. There is likely a direct correlation in our capacity for ownership and the degree to which we claim and receive God's love for us. There is no fear in love, and in being held in love, we are invited into the truest source of our freedom.

Step 5 Look to the Day Ahead. A prayerful immersion in God-directed reflection is not for its own sake, but for the sake of fuller engagement in our life orbits. Becoming contemplatives-in-action through discernment will lead to concrete steps that have their source in a Spirit-awakened recognition of what comes next. This step is nothing like a "to-do" list, but a guidance mechanism that grows out of God's desire(s) for us. This desire is certainly toward greater flourishing, but more importantly, toward a freedom to engage the needs at hand.

The *Examen* activates the awareness and willingness to act, to change, to work toward concrete life situations. These changes may be subtle, perhaps operating first from the level of attitude and perspective, but then expressed in concrete acts of love. We can be tempted to rest in the warm glow of prayerful presence, but St Ignatius declared that love must be manifested in deeds, not simply in words or good intentions.[30]

---

29. Manney, *Simple Life-changing Prayer*, 54.
30. Manney, *Simple Life-changing Prayer*, 67.

Even as these "steps" of the *Examen* are utilized, we must remember their purpose: to assist us in "finding God in all things." God is at work in us to awaken and guide all good and holy things that we are called to love, hold, and bless. The *Examen's* structure, helpful as it is, is intended to grow our capacity to perceive God's participation all the time, to "pray without ceasing." The *Examen* is thus for all times, places, persons, and situations. It is a particular way of "being with." For most of us, most of the time, we need the help of reminders, and a structure to support us. The *Examen's* living heart, however, is found in ever greater reliance on our Source.

Desolations and Consolations

In our survey of spiritual perspectives and practices that enhance spiritual formation, we recognized that our life in prayer encompasses all of who we are: Head (thoughts), heart (feelings), hands (actions). The Ignatian *Examen* clearly addresses all these vital elements in our spiritual growth and functioning. What is surprising about St Ignatius's method, however, is his granting a central place to feelings/affects in our daily life with God. His framework for this insight consists of the dual states of mind he calls "consolation" and "desolation"; he sees these as significant markers that help us recognize where we are in our relationship with God.

These notions represent the dynamic and active reflections of our relatedness within ourselves, and in concert with our life in God they describe the primary effect of orientations that reveal us to ourselves, and describe the state of spiritual harmony we are living. Our states of consolation come with feelings of peace, centeredness, joy, and purpose. Consolation takes us positively toward God and others in hope and love.[31] Its opposite is desolation, which draws us away from God's love and relatedness with others. In desolation we experience agitation, dejection, self-loathing, and spiritual emptiness. In consolation we find animation and consolidation of purpose. Consolation frees up and releases positive energy. Desolation sucks you dry.

As has been suggested, there is no "right" way to process each day through the *Examen*. Here again, we are reminded that it is not a rigid system, but a resource, a tool, for deepening and relating more effectively

31. Tetlow, *Always Discerning*, 170.

to self, God, and others.[32] Keeping in mind the flexibility of usage for this method, it is perhaps helpful to focus on a particular feeling or image that becomes noteworthy for us, perhaps because of its intensity, or the way it lingered in our consciousness and drew our attention. These movements can become useful springboards for reflection. Lingering with such moments takes us deeper into awareness; we are able to open up meanings that are normally tucked away beyond the reach of our self-reflection.

PRAYER AS INTERCESSION

The mode of prayer that prompts intercession rests in our capacity "to participate in the circulation of Grace through the great cosmic body of Christ."[33] Tilden Edwards thus captures the essence of intercession as arising out of the intimacy of God's Spirit with our own spirit. St Paul gives us the template for such intercession in Romans 8:26: "The Spirit helps us in our weakness; for we do not know how to pray as we should, but the Spirit itself intercedes for us with groanings too deep for words."

Intercession is prompted by God's work in us, and St Paul's words suggest that it is not built upon some higher knowledge or sophisticated analysis, but rather on a deep Spirit-awakened and Spirit-supported awareness of God's care for everyone. Our open hearts invite such solidarity, which intercession then compels.

The psychological parallel to intercession is empathy, which is not to be confused with other emotional states such as pity, sympathy, or "do-gooder" sentiments toward the suffering of others. Those impulses are predominantly ego-based sensitivities, in which our own agendas of needing significance, or desire for impact, predominate. In contrast, in intercession we are called as "vessels of the Spirit's intercession, reaching through us for the care and transformation of creation."[34] The theological and spiritual parallel to deep empathy is "mutual indwelling." In the words of Jesus found in John 15:4–7:

> Abide in me, and I in you . . . I am the vine, you are the branches; he who abides in me and I in him, he bears much fruit; for apart from me you can do nothing . . . If you abide in me, and my

32. Manney, *Simple Life-changing Prayer*, 44.

33. Edwards, *Living in Presence*, 108.

34. Edwards, *Living in Presence*, 108–109.

words abide in you, ask whatever you wish and it will be done for you.

A first glance at this passage might cause us to conclude that *our* wishes and desires in prayer are paramount, that *our* vantage points are so encompassing, that God is at *our* beck and call, and that *we* know best. Nothing could be further from the truth. The first invitation that intercessory prayer activates comes in the form of attitudes and actions arising from prayer. This will certainly include compassion that leads to action, but with a necessary deep degree of humility, and even an un-consciousness about our potential actions. Matthew 25:35–45 serves as a necessary counterpoint to the passage from John 15. Here, Jesus speaks to the unselfconsciousness of those who mobilized their intercession toward the sufferer who is hungry, the stranger, the sick, the prisoner, toward all those we are called to stay in solidarity with, seemingly espe-cially those with whom we do not normally associate. This passage from Matthew reveals how a prayerful Spirit-activated solidarity operates. A Holy Spirit awakened intercession is grounded in compassion as the fruit of awareness, without needing some personal rationale for doing so. Such intercession is a Spirit-activated and Spirit-sustained response that seeks God's desire in every situation, and not a response dependent on our assumptions.

The practices that support such Spirit-led intercession could include the following:

1. Cultivating openness to God Spirit.

2. Being honest with God about our petitions for ourselves; our true desires need to be named even as we affirm our deepest desire for God's will to be done.

3. Invoking intercession for others includes our desires for the situation(s), and especially as we affirm that God's will be done.

4. Becoming open to inclusion of concern for those with whom we differ and with whom we are in conflict or estrangement (God's desire is present to the encompassing reality of any situation, well beyond our own narrower vantage points).

5. Asking for guidance toward situations where action is called for on behalf of those we pray for.

SUMMARY

Our spiritual formation needs a sufficiently broad vision and breadth of perspective to embrace the complexity of ourselves and our place in the world. Spiritual formation, if it is to be sustained in our ever more complex and changing world, needs the "structural supports" of practices and disciplines that nourish and guide us along the way. Stumbling into times and phases of spiritual dryness, the woundings and traumas of life, will touch every person in varying degrees. God's Spirit has placed a seed in everyone from which that Spirit-awareness can grow, even if it has been profoundly neglected, traumatized, or violated. These spiritual habits can water the seeds long dormant, bringing them into the vitality of God's desire for us.

7

SPIRITUAL CHARACTER
AND THE SHAPING OF THE SOUL

A CRITICAL QUESTION: DOES spiritual formation make us better Christians, or even better persons? Maybe you have found yourself thinking that, after years of guiding parishioners as a pastor. Do spiritual practices make us better humans? Or should we take a more modest position? The early church fathers help us by turning the question in another direction. They relate spiritual character to the fundamental Christian anthropological concept of the "image of God." According to Basileus of Caesarea, the image of God is foundational for us to live in the Christian way:

> "Become perfect as your heavenly Father is perfect". Do you see
> how the Lord restores to us that which is according to the like-
> ness? "For he makes his sun rise on the evil and on the good,
> and sends rain on the just and on the unjust." If you become
> a hater of evil, free of rancor, not remembering yesterday's en-
> mity; if you become brother-loving and compassionate, you are
> like God. If you forgive your enemy from your heart, you are
> like God. If as God is toward you, the sinner, you become the
> same toward the brother who has wronged you, by your good
> will from your heart toward your neighbor, you are like God.
> As you have that which is according to the image through your
> being rational, you come to be according to the likeness by un-
> dertaking kindness. Take on yourself "a heart of compassion,
> kindness," that you may put on Christ.[1]

---

1. Harrison, *God's Many-Splendored Image,* 68–69.

The church fathers knew that spiritual formation contributes to our spiritual character, but it does not necessarily make us better than other (non-Christian) people. Rather, it makes us the persons that God has created us to be and the persons that Christ was willing to suffer and die for. We are persons made in the image of God and meant for becoming "Christ-like." In other words, spiritual character reflects a moral position and is about cultivating certain "virtues." In the end, however, it leads us to our purpose as humans in living a life in relation to our Creator and our Redeemer, who is also, by God's Spirit, our Renewing Agent.

This chapter introduces spiritual character, one of the four dimensions in the model of spiritual formation that we hope will help you to guide parishioners and those who you are called to care for in their journey with God. "Spiritual character" is a term that connects to other fields of thinking—namely, virtue ethics and positive psychology. Both fields are rich in literature and approaches. Yet this chapter suggests a different angle to spiritual character in the process of spiritual formation. Its primary concern is the nature of the relationship between a human being and God. Theological anthropology, the field that studies human beings as a theological topic, offers us another window to look at the persons that we accompany pastorally: people made in the image of God and journeying toward the likeness of Christ. Given that we are embodied persons, spiritual character is primarily about the soul and the shaping of our souls. The soul is that aspect of our humanity that relates us to God, both in being created and on our way to an enduring future. Spiritual character is about the shaping of our souls, in everyday life, in relation to the Triune God, and in view of an existence that transcends us to dimensions that we can never fathom.

Biblically speaking, the shaping of our soul is expressed with the help of several metaphors. To understand its richness, we will reflect on a few of these. We then focus on some aspects of the fruits of the Spirit to see how humans flourish by the work of the Spirit and through practices of spiritual formation.

BIBLICAL METAPHORS FOR THE SHAPING OF THE SOUL

We are "living souls." However, this does not mean that the soul is an immortal thing that constitutes our essence; an unchangeable and non-physical substance without beginning or end. This ancient Greek understanding still haunts Christian anthropology. This is not the place to enter the philosophical discussion on physicalism and the solutions that have been posed by Christian philosophers such as Nancey Murphy, who speaks about humans as "spirited bodies," or the arguments offered by other Christian philosophers such as Richard Swinburne in favor of a Christian type of dualism.[2] For Christians the resurrection of the body is the ultimate vision of the future of the Kingdom of God and every anthropological proposal that downplays our bodily existence should be approached with suspicion.

Further, according to both the Biblical and the Early Christian sources, we are more than our bodies. As "living souls" we are in a continuous process of transformation and this transformation is understood through a rich variety of terms and metaphors. These biblical metaphors point to diverse aspects of the shaping of the soul; we will consider a few of these, ranging from the basic anthropological terms (image of God, heart, and mind) to the spiritual processes of growth (sanctification). In between we find the dynamic between the work of God's Spirit (indwelling) and the human response to follow Christ (discipleship).

Likeness, Renovation, and Renewal

Acquiring a spiritual character is not simply a common human striving to becoming a better person; nor is it just a matter of practicing certain spiritual habits. Spiritual practices certainly support formation, as we illustrate elsewhere in this book. Biblical language grounds the shaping of the soul and spiritual character in creation, redemption, and renewal. Thus, to understand our human existence and spiritual growth, we need to think and speak in a threefold way. We can only understand our humanity from the One who gave us life and restores it—namely, the Triune God.

We are created "in the image of God." This phrase from Genesis 1:27 generated a good deal of speculation over what this image consists of. Does it concern our spirit or our morality? Does the image of God consist of our human capacity to relate to other beings? Rather than speculating in this way, we might think of the image of God as something that is in process. Let's continue listening to the early church fathers. Nonna Verna

2. Murphy, *Bodies and Souls*; Swinburne, *Are We Bodies or Souls?*

Harrison refers to Gregory of Nyssa's comparison to painters. Christ became incarnate and according to Paul's letter to the Colossians (1:15), he
was the "image of the invisible God." Harrison puts it this way:

> People can then be like students in an art class in which a fine
> painting is set before them and they each have the task of copy-
> ing it on their own canvases, attempting to bring forth the same
> beauty in their own art. Gregory says that likewise "every person
> is the painter of his own life, and choice is the craftsman of the
> work, and the virtues are the paints for producing the image." If
> we paint well, we become an image of Christ, who is the image
> of the Father, "as did Paul, who became an 'imitator of Christ'
> through his life of virtue." Thus we are called to use our freedom
> to choose Christ as our model and to produce his likeness in
> ourselves.[3]

From these thoughts we may gather two important impressions.
First, it is not enough to root our humanity in a single creative act of
God. Scripture teaches a process of growth, growth into the likeness of
Christ who is the definitive or perfect image of God. This point is even
stronger when we think about theologies that do not put "the Fall" or
"sin" between us and Christ. A medieval example is John Duns Scotus.
He taught that Christ would have become incarnate whether there was
a Fall or not. Even without sin, God would have communicated himself
perfectly by becoming one of us and thus bringing his image to light in a
more complete way than we could "paint" for ourselves. However, we live
in a world full of failure and sin. We are sinful human beings. Christ came
into a world in which the divine intentions in creation were greatly frus-
trated. His image in humankind needed a thorough recovery. Gregory's
line of thought of the human painter who paints toward the likeness of
Christ puts Christ in the center of the process of redemption and restoration. Spiritual character has to do with the likeness of Christ and spiritual
growth can only be achieved by looking at Christ. The restoration of the
image of God is due to Christ and his suffering and death. Indeed, this
restoration is due to his whole way of life.

The shaping of our souls in the form of Christ-likeness is explained
in various ways. Dallas Willard talks about spiritual formation as "the
renovation of the heart."[4] We need a renovation of our inner lives. This,
Willard says, is like "putting on the character of Christ"; it is moving from

3. Harrison, *God's Many-Splendored Image*, 69–70.
4. Willard, *Renovation of the Heart*.

radical evil to radical goodness. Willard draws an ingenious picture of the human inner life, that includes the heart, the will, and the mind, including thoughts and feelings. It is not necessary to decide on the correct terms here. The salient fact is that our inner lives need transformation. Character is not shaped externally. It is not just about a change in behavior. Spiritual character concerns our deepest desires and the choices of our heart.

The New Testament expression here is the "renewal of our mind," but "mind" should not be taken as referring to our rational capacities only. The phrase "renewal of the mind" occurs in Romans 12:1–2, but what it amounts to is explained in many other passages in the letters of Paul. According to the New Testament scholar, Tom Wright, this renewal of the mind runs deep in the Pauline letters. In Ephesians, Paul talks about putting away the old self and putting on the new self (Eph 4:22–24); in Colossians the old and the new are "renewed in knowledge according to the image of the one who created it" (Col 3:9–10).

Formation of spiritual character, or the "renewal of the mind" as we might call it, can be further understood in terms of its source (where it comes from), its goal (what it aims for) and its process (how it is developed). Derived from the Scriptural images such as the home (indwelling) and the journey (discipleship), Christian theology provides three fundamental answers. The renewal of the believer's mind comes from the indwelling of the Holy Spirit; it aims for living a life as a disciple of Christ; and the process of renewal is best understood through the notion of "sanctification." Let's unpack these three aspects a little.

Indwelling of the Holy Spirit

Our spiritual life starts with God. In creation as well as in redemption. It is not just a linguistic coincidence that the transformation of the human spirit and our spiritual character brings us into the realm of the third Person of the Trinity, the Holy Spirit. The relationship between God's Spirit and our human spiritual lives and souls is both intimate and distinct. Orthodox Christianity talks about "deification" to express the union between God and humans, closing the gap between the divine and the human realm as far as possible. Reformed Christianity, on the other hand, prefers the phrase "indwelling of the Holy Spirit."[5] Wesleyan Christians,

5. Leidenhag, *Demarcating Deification*.

for their part, stress that "God is the one who conforms and transforms us by the power of the Spirit."[6]

It is a movement from God toward us that initiates the renewal of the mind, that guides our spiritual life and that brings us to ultimate union with God. God's Spirit is the protagonist in our inner renewal. Going along with the Reformed expression, the "indwelling of the Spirit," we remember Christ's words in John 15, where he urges his disciples to remain in him and he will remain in them. This "remaining" is a spiritual reality, a reality that is created by the presence of the Spirit in a believer's life.

The indwelling of the Holy Spirit is vividly explained by Jonathan Edwards in his famous treatise, *Religious Affections:*

> The Spirit of God is given to the true saints to dwell in them, as his proper lasting abode; and to influence their hearts, as a principle of new nature or as a divine supernatural spring of life and action. The Scriptures represent the Holy Spirit not only as moving, and occasionally influencing the saints, but as dwelling in them as his temple, his proper abode, and everlasting dwelling place, 1 Cor. 3:16, 2 Cor 6:16, John 14:16, 17. And he is represented as being there so united to the faculties of the soul, that he becomes there a principle or spring of new nature and life. So the saints are said to live by Christ living in them, Gal 2:20. Christ by his Spirit not only is in them, but lives in them; and so that they live by his life; so is his Spirit united to them, as a principle of life in them; they do not only drink living water, but this "living water becomes a well or fountain of water," in the soul, "springing up into spiritual and everlasting life," John 4:14, and thus becomes a principle of life in them.[7]

Life as a Disciple

Spiritual character also concerns our everyday life. The indwelling of the Spirit and the renewal of our mind have an outward aspect. The renewal of the mind turns us into disciples or followers of Christ.

The image of the "disciple" is the biblical image of the person who hears the call of Christ, starts to follow the way of the Christ, and thereby enters an existence marked by constant challenge and spiritual

---

6. Leclerc and Maddix, *Spiritual Formation*, 12.

7. Edwards, *Religious Affections*, 200.

transformation. The book of Acts speaks about Christians as "those of the Way." Becoming a disciple is joining in a journey. This is not done in an individualistic way; it takes place in the community of disciples. Spiritual character may seem to refer to a feature of the individual believer, but it is deeply relational. Disciples shape their lives according to the teaching of the one they follow. The teachings of Jesus and the apostles shape our souls toward discipleship, they help us to grow in faith, in love and in hope.

According to Rowan Williams, the former Archbishop of Canterbury, faith, hope, and love are the "three indispensable qualities in the life of the Christian disciple."[8] He approaches the journey of the disciple as renewal of the mind from the perspective of the great spiritual writer, St John of the Cross:

> The distinctive and fresh insight that St John of the Cross offers is that if you put together understanding, memory and will with faith, hope and love, you have a perfect picture of where we start and where we finish. In the Christian life, faith (he says) is what happens to our understanding; hope is what happens to our remembering; and love is what happens to our wanting. So to grow as a disciple is to take the journey from understanding into faith, from memory into hope and from will into love. St John believed that in this process of Christian growing up, one of the most difficult things is the sense we will have that we have lost our bearings on the way. What we thought we understood we discover that we never did; what we thought we remembered is covered with confusion; and what we thought we wanted turns out to be empty. We have to be recreated in faith and hope and love for our understanding, our memory, and our will to become what God really wants them to be.[9]

Being a disciple is being on a journey. That means that spiritual formation is something that is never finished in this earthly life. The shaping of the soul is an eschatological process. Christians may long for a perfect life, but we will remain flawed disciples and travel with fellow disciples similarly flawed. Spiritual formation, in the model that we present in this book and more generally, is construed as journeying together and shaping our lives according to the teachings of the Scriptures. The image of the disciple thus naturally leads to another feature of the shaping of the

8. Williams, *Being Disciples*, 21.

9. Williams, *Being Disciples*, 21–22.

soul. Wesleyans and others refer to growth in holiness. "Sanctification" was the term used by the Wesley brothers "to describe the work of the Holy Spirit to free our lives from sin."[10]

Growing in Holiness: The Process of Sanctification

The notion of "becoming holy," or in theological language *sanctification*, runs deep in biblical thought. The spiritual character of the people of God is to be holy; the God of Israel says: "Be holy, for I am holy" (Lev 11:44). The Apostles quoted these words to characterize the spiritual character of the followers of Christ (1 Peter 1:16).

Becoming holy is one of the ways to understand spiritual formation. Sanctification, as it has also been called in the Christian tradition, is closely related to justification. Both becoming holy and standing rightly before God are about the restoration of the image of God and the renewal of the mind. Here the key questions are these: How do human beings participate in God's redemptive purposes? How is salvation appropriated by human beings? How, lastly, is the new life played out in concrete human existence? These questions are fundamental in working out the Christian understanding of salvation. Throughout the ages Christians have struggled to understand how God's holiness and justice relate to human beings becoming holy and escaping from bondage to the depressing influence of sin. This story has been told by various authors in great length and in great detail.[11]

If the renewal of the mind is about the inner transformation of the soul, and if being a disciple is the following of Christ in our everyday lives, growth in holiness and sanctification concern the deep relationship between humans and God. For some, growth in holiness means that we are less prone to sin, for others, holiness is something that can never be achieved in this life, but Christian theology always understands growth in holiness in terms of the undeniable bond between God the Holy One and human beings called to be holy because of God. Gerrit Immink provides a helpful perspective on the primacy of God in the process. He argues that:

> It would be incorrect to think that the difference between justification and sanctification is that in the first case God is the

10. Hauerwas, *Character Convergence*, 205.
11. McGrath, *Iustitia Dei*.

acting subject, while in the second the human being is the actor. Sanctification is just as much a matter of faith. In other word, we remain fully dependent on God's grace and live on the basis of God's compassion.[12]

Growth in holiness points to the mysterious space between the God who redeems and the created human being who is called to reflect God's image, to enjoy union with Christ, and to live with constant openness to the inner transformative work of the Spirit. This space is mysterious because it underlines the fundamental agency of the divine Spirit, who, as Chandler writes, "beckons humanity into a relationship with Christ as Redeemer, in order to transform the individual into greater depths of Christ-likeness in all life dimensions."[13]

However, becoming holy is deeply embedded into our humanity. That's why spiritual character is a feature of human beings. The spiritual is intertwined with our psyche, as the chapter on positive psychology emphasizes.

"Spiritual growth" is an agricultural metaphor that is best captured with the idea of the "fruit of the Spirit." Growth may not always mean "progress." However, it does mean "life." The shaping of our souls in the direction of being fully alive concerns all our relationships. Spiritual life bears the fruit *of the Spirit*, and it grows in our human existence in all relational directions, toward the self, toward God, toward our fellow humans, and toward the world. To this notion we now turn.

SPIRITUAL LIFE AND THE FRUITS OF THE SPIRIT

We find the fruit of the Spirit in Paul's letter to the Galatians. The famous passage in Chapter 5 binds together love, joy, peace, patience, kindness, goodness, faithfulness, gentleness, self-control. These traits are like grapes on a spiritual vine. The fruits of the Spirit vividly picture the new life in Christ through the Spirit. John Calvin, one of the Protestant Reformers, puts it like this: "Paul now informs us that all virtues, all proper and well-regulated affections, proceed from the Spirit, that is, from the grace of God, the renewed nature that we derive from Christ."[14]

12. Immink, *Faith*, 90–91.

13. Chandler, *The Holy Spirit and Christian Formation*, 4.

14. Calvin, *Commentary on Galatians and Ephesians*.

Spiritual formation is letting the fruits of the Spirit grow. So that the grace of God brings forth a flourishing life. The fruits are called virtues and affections by Calvin. This means that they are not abstract gifts; rather, they inhere in us. Just as our emotions belong to us, so the fruits of the Spirit spring from our souls; at the same time, they remain a gift of grace.

Thus, while the fruits shape our soul, they first and foremost refer to God. The fruits of the Spirit are God's gifts. Yet, the fruits are also about how we connect with our fellow human beings. So when Martin Luther in his commentary to Galatians explains the fruit of peace, he writes: "Peace towards God and men. Christians are to be peaceful and quiet. Not argumentative, not hateful, but thoughtful and patient."[15] It may not be central to the attention of the Reformers, but we cannot leave out our relationship to the wider world. The climate crisis urges us to rethink our relationship to the world and the fruits of the Spirit. Our relationship to the non-human world is part of spiritual growth. In this way, we understand the fruit of the Spirit holistically.

Let's consider three examples of the fruits of the Spirit in relation to how the soul is shaped through spiritual formation. The fruits show God's character, and they move us in relation to ourselves, in relation to our fellow human beings, and they open a perspective to the non-human world that we desperately need in the age of ecological crisis.

Faith

The Christian life starts with an act of faith. However, rather than being a single act of trusting God and God's promises, faith is about a habit, a continuing feature of the relationship between God and humans. When Paul explains the nature of faith, he points to Abraham: "Those who are of faith are blessed along with Abraham, the man of faith" (Gal 3:9). Paul reminds his readers of their father in the faith, who was called upon to continue to believe in God's promises his entire life. It is said of those who went out to see Jesus, that without seeing they believed because of his word.

According to the Christian understanding, faith is a central feature of spiritual character. There is a subtle interplay between a dynamic presence of faith in our Christian lives and a struggle to keep trusting God.

15. Luther, *Galatians*.

This interplay concerns all relationships that we have discerned above: with God, with ourselves, with fellow humans, and with the earth and all its inhabitants.

Faith is foremost about God and us. We put our trust in God because God is faithful. As a fruit of the Spirit, faith points to God as the One who can be trusted. This is the primary reality. God's words are truthful and God's promises will be fulfilled. According to Gerrit Immink, faith is first and foremost about God's communication with us; God is a speaking God:

> The relationship that expresses itself in our faith is characterized by the fact that God speaks, while we listen and respond . . . God speaks to us and promises his salvation. As the speaker, God is totally involved in this, for his faithfulness is the guarantee of the fulfillment of those promises.[16]

The fruit of faith is as much a gift from the Spirit as a reflection of the nature of God: God's faithfulness evokes trust on our part. When God's faithfulness evokes faith on our part, its significance is broader. First, in relation to the self, faith as fruit of the Spirit is about honesty. Being honest about oneself involves authentic self-awareness and self-reflection. In the Christian religion this should first be understood in reference to confession of sin. We are honest to God about the inner depths of our soul, including our deliberate faults, our tragic failures, and our culpable omissions.

In relation to our fellow humans, the fruit of faith evokes two responses. First, we refuse the temptation to approach our neighbors with an attitude of distrust and suspicion. Relationships with other human beings are characterized by faith if we approach them with confidence. Second, faith reflects the response of standing up against falsehoods. In the age of fake news, Christians display faith as the fruit of the Spirit when they refuse to join conspiracies and seek the truth, for themselves and for others.

Finally, faith is about the future of the world. Faith as a fruit of the Spirit celebrates truth and creates responsibility. This includes care for creation and a truthful relationship with the non-human world. We need faith in the complexity of today's ethical conundrums and in the overwhelming evidence of the critical state of our planet. At the same time, we must not lose trust in a future that we are secondarily responsible

16. Immink, *Faith*, 167.

for. God has the primary responsibility for it; we therefore know that the future is ultimately safe because of God's covenant with this world.

We put it this way on the prompt cards used in our model of spiritual formation: the fruit of faith makes us trust the love and grace of God that has been made known to us in Christ, in relation to God, to ourselves, to our fellow humans and to the non-human world.

Generosity

Research on generosity shows that there is a certain paradox involved: those who give without any expectation, receive much in return. By taking care of others, we take care of ourselves. This, researchers argue, is a sociological fact. Smith and Davidson make the important point that this virtue goes right to the heart of what it is to be human: "When generosity is embraced as a way of life, people increasingly live into the reality of what it means to be human, a fuller and truer sense of who human beings are and what we are capable of."[17]

Generosity consists of more than individual acts of giving. Generosity also touches the political domain. The moral philosopher, Martha Nussbaum, recalls Nelson Mandela's unusual generosity. She describes Mandela's attitude in his years of imprisonment as "non-anger." It was a way of doing justice in a generous way. In his captivity, Mandela did not consider certain roles or duties as below his dignity. Through introspection, he was able to adopt this attitude of "non-anger." "To Mandela, the angry and resentful approach is simply not appropriate to a leader, because a leader's role is to get things done, and the generous and cooperative approach is the one that works."[18] More than a virtue or an attitude, Nussbaum seems to suggest, generosity is also something pragmatic. It is something you do because it works. This may not sound very spiritual; it seems not to entail strong Christian convictions. Indeed, Nussbaum suggests the influence of the pre-Christian Stoic author, Marcus Aurelius.

This may be so, but it seems that the paradox of generosity is also acknowledged in Scripture. Proverbs 11 verse 25 says, "A generous person will prosper; whoever refreshes others will be refreshed." As a fruit of the Spirit, it stands against selfish ambition—one of the vices, the sinful

17. Smith and Davidson, *Paradox of Generosity*, 226.

18. Nussbaum, *Anger and Forgiveness*, 231.

desires.[19] Ben Witherington III identifies selfish ambition as a "social sin." Generosity is a social virtue; it is goodness directed toward others. Generosity, paradoxically, is both a turn toward the other and a turn toward the self. Generosity flows back to the giver.

This is also true of God. God's generosity is at the heart of the Christian faith. It is by grace that we live. The grace of God keeps us alive and through grace God grants us life. The incarnation is God's definitive act of generosity. By giving the divine self, God showed God's gracious and generous character. Christ is the embodiment of God's generosity. Through the gift of the Spirit and the fruits of the Spirit that grow minds in the process of being renewed, God's generosity returns to the giver. Our generosity toward one another starts with giving ourselves to God.

However, generosity is certainly not the current hallmark of the old centers of Christianity—namely, Western Europe and the regions of the world that culturally reflect the values and the economic status of what is called "the West." In this age, the old centers of Christianity are not particularly known for their generosity. One need only think of the growing gap between rich and poor and the endless stream of refugees—a sad political and humanitarian reality that results from global economic disbalance and political interferences in other countries. The modern post-Christian world is similarly not known for its generosity with respect to the exploitation of the earth. It is true that major transitions are taking place. Nevertheless, our attitude to the non-human world needs to be much, much more generous. We constantly need to rediscover the depth of God's grace toward us in order to act from grace ourselves, toward others and toward the world. We express it this way on the prompt cards that are used in our model of spiritual formation: The fruit of generosity is a reflection of God's generosity to us; giving good things to others freely and abundantly.

Joy

The third fruit of the Spirit that we look at to understand spiritual growth and the shaping of the soul is joy. The Scriptures are full of joy. Joyful Psalms sing the praises of God. But joy is much more than a mere expression of a positive attitude.

---

19. Witherington, *Grace in Galatia*, 402.

The English writer C.S. Lewis gave his autobiography the title, *Surprised by Joy*. Lewis was married to Joy Davidman, but the autobiography is not about his marriage but about his early life, leading to his conversion to Christianity. Joy, for Lewis, has to do with desire, with yearning. Joy cannot be grasped. Alister McGrath, Lewis' biographer has this to say: "This sense of yearning was so powerful and so desirable that Lewis returned again and again to what he thought were its sources. Yet joy proved resistant to his attempts at control; the more he actively sought to secure it, the less he managed to grasp it. It lay beyond his control."[20]

Joy is first an experience. It cannot be organized. It is a gift, a grace. Hence, joy as a spiritual fruit, like all the others, starts with God. God is the surprise that encounters us, that fills us.

Whomever writes about joy cannot leave suffering behind. Mary Moschella quotes Jürgen Moltmann: "How can we laugh and rejoice when there are still so many tears to be wiped away and new tears are being added every day?"[21] In responding to Moltmann, Moschella provides a valuable perspective from the field of pastoral studies. Pastoral studies "often seem to get stuck in the proclamation of radical suffering, violence and evil . . . it becomes all the more important to discover pathways back up toward experiences of grace, hope, and joy."[22] The path to spiritual formation shapes the soul in a world of suffering and evil. The intent, though, is not to focus on evil, but rather to live a joyful life. In summing up her position, Moschella offers three perspectives: respond, resist, and rejoice. We must "respond to suffering and resist injustice and yet remember to rejoice in God's goodness, beauty, and love."[23] From the first disciples and their suffering, we learn that joy is indeed a matter of spiritual character. It may even be called an "extraordinary achievement" because to experience joy in circumstances that call for courage and perseverance does not reflect what many take to be the natural occasions for joy.[24]

Though joy is a human emotion, Moschella writes also about the gladness of God. Similarly, Klaas Bom argues that we cannot refer to joy as an anthropological feature, as an aspect of spiritual character, for

---

20. McGrath, *Intellectual World of C. S. Lewis*, 110.

21. Mary Clark Moschella, *Caring for Joy*, 114.

22. Mary Clark Moschella, *Caring for Joy*, 115.

23. Mary Clark Moschella, *Caring for Joy*, 228.

24. Roberts, *Spiritual Emotions*, 122.

example, without also speaking about divine joy. Bom presents the voices of a 17th Century French Catholic (Blaise Pascal), a 20th Century Dutch Reformed person (A.A. van Ruler), and contemporary Latin-American Pentecostals. These voices show that Christian joy is founded in God's being. Divine joy is Trinitarian; it is "attached to the Creator, focused on the love of and consolation through Christ, and expressed through the Holy Spirit."[25]

According to Pamela Ebstyne King and Frederic Defoy, joy needs to be understood as a psychological habit. They list various understandings of joy, with "the common denominator that joy is an emotional response to something good."[26] Though interested in the psychology of joy, they connect to important Christian beliefs, namely that joy as ultimate goodness is theological and concerns God's purpose for humanity, and that joy is not fully realized in this world and is therefore an eschatological reality. Joy is clearly central in spiritual character and discipleship.

How should we categorize joy? Is joy an emotion, a desire, an experience, or a virtue? Perhaps joy is an act. We engage in the act of rejoicing. It is something we do, naturally, in response to God's love for us. As we capture it on the cards that are used in our model of spiritual formation: The fruit of joy is rejoicing in the grace and love of God. Joy that flows from the knowledge that in the good times and in the bad, God is with me, those I love, and all God's children.

SUMMARY

In this chapter we explored spiritual character, one of the four dimensions covered by our model of spiritual formation. "Spiritual character" is a term that connects to other fields of thinking—namely, virtue ethics and positive psychology. We offered a different angle to spiritual character. The primary focus, we argued, is the nature of the relationship between a human being and God. Theological anthropology gives us another window to look at the persons that we accompany pastorally: people made in the image of God and journeying toward the likeness of Christ. Given that we are embodied persons, spiritual character is primarily about the soul and the shaping of our souls. Spiritual character is about the shaping of our souls, in everyday life, in relation to the Triune God, and in

25. Bom, "Joy, Joy, Joy," 226.
26. King & Defoy, Joy as a Virtue, 309.

view of an existence that transcends us to dimensions that we can never fathom. Hallmarks of the spiritually shaped soul—faith, generosity, and joy—were discussed. All are socially oriented, but the primary orientation is to God and God's grace, given freely in Christ through the power of the Spirit.

8

CONNECTING WITH A
CONTEMPORARY PERSPECTIVE

Positive Psychology as a Pastoral Resource

IN THE FIRST CHAPTER, we showed that our approach connects with an ancient Christian tradition, according to which the pastor's primary calling is to spiritual and moral guidance. Our model also links with a contemporary school of theory and practice—namely, positive psychology.

There has been a tendency for pastoral theologians to uncritically borrow from the human and social sciences. We have chosen to incorporate into our spiritual formation process some of the core strengths and virtues advocated by the positive psychology movement. It behoves us to make a theological argument for the appropriateness of doing so. A central issue that needs to be confronted head-on is the optimistic, sunny view of the human person that positive psychology works with. Positive psychology does not recognize the Christian notion of a flawed, sinful self that is unable to improve itself through will and effort alone. On the Christian view, humans must rely on the empowerment of the Holy Spirit and the redemptive force of divine grace. Clearly, positive psychology cannot endorse this anthropology. Indeed, no secular system of psychology can. A fundamental challenge for anyone who wishes to achieve an integration of psychology and theology is that the fields have two quite different objects for investigation. Psychology, by definition, is the study of the *psyche* (the original meaning was soul, but it is now understood as mind); theology, by definition, is the study of God. Therefore, there will necessarily be some fundamental differences between the two systems. Despite this, we contend that "an exchange of gifts"[1] is possible. Positive psychology sends us back to a biblical gift that some of us have downplayed or even dismissed—namely happiness. In both the Hebrew Bible and in the gospels, eudaimonic[2] happiness is an important theme.

This new psychological movement also stimulates us to think about what a positive theology might look like. Many in the Evangelical, Lutheran, Reformed, Wesleyan[3] and Roman Catholic traditions have embraced a pathology-oriented anthropology. On this view, the consequence of the Fall is that humans have become hopelessly mired in sin and their only consolation in desolation is saving grace. Christian theology, for its part, seeks to remind those in the positive psychology movement that the final goal of human life is not *eudaimonia* in the here and now. Further, a state of blessedness on earth can only be partially established through an individual's effort, no matter how noble and altruistic they happen to be. *Eudaimonia* is fully realized through commitment in this life to cooperate with God in God's project of establishing the divine Reign, and beyond the temporal through the beatific vision secured by grace through faith.

The tasks taken up in this chapter are fivefold. First, we present an overview of positive psychology. Second, the work of those who argue that happiness is a prominent theme in the Bible is discussed. Next, an outline of a "positive theology" is developed. Fourth, following on from this theological conversation, an argument is made for communion (giving and receiving love) as the ideal for *agape* rather than self-sacrifice and self-denial. Finally, the theological reason for including optimism in the psychological well-being domain and hope in the spiritual character field is presented.

---

1. The term comes from an article by Ellen Charry and Russell Kosits. See Charry & Kosits, "Christian Theology and Positive Psychology."

2. Aristotle averred that the goal of human life is *eudaimonia*, blessedness or happiness (see below). He argued it is secured through a life of virtue.

3. Wesley's own position notwithstanding.

OVERVIEW OF POSITIVE PSYCHOLOGY

In his book entitled *Authentic Happiness*, Martin Seligman explains why this state is so crucial for human beings: "[F]eeling positive emotion is important, not just because it is pleasant in its own right, but because it *causes* much better commerce with the world. Developing more positive emotion in our lives will build friendship, love, better physical health, and greater achievement."[4] In this focus on psychological well-being, attention is given to character strengths, optimism, life-satisfaction, self-esteem, and self-confidence.

A helpful overview of the approach is found on the website of the Positive Psychology Center at the University of Pennsylvania (Seligman's home institution):

> Positive Psychology is the scientific study of the strengths and virtues that enable individuals and communities to thrive . . . This field is founded on the belief that people want to lead meaningful and fulfilling lives, to cultivate what is best within themselves, and to enhance their experiences of love, work, and play.
>
> Positive Psychology has three central concerns: positive emotions, positive individual traits, and positive institutions. Understanding positive emotions entails the study of contentment with the past, happiness in the present, and hope for the future. Understanding positive individual traits consists of the study of the strengths and virtues, such as the capacity for love and work, courage, compassion, resilience, creativity, curiosity, integrity, self- knowledge, moderation, self-control, and wisdom. Understanding positive institutions entails the study of the strengths that foster better communities, such as justice, responsibility, civility, parenting, nurturance, work ethic, leadership, teamwork, purpose, and tolerance.[5]

In *Authentic Happiness*, Seligman argued for an understanding of happiness that incorporates three elements: positive emotion, engagement, and meaning. By the time *Flourish: A Visionary New Understanding of Happiness and Well-being* was published, his thinking had evolved.[6] While he continued to emphasize the role of choice, he moved to

4. Seligman, *Authentic Happiness*, 76.

5. Seligman, Positive Psychology Center homepage. Retrieved from http://www.ppc.sas.upenn.edu, July 24th, 2020.

6. Seligman, *Flourish*.

consideration of a more complex concept—namely, well-being. Well-being, in turn, is measured by flourishing. From this time onwards, well-being rather than happiness is established as the focus of much of the research in positive psychology. Seligman contends that for human beings to flourish five elements must be in place. He refers to a PERMA model: 1. Positive emotion, 2. Engagement, 3. Positive relationships, 4. Meaning, and 5. Accomplishment.

(P) **Positive Emotion.** Included in this category are studies of subjective well-being and life satisfaction, research on positive affectivity, and positive emotions. A prominent example of research on positive emotions is the work of Barbara Fredrickson.[7] Fredrickson's research had a profound effect on Seligman in the early days of the pursuit of his new passion, and it has continued to do so. Positive emotions include joy, interest, contentment, and love. The research by Frederickson demonstrates that positive emotions have their own complex characteristics. Positive emotion cannot simply be equated with the absence of negative emotions. It not only feels different; it also has different psychological functions. Frederickson's "broaden and build" model examines how positive emotions lead to actions that build personal resources in the long-term.[8] Negative emotions are usually associated with specific action: fear drives us to flee, while anger puts us on the attack. Positive emotions, on the other hand, are less tied to specific actions or life-threatening situations and lead to broader, more flexible response propensities. In this way, they offer us a wider array of cognitive and behavioral options. For example, joy leads into play, interest drives the desire to explore, and love is behind our enjoyment of those we are close to.

(E) **Engagement.** The most well-known work in this category is that done on flow and creativity by Mihaly Csikszentmihalyi. His very popular book, *Flow: The Psychology of Optimal Experiences*,[9] was published before the formal development of positive psychology, but it nevertheless constitutes a very important contribution to the movement. The concept of flow emerged from many years of research on the positive aspects of human experience and it is defined as "the process of total involvement with life," which is generally accompanied by joy and creativity.[10] Seligman

---

7. See Fredrickson, "What Good are Positive Emotions?"; Fredrickson, "Role of Positive Emotions."

8. See Fredrickson, "What Good are Positive Emotions?"

9. Csikszentmihalyi, *Flow*.

10. Csikszentmihalyi, *Flow*, xi.

puts it this way: "You go into flow when your highest strengths are deployed to meet the highest challenges that come your way."[11] Csikszentmihalyi, like others in this psychological school, grounds his concept in Aristotle's view of happiness (*eudaimonia*). When "in the flow," a person is so completely absorbed in what they are doing that they lose their sense of time, and the activity is experienced as intrinsically rewarding.[12]

(R) **Positive Relationships.** There is a large body of research in positive psychology dedicated to traits and behaviors that foster positive relationships such as love, compassion, altruism, and empathy. Christopher Peterson, another one of the pioneers in positive psychology, captures the role of relationship very succinctly: "Other people matter."[13] Love is identified as a character strength, or positive trait, that is expressed in caring relationships with others.[14] It is defined as a "cognitive, behavioral, and emotional stance toward others." Love occurs within reciprocated relationships and incorporates romantic love, friendship, and the love between parents and children. A distinction is made between love in interpersonal relationships and in altruistic concern for others. The latter orientation is captured by words such as "kindness, generosity, nurturance, care, compassion, and altruistic love."[15]

(M) **Meaning.** Meaning in this context is defined as "belonging to and serving something that you believe is bigger than the self."[16] It goes without saying that this is not an entirely new concept for psychology. It is closely related to Erik Erikson's concept of generativity.[17] *Generativity* refers to "making your mark" on the world by establishing and guiding the next generation, as well as creating and accomplishing things that leave the world in a better state than you found it. Generative adults bring improvement to their world and find meaning through this pursuit. Meaning-making is obviously also connected to Viktor Frankl's logotherapy.[18] According to this theory, most psychological disorders result from failure to meet our basic spiritual need for meaning. Psychological

11. Seligman, *Flourish*, 37.

12. See Nakamura & Csikszentmihalyi, "Flow Theory and Research."

13. Peterson, Foreword. In *Oxford Handbook of Positive Psychology*, xxiii.

14. Peterson & Seligman, *Character Strengths and Virtues*, 304.

15. Peterson & Seligman, *Character Strengths and Virtues*, 326.

16. Seligman, *Flourish*, 17.

17. See Erikson, *Identity*, 138–139.

18. See Frankl, *Man's Search*.

well-being requires letting go of materialistic pursuits and embracing self-transcendence. The essence of logotherapy is awakening people's sense of the need of, and responsibility for, finding meaning in their existence.

(A) Accomplishment. This refers to pursuing competence, success, and mastery for its own sake, in a variety of activities, including work, sports, and hobbies. It is closely linked to goal pursuit. It's important to set realistic goals. Simply putting in the effort to achieve these goals results in a sense of satisfaction. When a person finally achieves them, there is a sense of pride and fulfilment. Accomplishment is also closely associated with the flow experience. As Krueger puts it, "[E]ngagement in the sense of flow (i.e., being absorbed in the process of doing the work ...) already implies accomplishment. Flow foretells success because the task is, by definition, tractable." [19] Seligman contends that accomplishment is something that people seek even in the absence of other aspects of the full life, such as positive emotion, engagement, and meaning.[20]

Below we offer a fully developed evaluation of positive psychology from a biblical and theological perspective. However, we cannot let the statement on accomplishment go without critical comment. The state of being in the flow, together with accomplishing goals in various domains of life such as education, work, and sport clearly enhances personal well-being. It is a great feeling to have worked hard and used your gifts and personal resources with skill, focus, creativity, and imagination to achieve the desired result. For the Christian, however, there are higher values involved. Service is one of these. The call to servanthood, it goes without saying, is a strong motif in the New Testament. Jesus told the disciples that "the Son of Man came not to be served but to serve" (Mk 10:45). In 1 Peter 4:10 it is stated: "Like good stewards of the manifold grace of God, serve one another with whatever gift each of you has received." Our Christian vocation—and here the focus is on work and ministry, both paid and unpaid, rather than sport or hobbies—is to use our gifts creatively and conscientiously for the good of others. Service to individuals and the community is the ultimate goal. A feeling of emotional well-being is a by-product of using our gifts in the service of others.

We also recognize that in most, if not all, of the cultural contexts we represent happiness is commonly associated with accomplishment, success, status, and prestige. While happiness is quite a strong theme in the

---

19. Krueger, "Seligman's Flourish," 122.

20. See Seligman, "Authentic Happiness."

Bible, it is most often placed in a spiritual rather than a material frame. It is to an in-depth consideration of this fact that we now turn.

HAPPINESS IN THE BIBLE

One member of the team, Neil Pembroke, had the opportunity to present two papers on the research project sitting behind this book at a one-day symposium on Christian formation in the parish at Ridley College, Melbourne Australia, in early March of 2020. Ridley is an Anglican theological college in the evangelical and Reformed tradition. The aspect of the program that the team has developed that was the most disconcerting for the two Anglican priests who responded to Neil's papers—and also for a number of the symposium participants—was the incorporation of positive psychology. In particular, the focus on happiness and flourishing was vigorously challenged. The view expressed was that the aim of the Christian life is spending oneself in serving others and in witnessing to the Gospel. Indeed, if we look to the example of the apostle Paul, we see a missionary life marked very often by turmoil, hardship, and suffering. In this scenario, what could the pursuit of happiness possibly mean? The respondents to my paper argued that living faithful to Christ and to his commission to bring others to Christ is hard and demanding; the positivity associated with that is joy rather than happiness. It is our view that the Bible promotes both joy and happiness as very real possibilities for Christians. In what follows, attention is given to both the Wisdom tradition and the gospel of Luke.

We begin with a discussion of happiness in the Book of Proverbs. Martin Seligman identifies three forms of life that produce happiness and well-being.[21] The first is the pleasurable life. Here the focus is on pleasing experiences and sensations that secure a sense of well-being. Attention is directed to the present moment and the gifts that it offers. The good life, the second form of life, is one dedicated to inculcating personal virtues. Here there is an alignment with the Aristotelian vision: a life of virtue results in *eudaimonia*. The final way of life is a meaningful one. Meaning is established through embracing a cause that transcends an individual's own life. In dedicating one's life to a greater cause or purpose, a sense of meaning is secured. It is the second form of life—the good life—that Proverbs is oriented to. Carol Newsom argues that the eudaimonic vision

---

21. See Seligman, "Can Happiness be Taught?"; Seligman, *Authentic Happiness.*

of happiness we find there is established on the belief that the world has a relatively predictable and set order that can be grasped by the person of wisdom.[22] What we find in Proverbs is a father's guidance to his son concerning the attitudes, disciplines, and actions that lead to human flourishing. Molding one's life around wise thinking and acting leads to the good life in the moral sense and in the sense of personal fulfilment.

Newsom emphasizes the fact that it is eudaimonic rather than hedonistic happiness that is the focus of Proverbs.[23] Indeed, the Book shines the light very clearly on the non-hedonic aspects of acquiring wisdom through its repeated references to the personal discipline that an individual must embrace. Proverbs is primarily concerned with the satisfaction and sense of fulfilment that come from the confluence of disciplined and virtuous character, on the one hand, and diligence in carrying out one's tasks, on the other (something Seligman, Csikszentmihalyi and others in the positive psychology movement fully endorse). Wise living has its rewards. Those rewards are, first, prosperity and a sense of security and stability in a world of turmoil, and second, approbation from the community and from on high.

We also find reflection on the conditions required for happiness in the gospels. Luke, for example, makes a number of references to the joy, celebration, and blessing to be enjoyed by the followers of Christ. Joel Green argues that happiness comes into sharp focus in three sections of the Third Gospel.[24] In Luke 1–2, the entry into the world of John and Jesus are happy events that are cause for celebration not only for their parents and circle of family and close friends, but also for all people. This is evidenced in the announcement of the angels to the shepherds after the birth of Jesus: "I am bringing good news to you—wonderful, happy news for everyone: Your savior is born today in the city of David; he is Christ the Lord" (Lk 2:10–11).

Luke paints a picture of Jesus as viewing the world and God's Realm very differently to the Pharisees and scribes. This comes into focus in Luke 15 (Green's second section). Here Jesus' way of acting draws sharp criticism and rebuke from his adversaries. They are critical of the fact that Jesus shares in table fellowship with tax collectors and sinners. Jesus responds to them by telling three parables about finding something

22. See Newsom, "Positive Psychology and Ancient Israelite Wisdom."

23. See Newsom, "Positive Psychology and Ancient Israelite Wisdom," 123.

24. See Green, "We Had to Celebrate."

that has been lost—a lost sheep, a lost coin, and a lost son. The ultimate point in all of these stories is that celebration at table is the right response because it reflects the celebration taking place on high. It is only right, says Jesus, that human happiness mirrors God's own happiness. We will make the same point below in developing a positive theology. But before getting to that, it is necessary to briefly mention the "happy dispositions" in Luke 6:20–26—Green's third and final section.

In this segment of the Third Gospel, Jesus identifies certain dispositions that are established in the blessed ones. He wants to make it clear that the way to happiness is not by committing oneself to finding it. Rather, happiness is the by-product of committing to God's royal rule revealed in the teaching and mission of Jesus. That is, the context for happiness according to Luke is eschatological. With the coming of Jesus, and his death, resurrection and exaltation, a new era has begun. Those who commit their lives to God's mission in the world as revealed by Jesus will flourish in this eschatologically ordered world.

In our view, theologians in the classic tradition represented by Augustine, Anselm, and Calvin have paid too little attention to the theme of happiness in the Bible. The focus has been largely on the tragic nature of the human condition—original sin—and happiness as an eschatological reality, on the one hand, and on selflessly spending oneself and embracing suffering in service and witness to Christ, on the other. It is no part of our intention to turn a blind eye to sin and the dark side of human nature. Nor do we overlook the fact that suffering for the sake of Christ and his call to love is sometimes necessary and inevitable. What we offer by way of seeking to critically correlate the Christian heritage with positive psychology is a positive theology that complements, rather than replaces, the dominant theological tradition. Our argument is that there is a happiness-driven complement to pathology-focused theology, and an understanding of *agape* as communion that sits beside a view of Christian love as self-sacrifice.

TOWARD A "POSITIVE THEOLOGY"

In the history of Christian thought, happiness has most often been viewed as a heavenly reward. That is, it is an eschatological rather than a present hope. The eschatological perspective on happiness is central in Augustine's thought. According to him, the unpredictable, uncontrollable, and dangerous side of life means that it is futile to look for happiness in this world. The attempt to secure material goods is a vain search for happiness because wealth, health, status, power, and friends can all be lost. Life in this world is filled with uncertainty and insecurity; the only dependable reality is the grace of God and the hope of eternal glory. Further, though virtue may sometimes triumph over vice, such fitful moral victories are hardly the basis of lasting happiness. That must wait until all vice is vanquished in the eternal kingdom.[25] Indeed, not even virtuous living can lead to an assurance of future happiness. All humans are subject to divine wrath and the punishment that comes with it. It is only through divine grace that some are elected to eternal happiness. In sum, Augustine argued for pinning one's hopes on celestial rather than terrestrial happiness.

In the Middle Ages, under the influence of Augustine's theology, all hope of temporal well-being was given up and attention was turned squarely to divine displeasure over sins and how they could be forgiven. The priest had the power to absolve sin and thereby offer the hope of salvation and heavenly reward. Christians—the overwhelming majority in medieval Europe—were driven by fear of hell and social harmony was thus maintained.

Anselm's aim in *Cur Deus Homo* was to call the faithful to a life of righteousness, while guarding against the despair that comes with inevitable failure in this regard. God requires his creatures to be fully righteous, but the power of sin is so strong that no one can achieve this. Anselm offered hope for all those caught in this vicious predicament by arguing that God the Son freely gave up his life in our place to satisfy the demand that sin be punished. In this way, the view was firmly established that *agape*—perfectly exemplified by Christ on the Cross—requires selflessly giving of oneself for others. Below we make a case for agape as communion rather than self-sacrifice. For now, we need to conclude this overview of the theological school of thought that happiness is an eschatological reality.

John Calvin was profoundly influenced by the Augustinian perspective that human beings are dominated by the power of sin. While he, like Augustine, accepted that the Genesis 1 declaration of the *imago Dei* confers dignity on the human, he was strongly of the opinion that the divine image is now very badly tarnished due to the powerful influence of sin (the Genesis 3 story). Full terrestrial happiness is an illusory hope

---

25. See Augustine, *City of God*, 19.27.

in this theological schema. The depth and power of original sin means that the best one can hope for is fleeting moments of joy and happiness. The only true happiness available to humans in this life flows from the confidence that one's sins are forgiven because Christ died in our place and paid the penalty for us. Absolute happiness is postponed until one inherits eternal glory.

Though John Wesley accepted the doctrine of original sin, he differs from Augustine and Calvin in his view that God desires genuine temporal happiness for God's creatures. The important Wesley scholar, David McEwan, makes this abundantly clear in his fine book, *The Life of God in the Soul: The Integration of Love, Holiness and Happiness in the Thought of John Wesley.*[26] The central question that McEwan addresses is this: How did Wesley respond to the issue of the extent to which in this fallen world with all of its attendant corruption, misfortune, pain, and suffering Christians can expect to experience genuine and lasting happiness? His answer is that as Wesley wrestled with this deeply challenging question over the course of his ministry, he came to see that to the extent that we reflect the essential nature and character of God in the way we live, we will experience genuine happiness. The nature and character of God in essence is love. We were created in love to love both God and neighbor. When we do all things in love, we reflect the nature and character of God, and the result is genuine happiness.

McEwan observes, as we also have, that as long as Christianity has been around, there have been those who hold to the view that being a disciple of Christ is a grim business. We are called to self-denial and cross-bearing; we shouldn't expect to be happy. But Wesley believed that the fruit of living in love of God and neighbor is an enduring state of enjoyment and contentment. God is not the ultimate kill-joy. Rather, God intends that we enjoy our lives.

Wesley realized that living in love means that sometimes we need to do things that are hard, that cost us something (once again, something that we have also recognized). McEwan takes up the issue of connecting choosing what is painful, on the one hand, and God's intention that we enjoy our lives, on the other, in his chapter on helps in spiritual formation. He shows how Wesley took the view that freely choosing to embrace the Cross is a necessary condition of loving God and neighbor. Pleasing ourselves, choosing only pleasurable activities, blocking our ears to the

26. McEwan, *Life of God in the Soul.*

call of God and neighbor, is not consistent with Christian maturity. In order to be perfected in love, in order to experience the wholeness that is inextricably bound up with happiness, we sometimes need to choose to do things that cost us personally. Wesley's point, one that McEwan brings out so clearly, is that self-protection and egoism may seem like routes to happiness, but selfishness can only end in emptiness and self-diminishment. The path of holiness and love is the path to genuine happiness. How could it be otherwise when we were created to reflect the nature and character of God?

Ellen Charry is also drawn to the idea that God intends for humans to be genuinely happy, both in this life and in the next.[27] Charry develops what she calls a "positive theology." She argues, first, that, through our baptism and our faith in Christ as our Lord and Savior, we are established in an identity as the ones who are unconditionally loved by God and fully assured of God's healing and forgiveness.[28] For those whose identity is grounded in the *en Christo*, there is the happy and joyous reality of a divine promise to never let us go. Christians are able to forgive themselves for selfishness, greed, apathy in the face of suffering and injustice, failures in love of God and neighbor, and more, because they are assured of God's infinite love and mercy. Living as a godly self lovingly established by God means that there is the confidence that comes with knowing that each time we fall God will pick us up, and each time we are busted by sin we will be healed. Because of the power of darkness in us, we are locked in a struggle between the self that bends us away from God's good will (the "law of sin") and a righteous self who loves the divine will (Rom 7:14–25). In spite of this, the identity we have in virtue of our baptism into Christ's death and resurrection means that we have cause for genuine self-confidence, self-love, and self-prizing.

Charry's second take on positive theology is based in the position—affirmed by many other leading contemporary systematic theologians—that God is not actually immutable and impassible as Aquinas and the other scholastic theologians thought. God experiences emotion.[29] The biblical picture is of a God who grieves, feels sad, feels joyful, gets angry and jealous, and who suffers (we will take up this theme again below). The view of God as unable to experience emotion has more to do with

27. See Charry, "Positive Theology: An Exploration"; Charry, "Necessity of Divine Happiness."; and Charry & Kosits, "Christian Theology and Positive Psychology."

28. See Charry, "Positive Theology," 290.

29. See Charry, "The Necessity of Divine Happiness," 238–241.

the philosophical argument that if God were to experience an emotional state the result would be a change in God that could only mean loss of divine perfection (the idea of change to a higher degree of perfection is incoherent) than it does with a straight-forward reading of the story of God's engagement with Israel and with the whole world in and through Christ.

Charry accepts that the Bible paints a picture of God experiencing an array of emotions. One of these emotions is happiness over human flourishing. She argues that when we view it this way, the profound and pervasive human anxiety over the fact that we can never please God gets turned upside down. When God sees humans flourishing as they experience a deep sense of fulfilment, meaning, and purpose, God is well-pleased. It warms God's heart, so to speak, to see the work of God's hands living full lives. Irenaeus famously said that the glory of God is the human totally alive. Speaking against a pathology-driven theology, Charry makes this statement: "Surely divine encouragement is more effective than punishment (or its threat) in service to creation's flourishing. And if human flourishing is more delightful to God than its perishing (cf. Ezek 18:23, 33:11), theologians would do well to attend to God's and our mutual delight in one another more than to God's displeasure at our failures and our consequent guilt and distress."[30] Through baptism and the act of faith we become participants in the drama of salvation. What this means is that the Christian is drawn into "God's happy project of loving creation into flourishing."[31]

Clearly, much more work is required to construct a comprehensive positive theology. However, given the scope of this book, we must be content with this sketch. The aim is simply to present a compelling theological rationale for our decision to incorporate positive psychology into our whole-person approach to spiritual formation.

COMMUNION AS THE IDEAL FOR AGAPE

In discussing pathology-driven theology above, we noted that a companion position of this approach is that followers of Christ are called to spend themselves in service of others in imitation of Christ, who chose the way of the Cross in service of humankind and its salvation. It is abundantly

30. See Charry, "The Necessity of Divine Happiness," 246.

31. See Charry, "The Necessity of Divine Happiness," 247.

clear that self-sacrifice is sometimes required of Christians as they live faithful to the love command. Scenarios such as supporting a spouse through a period of mental illness, caring for an adult child living with disability, taking on suffering in witnessing to the gospel, standing with the oppressed and marginalized despite the vilification come to mind. However, we hold that the ideal for *agape* is not self-sacrifice but rather communion—giving and receiving love in a spirit of reciprocity. Here we follow the line developed by the theological ethicist, Stephen Post.

According to Post, mutual love or reciprocity is the only appropriate basic norm for interpersonal relations.[32] He also refers to this mutual love as "communion." He argues that there is a "true" self-love that is expressed through a desire for a triadic fellowship involving God, self, and other(s).[33] An individual pursues their own needs and aspirations, but only in the context of a loving commitment to the needs and aspirations of those with whom they share life. Such a reciprocal love, argues Post, is not inferior to selfless love, as many believe:

> The moral excellence of communion (giving and receiving love) is too often lost sight of . . . Frequently selfless love . . . is thought to be ethically superior to communion and alone worthy of the designation "Christian." The equilibrium of communion that allows each participant to find fulfillment through the process of mutuality is set aside to make room for the rare genius of selflessness. However, in our view, a "true" or proper self-love defined as the pursuit of one's own good within the context of triadic communion can be distinguished from both selfishness (the pursuit of one's own separate interests) and self-infatuation . . . [34]

Post argues, then, that it is legitimate to pursue your own good within the context of a triadic fellowship. Such self-love must be distinguished from both selfishness and self-infatuation. Selfishness means pursuing your own interests without due regard for the interests of others. But the person who is committed to a life of communion pays due attention to the needs and desires of others. A person who is self-infatuated, on the other hand, simply cannot manage fellowship with others. They are so attracted to self that they find no interest in getting to know others in any depth. The good of personal fulfillment, by contrast, is pursued through a

32. Post, "Inadequacy of Selflessness," 213.

33. Post, "Communion and True Self-Love," 345.

34. Post, "Communion and True Self-Love," 345.

relationship of reciprocity. You desire fulfilment for yourself, but you are equally concerned with helping others find it.

Post's basic argument is that the ideal of a love stripped of all self-concern is grounded in a mistaken conceptualization of divine love. Self-concern, it is important to recognize, is very different from selfishness. There are legitimate concerns that the self has and these need to be taken care of. A central concern that God has is the mutual good of communion with human persons.

Post turns to both the Hebrew and the Christian scriptures to demonstrate that God is not disinterested in the way God loves humankind. In the Bible we find a picture of a God who grieves (something we have also noted). YHWH "was sorry that he made humanity on earth," we read in Genesis, "and he was grieved at heart" (6:6). Why is God grieved? Because God reaches out in love calling humanity into communion, and time and again people reject that call. If God's love was disinterested, this grieving would make no sense. But if we take God's deep concern for the mutual good of fellowship seriously, we also give due credit to the important human vocation of soothing divine pain through promoting that fellowship.

Post uses Abraham Heschel's discussion in *Between God and Man* to discuss this vocation. The Israelite prophets, Heschel says, had as their goal the mitigation of the divine *pathos* that is associated with rejection by humans. In calling the people to turn away from their sin and turn anew to God and to the divine will and purpose, they were attempting to change God's *pathos* into joy. According to Heschel, it is simply not possible to find the ideal of selfless love in the Hebrew Scriptures. What we find, instead, is a profound valuation of a reciprocal relationship of love between God and humanity. Communion between YHWH and Israel is the preferred vision and ultimate aim as far as the writers of the Hebrew Scriptures are concerned. Certainly, there is no place for egocentricity with the "I" at the center of the universe. But self-concern is quite distinct from selfishness. A passionate concern for the mutual good of fellowship is not only legitimate, it should be vigorously pursued. Post thus contends that mutuality rather than mere giving is the goal of love.[35] YHWH gives fully of the divine self, but YHWH also desires a response of love. The Hebrew Bible reveals a God "on the make," if you will.

35. See Post, "The Inadequacy," 216.

Heschel, Post notes, amasses a vast array of scriptural references to support this contention. Here are just a few of his examples. "You hunt me like a lion" (Job 10:16). "The voice of the Lord cries to the city" (Micah 6:9). And finally, the Lord calls out, "Where are you?" (Gen 3:9). These texts point to the fact that God is unwilling to be alone and pursues humans in the hope of establishing fellowship with them.

We have established that God's love for us is not disinterested, but what about the call to imitate Christ? Surely Christ is the model of a life totally devoid of self-interest and self-love? Post argues that while the Christ of the gospels is never selfish, it is misleading to suggest that he has no self-concern. The concern Jesus has is the same as that of the Father: to call humans into communion. Once this goal was lost and those who valued power and privilege more than fellowship with God began to exert their influence, the way of the Cross was established as the way of salvation. God's hope in Christ was for everyone to hear the invitation to be part of the Realm of God and to accept it. The fact that certain powerful ones did not and moved so viciously against Jesus meant that God's saving love, originally channeled through Jesus' healing and preaching ministry, would now be focused on the Cross.

Does it follow that the Cross is thereby established as the ultimate exemplar of all love? If the answer is "yes," it follows that self-sacrifice rather than mutuality is the final aim of love. Post contends that it is not necessary to go down this path. Following Richard Westley, he takes the view that the Cross is only one dimension in the salvation event:

> [T]he deepest desire of [Jesus'] heart was that people would respond to his proclamation and have a change of heart. But if he knew that the human race could only be saved on the condition of his own bloody murder, then he could not want "everyone" to be transformed by his message. If everyone responded . . . there would be none left to administer his violent death. To hold that it was only through his passion and death on the cross that we are saved amounts to nothing less than saying that Jesus was a hypocrite about his preaching.[36]

If the Cross is one (albeit central) dimension of Christ's saving work rather than the totality of it, then there is no requirement to hold up self-sacrifice as the Christian ideal. In sum, the theological line that we take is that while Christians are called to take up a stance of self-denial when

---

36. Westley, *Redemptive Intimacy*, 114–115; cited in Post, "The Inadequacy," 220.

it is required by the demands of love, the *ideal* is communion (giving and receiving love in a spirit of reciprocity). Humans flourish when they share in relationships of loving communion.

The final task in this chapter on positive psychology in theological perspective is to provide a warrant for the choice we made to assign optimism to the psychological well-being domain and hope to the spiritual character set. To assist us here, the work on hope by a pioneer of the positive psychology movement, C.R. Snyder, is analyzed.

OPTIMISM AND HOPE IN THEOLOGICAL PERSPECTIVE

Snyder and his associates take a goal-based approach to the psychology of hope.[37] In their early work, they defined hope as "a cognitive set that is based on a reciprocally-derived sense of successful agency (goal-directed determination) and pathways (planning to meet goals)."[38] Here the three essential components in the theory— goals, pathways, and agency—are identified. Now of course one might say that the definitions of hope presented above also suggest that goal-directed behavior is central. The goal of the person in a situation of deprivation is clear enough: it is to get out of it. They feel trapped in the darkness; their aim is to escape into the light. However, this approach will not satisfy Snyder and his associates. They contend that the goals referred to must be quite specific in order to develop an adequate psychology of hope. "If you recall the historical skepticism aimed at hope," they write, "it often appeared to result because it was vague and lacked an anchor. Goals provide the endpoints or anchors of the mental action sequences; they are the anchors of hope theory."[39] Two different types of goals are identified.[40] First, there are positive "approach" goals. Examples include a writer wanting to get a publisher for a book, and a dieter desiring to maintain their newly acquired slim figure. In the second category, we find "avoidance" goals. The defining feature of this type of goal is a desire to avert a negative outcome. For instance, a regular

---

37. See Snyder et al., "The Will and the Ways"; Snyder, Cheavans, & Sympson, "Hope: An Individual Motive"; Snyder, "Hypothesis"; and Snyder, Cheavans & Michael, "Hope Theory."

38. Snyder et al., "The Will and the Ways," 571.

39. Snyder, "Hypothesis," 9.

40. See Snyder, Cheavans & Michael, "Hope Theory," 105–106.

beachgoer may use sunscreen lotion in an attempt to avoid developing skin cancer.

Goals cannot be achieved without a strategic approach. In order to attain the end-points that we desire, we need to plan. That is, we need to map the path that we are going to follow. "Pathways thinking taps the perceived ability to produce plausible routes to goals."[41]

Agency, lastly, is the motivational component; it drives people along the routes to their goals. It requires mental willpower to engage in a sustained approach to achieving a desired end-point. Agentic thinking "provides the spark for a person's goal pursuits."[42]

Experience indicates that it's not that often that we find a trouble-free, easy, or direct route to our cherished goals. Along the journey we usually encounter some obstacles. The high-hope person, Snyder et al. point out, has both the capacity to envision pathways around a blockage, and the requisite mental strength to keep pushing forward.

One question that immediately presents itself upon reviewing the Snyder et al. approach is whether the experience they describe is really hope. It seems more like optimism to us.[43] Optimism is usually construed as a feeling or conviction that I will prevail in my quest, despite the obstacles in my path. In his survey of the psychology of optimism, Christopher Peterson has this to say:

> Optimism enters into self-regulation when people ask themselves about impediments to achieving the goals they have adopted. In the face of difficulties, do people nonetheless believe that goals can be achieved? If so, they are optimistic; if not, they are pessimistic.[44]

Given this interpretation of optimism, it's not surprising that Peterson includes the work of Snyder and associates in his survey. In reviewing their goals-pathways-agency approach, it seems clear that what they are describing is more an optimistic outlook than the experience of hoping. It's important to avoid confusing the two terms. They are closely related, but they can also be distinguished. Gabriel Marcel makes a distinction between hope and optimism that is germane to our area of interest. The differentiation that he posits revolves around the I-We axis. Optimism

41. Snyder, "Hypothesis," 9.

42. Snyder et al., "Hope: An Individual Motive," 108.

43. Cf. Hobfoll et al., "Fact or Artifact," 85.

44. Peterson, "Future of Optimism," 47.

operates in "the province of the 'I myself'."[45] *I* make the judgment that *I* have the personal resources to overcome the roadblocks on the path to my goal. Hope, on the other hand, is sustained in a relational context. Marcel avers that the most adequate expression for hoping is "I hope in thee for us."[46] For him, the fact that hope is indissolubly bound up with communion is so true that he wonders "if despair and solitude are not at bottom necessarily identical."[47] Marcel views the despairing person as a neighbor, as one who addresses him with a particular appeal for help. He puts it this way:

> Assume that [the despairing person] asks the question: 'Do you pretend that it is in my power to hope, although all the exits seem to me closed?' Doubtless I will reply: 'The simple fact that you ask me the question already constitutes a sort of first breach in your prison. In reality it is not simply a question you ask me; it is an appeal you address to me, and to which I can only respond by urging you not only to depend on me but also not to give up, not to let go, and, if only very humbly and feebly, to act as if this Hope lived in you; and that means more than anything else to turn toward another—I will say, whoever he is—and thus to escape from the obsession which is destroying you.'[48]

Optimism and hope are distinct (though closely related) phenomena. I am optimistic because I trust in myself and in the resources at my disposal. I am hopeful because the other has heard my appeal and entered into a loving solidarity with me. Here a biblical note is sounded.

BIBLICAL PERSPECTIVES ON HOPE

The biblical view is that hope is something that we do together. At the center of the community of hope that the Hebrews and the earliest Christians form is God. Hope joins us one to another; God is "the guarantee of the union which holds us together."[49] The central theme in the grand narrative of the Bible is the self-communication of God. God is a witness to human history. Witnessing can be a passive activity. A person may

45. Marcel, *Homo Viator,* 34.
46. Marcel, *Homo Viator,* 60.
47. Marcel, *Homo Viator,* 58.
48. Marcel, "Desire and Hope," 285.
49. Marcel, *Homo Viator,* 60.

witness an event and do little or nothing in response to it. God, however, is an active witness. God is *agape* and it is the nature of *agape* to desire the best for others and to actively give of self in securing this desideratum. In the Scriptures we find story after story of God's healing and liberating engagement with individuals and communities.

It is because God is an active witness that the people learn to trust and to hope. All of the major events recorded in the Bible can be construed as narratives of hope. The Genesis narratives revolving around Abraham, Isaac, and Jacob, first, should be read as testimonies to hope.[50] What these stories attest to is that the identity and the future of the People of God are intimately bound up with the promises of God. The people are invited to imaginatively project into a future in which God will ensure a long line of descendants, greatness as a nation, a new land, and, through them, a blessing to the nations. They come to know YHWH as the God who is faithful in keeping promises. Their hope, then, is something that builds over time. It is constructed on the foundation of memory. The stories that fund the communal memory are stories of the mighty acts of a God for whom no barrier is too high, no obstacle too large.

That paradigmatic story of hope, the Exodus, began with a cry of pain.[51] After a long period of containment and control, oppressed persons come to a point of simply accepting that what they experience is the way life is. They allow themselves to be molded by the order that has been constructed by their overlords. But something happened to change the situation for the Hebrew slaves in Egypt. They were no longer content to passively embrace the world that had been shaped for them by those in control. In finding a voice for their grievance and distress, they made a start on the road of defiance and protest. There is hope in protest.

The situation for the Hebrew slaves was radically changed because they dared to cry out. Their cries reached the heavens and the heavens responded. The cry of distress was not addressed to YHWH, but YHWH nevertheless heard it and acted decisively to set this people free.

The prophetic texts of the eighth to the sixth century BCE also center on the themes of promise, hope, and trust. The poems that we find there take us into the future God has prepared for the people. It is true that many in the community of the time could not see past the order of things that they were caught in. Whether the order was established

---

50. Cf. Brueggemann, *Hope within History*, 73.

51. Cf. Brueggemann, *Hope within History*, 16, 20.

around injustice and idolatry in the community, or around the oppressive practices and controlling interests of aggressive nations, what is currently in place is what many accepted as the norm—or at least as simply the way things are and will always be. There is nevertheless a shaft of hope that penetrates into the darkness as the prophets declare, "Behold, the days are coming." A new order is on the way. The drive into a new and better world, the prophets declare, comes from nowhere else but the mystery of God.

In the Christian Scriptures, God-with-us is given an ultimate expression in the person and work of Jesus Christ. The hope of Jesus, our hope, is centered on the coming reign of God. "Jesus came to Galilee, proclaiming the good news of God, and saying, 'The time is fulfilled, and the kingdom of God has come near; repent, and believe in the good news'" (Mk 1:14–15). We have seen that captivity is a central image for the deprivation that necessitates the sustaining power of hope. The reign of God is characterized by the release from all forms of bondage:

> The Spirit of the Lord is upon me,
> because he has anointed me to bring good news to the poor.
> He has sent me to proclaim release to the captives
> and recovery of sight to the blind,
> to let the oppressed go free,
> to proclaim the year of the Lord's favor (Lk 4:18–19).

In his healings and exorcisms, in his words of affirmation and forgiveness, in his befriending of the outcasts, in his challenge to unjust and oppressive practices, Jesus inaugurates a reign of love, freedom, and righteousness. The hopeless feel trapped; everywhere they look all they see is a "No Exit" sign. Jesus embodied the *agape* of God. Love takes as its mission showing trapped people the way out. Love takes those who are trapped in sin, suffering, and injustice through the door that opens on to a new and brighter future—one characterized by peace, healing, and freedom. The resurrection is the definitive statement on this future. It is a foretaste of the glorious existence that awaits us. We hope for a measure of freedom now, but our ultimate hope is for the end time when God "will wipe away every tear" (Rev 21:4).

With the fact that optimism and hope, while closely related, need to be carefully distinguished in mind, we opted to place optimism in the psychological well-being domain and hope (one of the three theological virtues) in the spiritual character set. Optimism is associated with confidence in an individual's ability to find a way around obstacles to achieving a goal that has been set. Hope in the biblical perspective is something we do together under God.

SUMMARY

Many Christians take a very earnest and dour, almost glum, approach to following their Lord and shape their spirituality around cross-bearing and the attendant suffering. It is certainly true that there are occasions when the Christian is called upon to take up their cross and follow. However, it is also important to take cognizance of the fact that in both the Hebrew Bible and the Christian Scriptures the happiness of the faithful is a prominent theme. One only need look to Wisdom literature and the gospels.

It is on this basis that a positive theology is built. Those whose privilege it is to be baptized and to live through faith in Jesus as Lord celebrate life because they are secure in their identity as children of God and sisters/brothers of Christ. Those in God's family are assured of renewal, healing, and forgiveness when they stumble and fall. Looking with confidence to the love, mercy, and forgiveness of God supports us in forgiving ourselves and looking beyond the sinfulness and infidelity to that side of us that is truly good, right, and worthy. Moreover, the very fact that God finds joy and happiness in human flourishing means that, far from seeing it as a selfish and unworthy aim, we are entitled to value it and to seek to actualize it.

The alternative to positive theology is a pathology-driven type. A companion position of this approach is that followers of Christ are called to continually spend themselves in service of others in imitation of Christ, who chose the way of the Cross in service of humankind and its salvation. We have argued that while self-sacrifice is sometimes required of Christians as they live faithful to the love command, the ideal is communion—giving and receiving love in a spirit of reciprocity.

Finally, through critical reflection on hope as construed by certain positive psychology theorists, we put the view that what is really being talked about here is optimism. Hope is a central biblical theme and one of the three theological virtues. It is also something that is best done in community. A Christian is grafted into the Vine in baptism; faith, hope, and love are what we do together. Such reflection indicates why the decision was made to place optimism in the psychological well-being domain and hope in the spiritual character category.

9

VIRTUE AND SPIRITUALITY

IN THE GOSPELS, WE encounter Jesus' ministry of calling people to turn from the darkness and embrace the light. The earliest gospel, Mark, opens with an exhortation to repent as the Kingdom of God is at hand. Jesus casts his ministry as freeing people from the life-denying forces of vice and cruelty. The spiritual path that he offers involves renouncing sin and evil and opening yourself to the sanctifying power of God. As we saw in Chapter 1, the Church Fathers similarly thought of the moral and spiritual aspects of our lives as inextricably bound together. Gregory of Nazianzus contended that the spiritual life—which he understood to consist primarily of contemplation, sharing in the sacraments, and meditation on Scripture—incorporates moral improvement. Ambrose held that the pastor guides his people not only as a physician of souls but also as a teacher. Through his preaching, especially, the pastor draws his people into the Christian spiritual and moral ideal. There is a number of important contemporary thinkers in both moral and spiritual theology who strongly endorse the approach of the Fathers.[1] We are persuaded by this line of Christian thought; we included moral character as one of the four areas in our spiritual formation process.

1. See, for example, Austin, "Spirituality and Virtue"; Keating, *Spirituality and Moral Theology*; Keenan, "Catholic Moral Theology, Ignatian Spirituality"; O'Keefe, "Catholic Moral Theology and Christian Spirituality"; O'Keefe, *Becoming Good, Becoming Holy*; Rehnman, "Virtue and Grace"; Sedgwick, *Christian Moral Life*; Spohn, "Christian Spirituality and Theological Ethics"; and Van Slyke, "Understanding Moral Dimension."

This decision was relatively easy. The choice of an approach to the moral life exercised our minds quite a bit more. There were three main systems to choose from: deontological ethics, utilitarian ethics, and virtue ethics. It was of course the third that was chosen. We go into the reasons more fully below. For the moment, it's enough to say that we are persuaded by the argument that of the three a virtue or moral character approach aligns best with Christian spirituality.[2] To set the scene for that discussion, we need to say a little bit about each moral system, beginning with utilitarianism.

THREE MORAL PHILOSOPHIES

The English philosopher, Jeremy Bentham, was a pioneer in utilitarian philosophy. He thought that the principle of social utility furnishes objectivity and certainty in moral thought. "Nature has placed mankind under the governance of two sovereign masters, *pain* and *pleasure*. The *principle of utility* recognizes this subjection . . . An action may be said to be conformable to the principle of utility . . . when the tendency it has to augment the happiness of the community is greater than any it has to diminish it."[3]

The basic criterion of what is morally right, wrong, or obligatory in utilitarian theories is the *consequences* which flow from particular rules or acts. That is, they have a teleological frame of reference. The ultimate end posited is the greatest general good. A rule or action is right if and only if it can be assessed as likely to produce at least as great a balance of good over evil for the community as any alternative. It is important to recognise that the good referred to here is non-moral good: food, shelter, health, etc.

Deontologists argue that the main focus should be on those universal principles that establish what is right or obligatory, rather than the goodness or badness of consequences. A deontological approach is often called "formalistic," because its central principle is that an action must conform to some rule or law.

Deontological ethics has its roots in the moral philosophy of Immanuel Kant. As an Enlightenment thinker, he was inspired and guided

2. See, for example, Spohn, "Christian Spirituality and Theological Ethics"; Austin, "Spirituality and Virtue"; and Van Slyke, "Understanding Moral Dimension."

3. Bentham, *Introduction to Principles*, chp II, xiv. Cited in Kainz, *Ethics*, 78.

by one of the movement's cherished principles—namely, autonomy. Kant rejected a divine command approach to ethics. In his view, persons are not obligated to do what they are commanded to do, even if that command comes from God. It is either the case that a right action is right because God approves or commands it, or that God approves or commands a right action because it is right. Kant affirms the second option. If it is the case that we only do what is right because God commands it, there is little or no moral validity to our actions. If the main reason that I act in a moral way is because I believe that God will reward me for doing so, there is little intrinsic value in my action.

The next question is this: If I cannot simply depend on knowledge of divine commands to tell me what is right and good, on what basis can I establish what constitutes a moral action? Kant answers by saying that moral action has as its only motive to act for the sake of duty. That is, it is not the consequences of an act that make that act moral but the motive behind it. I therefore need to have the right intention. The right intention is to act for the sake of duty. My duty lies in obeying those rules generated by the categorical imperative. The term *imperative* points to the fact that for Kant moral action takes the form of a command. According to the categorical imperative, I ought never to act except in such a way that I can also will that my maxim become a universal law.

The central feature of this definition is the requirement of universal applicability. The question a person needs to ask, then, is this: Can this moral principle be universally applied? Any principle that becomes contradictory when it's applied universally is ruled out. Examples are these: "Always break your promises" (the contradictory result is that promises never mean what they purport to mean), and "Always accept help but never give it."

The third system is virtue ethics. Given that this is the approach we settled on, this is covered in more detail. A very significant figure in the history of Christian virtue ethics is Thomas Aquinas. The approach goes back as far as Aristotle. Leading contemporary virtue ethicists include Jean Porter, Stanley Hauerwas, Christine Swanton, William Spohn, and Joseph Kotva. Virtue, according to Aquinas (and following Aristotle), is that which makes the agent good and their acts also good.[4] Here we are primarily attending to the formation of moral character, rather than

---

4. Aquinas, *Summa Theologica* I-II.56.3.

to either consequences of moral decision-making or universal moral principles.

Aristotle viewed human beings, along with all other creatures, as having a specific nature. It is in the nature of human beings and all other creatures to move toward a specific *telos* or goal. The human by nature, then, has an orientation to a good end. This good, says Aristotle, is *eudaimonia*. When it comes to Greek, or any foreign language for that matter, finding precise correlates in English is often a problem. *Eudaimonia* is usually taken to mean happiness, blessedness, and prosperity. Alasdair MacIntyre offers a fuller definition: "It is the state of being well and doing well in being well, of a man's being well-favored himself and in relation to the divine."[5] The virtues are those dispositions that enable a person to attain *eudamonia*; the lack of which will frustrate their movement toward that *telos*. Put simply, because of the way we are made we have a goal that we instinctively aim for—happiness—and virtue helps us to get there. It is worth noting here that the positive psychology movement has appropriated the Greek word in describing what is meant by happiness. It aligns itself with Aristotle's understanding that happiness—i.e., it is the result of living a life of virtue.[6]

A fundamental concern for Aristotle in his *Nichomachean Ethics*[7] is to establish which division in the soul—passions, faculties, or states—a virtue fits into. That is, he wants to know what kind of human capacity an excellence (the Greek word *arête* means "excellence") really is. What Aristotle calls the passions we moderns think of as intense emotions (he refers to "pleasures and pains"). Though the emotions are important in the moral life, it is evident that more is involved in the cultivation of virtue. For this reason, this first candidate gets ruled out. Our mental faculties, for their part, allow us to know that we are feeling this or that passion, but such knowledge cannot take us to the heart of what it is to be virtuous. Thus, there is only one candidate left—namely, the states. To be a person of moral character is to live in a state of virtue. Aristotle was a practical thinker, and as such he construed the virtues as capacities that help a person do their work well. But they must also be viewed on another level. Not only do the excellences help us do good work, they also produce within us a *state* of goodness. We're able to do good work

5. MacIntyre, *After Virtue*, 148.

6. See, for example, Franklin, *Psychology of Happiness*.

7. The text of the *Nicomachean Ethics* used is the Revised Oxford Translation. See Aristotle, *Nicomachean Ethics*.

because we are virtuous persons. "[E]very excellence both brings into good condition the thing of which it is an excellence and makes the work of that thing be done well . . . Therefore . . . the excellence of man also will be the state which makes a man good and which makes him do his own work well."[8]

As intimated above, Aristotle assigns an important role to feelings of pleasure and pain in cultivating virtue. He writes: "We must take as a sign of states the pleasure or pain that supervenes on acts; for the man who abstains from bodily pleasures and delights in this very fact is temperate, while the man who is annoyed at it is self-indulgent, and he who stands his ground against things that are terrible and delights in this or at least is not pained is brave, while the man who is pained is a coward."[9] This is a controversial element in Aristotle's theory. A Kantian, for example, would deny that moral action is in any way related to feelings. Remember that his emphasis is on *deon*, obligation or necessity. The morally good person has the good will sufficient to do their duty simply because it is their duty. Nonetheless, it's a crucial element in Aristotle's account of moral excellence. He strongly rejects the view that the feelings associated with good and right acts are of no consequence in the moral life. A good person is the one who "rejoice[s] in noble actions," who "enjoy[s] acting justly."[10] It is not enough, however, to describe the excellences of character in terms of feeling and desire. Action and truth are also controlled by thought and choice. In any given situation requiring moral action, the virtuous person must choose how they will act to attain the good.

Choice is obviously linked to voluntariness. Aristotle observes that choice "seems to be voluntary, but not all that is voluntary seems to be an object of choice. Is it, then, what has been decided on by previous deliberation? For choice involves reason and thought."[11] Choice is "deliberative desire of things in our power; for when we have decided as a result of deliberation, we desire in accordance with our deliberation."[12] The expression "deliberative desire" has important connotations, combining as it does the factors of rationality and feeling. Aristotle is very aware of the interdependence of reason and desire. Reason alone can't move a

---

8. Aristotle, *Nicomachean Ethics* 1106a 15, 21

9. Aristotle, *Nicomachean Ethics* 1104b 4–10

10. Aristotle, *Nicomachean Ethics* 1099a 16–19

11. Aristotle, *Nicomachean Ethics* 1112a 15–17

12. Aristotle, *Nicomachean Ethics* 1113a 10–13

person to act. A person turns their mind in a certain direction because
they want to. Desire alone is insufficient to determine conduct; it must be
formed by reason. While Aristotle makes it clear that reason and desire
are indissolubly linked in the context of action, he fails to state precisely
how they relate to each other. It has been suggested that he needs the
concept of intention to complete this segment of his theory. The idea of
intention draws in the will.[13] Moreover, will is stronger than desire.

There is a significant difference between saying that I have the *desire*
to go for a one mile jog this afternoon, on the one hand, and that I *will* go
for one, on the other. The exercise of will is more powerful than the presence of desire. We would all be better people if we could follow through
on all our good intentions! Below we will see that Thomas Aquinas was
very aware of this fact; he introduced the important component of will
into his theory of virtue.

The capacity for making a good choice is possible because a person
has attained the virtue of practical wisdom (*phronesis*). A person of practical wisdom possesses both true reasoning and right desire.[14] Reason
and desire are harnessed in deliberating well in order to establish those
passions and actions which conduce to the good life. According to Aristotle, in relation to passions and actions there is excess, defect, and the intermediate or mean.[15] It is possible to feel fear and confidence, anger and
pity, and in general pleasure and pain too strongly or too weakly. Moral
excellence, however, involves feeling the passions "at the right times, with
reference to the right objects, towards the right people, with the right
aim, and in the right way."[16] This is the intermediate. The situation is
similar in relation to action. Judgment is required in matters pertaining
to moral excellence to establish the mean. Thus, the person possessing
moral excellence and the capacity for right deliberation will establish
courage as the mean between fear and rashness, liberality as the mean between prodigality and meanness, proper pride as sitting midway between
empty vanity and undue humility, to name just a few of the possibilities.

The person of virtue uses reason to order and tame the passions
and appetites. Reason can never be the slave of passion. The moral life is
fundamentally about excellent deliberation ordering the passions and so

---

13. See Hauerwas, *Character and Christian Life*, 54.

14. Aristotle, *Nicomachean Ethics* 1139a 23–25

15. Aristotle, *Nicomachean Ethics* 1106b16–28

16. Aristotle, *Nicomachean Ethics* 1106b 21–22

moving the moral agent toward attainment of the good. Indeed, moral excellence and practical wisdom are indissolubly linked. Moral excellence establishes the right end for the human, and practical wisdom indicates the means for achieving that end.[17] Making the right choice requires both practical wisdom and moral excellence. It's not possible, therefore, for a person who is morally deficient to exercise practical wisdom. This Aristotle makes clear in an important passage in the *Nicomachean Ethics*:

> [I]f the acts that are in accordance with the excellences have themselves a certain character it does not follow that they are done justly or temperately. The agent also must be in a certain condition when he does them; in the first place he must have knowledge, secondly he must choose the acts, and choose them for their own sake, and thirdly his action must proceed from a firm and unchangeable character.[18]

The choice of what appears to be a virtuous act does not in itself guarantee that this act is in fact virtuous. A soldier may, for example, stand firm in the face of an enemy onslaught not because he's courageous, but rather because he's so overwhelmed with fear and terror that he cannot move! It is only a choice made in the context of a virtuous character which establishes an act as morally excellent. Actions may rightly be called just and temperate when they're done as just and temperate persons do them.

Choice and practical wisdom are clearly key concepts in Aristotle's theory of moral virtue. So, finally, is the idea of training. Through the use of practical wisdom, the moral agent is able to establish those passions and actions which over time are formative of character. It is in acting virtuously that a person eventually comes to possess this or that virtue. Just as a person becomes a lyre player by playing the lyre, one becomes just by doing just acts, brave by doing courageous acts, and so on.[19]

Taking all this into account, what then is a virtue for Aristotle? It is "a state concerned with choice, lying in a mean relative to us, this being determined by reason in the way in which the [person] of practical wisdom would determine it."[20] In looking at Aquinas' theory, we'll see most

---

17. Aristotle, *Nicomachean Ethics* 1145a 4–6

18. Aristotle, *Nicomachean Ethics* 1105a 2–1105b 1

19. Aristotle, *Nicomachean Ethics* 1103a 31–1103b 1

20. Aristotle, *Nicomachean Ethics* 1106b 36–1107a 1

of these themes emerging, but they will be re-shaped through theological reflection.

Thomas Aquinas follows Aristotle in positing that the human is oriented by nature to a *telos*. However, while Aquinas agrees that happiness is the proximate end for human beings, he insists that our ultimate end is supernatural. Further, he does something that his teacher was unable to do, and that is describe the role of the will in moving a person toward that goal. Those individuals who have the theological as well as the natural virtues are moving toward the ineffable glory of the beatific vision.

For Aquinas, there's one overarching, ultimate end to which the actions determined by will and reason are oriented. In his *Commentary on Nicomachean Ethics*,[21] Aquinas argues that where there are several goods identified, it is necessary to transcend the plurality to establish a superordinate end.[22] There is a unity in human nature; it follows that the human person's ultimate end must be one. Not everyone will agree with this position. Some may argue it is possible to construe the tendency to focus your actions on the one superordinate goal, even if it is a noble one, as distorted and unbalanced. Such an approach, on this view, is narrow and obsessive. Might it not be preferable to structure your life around a series of interconnected goals? Jean Porter suggests that Aquinas really intends something like this.[23] The one end incorporates different goods, pursued and enjoyed in a harmonious fashion. Thus, we can think of a superordinate goal and certain subordinate goals. Along this line, Aquinas says that the human person, if not directly seeking the perfect good—their ultimate end—is seeking a good "as tending to that, for a start is made in order to come to a finish . . . "[24] A well-balanced person, for example, will have fun and recreation as one of their subordinate goals. They are aware that it is very difficult, if not impossible, to love God and neighbor fully if life is filled up with duty and responsibility. Such an approach to life leads to staleness, frustration, and boredom. This is hardly the ground out of which a life of love and service is likely to spring.

Aquinas believes that every person naturally acts in such a way as to pursue what they perceive as the good.[25] Clearly, it is possible for a per-

21. See Aquinas, "Commentary."
22. Aquinas, "Commentary" I, lecture 9.
23. See Porter, *Recovery of Virtue*, 78.
24. Aquinas, *Summa Theologica* I-II.1.6.
25. Aquinas, "Commentary," 22.1.c.

son to be mistaken about what is good for them. But no one intentionally acts against the good. As Ralph McInerny expresses it:

> If we come to see that not-A rather than A contributes to our happiness, we have the same reason for doing not-A that we thought we had for doing A. We did A in the mistaken belief that it was good for us; when we learn that our judgment was mistaken, we do not need any further *reason* for not seeking A. We already and necessarily want what we think is good for us, and we now see that A is not.[26]

"A" might be attempting to devote virtually all my free time to devotional activities and good works. The thinking is that in this way I will grow in holiness and experience a state of happiness that only the saints know. After a time, though, I find that rather than experiencing a new level of peace and joy, I simply end up feeling jaded and sad. The saving grace comes when I discover the wisdom of "not-A": achieving a balance in my life. I realize that in order to reach my superordinate goal of a deep union with God it's essential that I take a break to enjoy myself as well as devoting myself to serious Christian activity.

In sum, humans are essentially oriented to the good; they choose acts which their reason tells them will move them toward the goal of happiness. Virtue, according to Aquinas (and following Aristotle), is that which makes the agent good and their acts also good.[27] It is virtue, then, that disposes a person to act well, in accordance with their essential orientation to the end for which they were created. The question is, though, how does a person acquire virtue? Aquinas asks whether a virtuous disposition can be acquired through a single act.[28] Clearly this is not possible. In order for virtue to become established in a person, reason must achieve mastery over "the appetitive faculties" (our passions and desires). Now there is a whole range of situations involving a vast number of factors in which the desires come into play. It is not possible to establish right and good judgements in all these complex and diverse situations "in an instant," so to speak. The virtuous disposition develops over time; it is a *habit*. It is a complicated business managing desires in order to establish virtue. A young business executive, for example, finds that there is a number of ways in which she can advance herself at the expense of

26. McInerny, "Ethics," 201–202.

27. Aquinas, *Summa Theologica* I-II.56.3.

28. Aquinas, *Summa Theologica* I-II.51.3.

others. She resists the temptation for a whole year and feels that she can now say that she has the virtue of justice. The problem is, though, that the temptation can surface in so many different forms. It is only through breadth of experience and through consistently choosing the right and good path that the virtue takes root. Aquinas would say, "You've made a start, but you have not yet faced enough tempting situations to be able to say that the habit of justice is formed." More formally, he puts it this way: "The rational powers, proper to a [person], however, are not determined to one act, but rather in themselves are poised before many. It is through habits that they are set towards acts . . . Human virtues, therefore, are habits."[29]

As Hauerwas points out, though, Aquinas' notion of a habit is quite different from our modern idea.[30] We tend to think of a habit as something automatic, a rather mechanical function. For example, a person has the habit of each day buying a newspaper on the way home from work, reading it, and then walking the dog. For Aquinas, in contrast, a habit is a disposition to act well (or ill). Thus, when he speaks of a virtue as a habit, he refers to a well-established disposition to act for the good. Habits are a "readiness for action."[31]

We saw in our discussion of Aristotle's account of the virtues that his theory suffers through the lack of appreciation for the role of the will in relation to action. Aquinas, on the other hand, assigns a very important place to will in his moral psychology and, pertinent to our inquiry, in his theory of the virtues. He says that the intellect is moved by the will, as are all human faculties.[32] A person turns their mind in a certain direction because that is what they want to do. The intellect, in this sense, is subordinate to the will. Thus, will is the subject of "virtue in its unqualified sense."[33] The moral virtues are oriented to the will; the intellectual virtues to the rational powers. "The subject of a habit which is called virtue in a certain respect can be the intellect [practical or speculative] . . . The subject of a habit which is downrightly called virtue, however, can only be the will . . . The reason for this is that the will moves to their acts all

29. Aquinas, *Summa Theologica* I–II.55.1.

30. Hauerwas, *Character and Christian Life*, 69–70.

31. Hauerwas, *Character and Christian Life*, 70.

32. Aquinas, *Summa Theologica* I–II.56.3.

33. Aquinas, *Summa Theologica* I–II.56.3.

those other powers that are in some way rational . . . "[34] Put differently, it's a virtuous thing to use our rational powers to work on the various intellectual and practical challenges life throws up. But the moral life proper requires the exercise of the will. If we want to be persons of strong moral character, we need a consistent and strong intention to act for the good.

Aquinas, however, is not only interested in the way in which reason and appetite are well disposed in a person. His theological orientation leads him to ask how the supernatural virtues—faith, hope and love—are related to acquired virtue. His answer is that these infused or supernatural virtues, under the influence of the grace of the Holy Spirit, produce the intellectual and moral virtues.[35] A fundamental theological principle undergirding Aquinas's moral theory is the grace of the Spirit moving a believer to act for the good. Here the gifts of the Spirit play a crucial role. Grace and the gifts are indissolubly linked in Thomas' theological ethics. There is a "supernatural flow system," if you will, that Aquinas constructs in his theological ethics. At the head of the system is grace, from which the infused virtues flow;[36] the gifts of the Holy Spirit emanate from the infused virtues as effects; and the gifts, finally, are the source of the intellectual and moral virtues.

Aquinas understands the grace of the Holy Spirit—that supernatural help that is the ultimate source of the moral life—primarily as a motive force. While it is quite appropriate to construe grace in Aquinas's thought as "a special life principle"[37] or as "a new mode of existence,"[38] the most characteristic depiction of grace is a supernatural help that moves the believer to their proper end in God.[39] Grace is defined by Aquinas in the treatise on virtue in the *Pars Secunda Secundae* as a "supernatural principle moving one interiorly."[40] In the treatise on grace, it is similarly referred to as that which "moves the soul inwardly."[41] The treatise on grace, in fact, is filled with references to God moving the soul so that it is inclined to act righteously.

34. Aquinas, *Summa Theologica* I–II.56.3.

35. Cf. O'Meara, "Virtues in Theology of Aquinas"; Torrell, *Saint Thomas Aquinas*, 155; Meinert, *Love of God*; and Spezzano, "Grace of the Holy Spirit," chapter 3.

36. Aquinas, *Summa Theologica* I–II.110.3.ad 3.

37. O'Meara, "Virtues," 258.

38. O'Meara, "Virtues," 259.

39. Cf. Oliver, "Sweet Delight of Virtue."

40. Aquinas, *Summa Theologica* II–II.6.1.

41. Aquinas, *Summa Theologica* I–II.109.6.corp.

It may seem strange to us moderns to think of divine grace in terms of causing movement in the soul. We have become accustomed to thinking of movement, with Descartes, as simply "the action by which some body is transferred from one place to another."[42] Aquinas, in contrast, thought of motion in an Aristotelian sense as broadly any kind of change. A cold thing becoming hot, an ignorant person becoming learned, and a puppy growing up are all examples of motion. Aquinas considers that humans, mired as they are in their postlapsarian corrupted condition, are incapable through their own resources of moving from a sin-dominated state to one infused with virtue. The grace of the Spirit is the supernatural help that is absolutely necessary in moving sinful humans to their ultimate end in God. As indicated above, it is necessary to tie grace and gifts of the Spirit together in reading Aquinas on virtue. It is the gifts that provide the perfection of the moved thing or "mobile" (the believer) in relation to the mover (the Spirit). That is, the gifts modify the soul of the believer so that it has an aptitude to be moved by grace.

In sum, Aquinas, first, views grace primarily as a motive force, and second, assigns the grace of the Spirit and the gifts of the Spirit pivotal roles in a supernatural flow system that begins with grace and moves via the agency of the gifts to a life of moral habitude (a readiness to act in a moral way). The relationship between the infused virtues and the acquired virtues that are constitutive of our moral character looks like this: The grace of the Spirit infuses faith, hope, and love (the theological virtues), which in turn generate the gifts of the Spirit, which, finally, work together to produce moral character.

In surveying the way Aristotle and Aquinas treat the virtues, we have noted some important differences. Aquinas assigns an important place to the role of the will in ordering the passions; he places a supernatural *telos* above the proximate end of temporal happiness; and he assigns a crucial role to the grace of the Spirit in moving people from a sinful state to one of moral habitude. A survey of other important virtue theorists would identify still more differences in emphasis and interpretation. Anyone interested in developing a system of virtue ethics is very quickly confronted with the question of whether or not it's possible to identify a unitary concept capable of tying together the vast array of interpretations. Alasdair MacIntyre sets himself this task in his influential and eloquent work, *After Virtue*. But getting into that complicated discussion is beyond

---

42. Descartes, *Principles of Philosophy*, Part II, § 24.

the scope of this chapter. Our survey of the virtue ethics of Aristotle and Aquinas at least gives a reasonably good sense of what the concept of moral character means in the virtue ethics tradition, in general, and in the Christian version, in particular.

VIRTUE ETHICS AS THE BEST FIT
WITH SPIRITUALITY

Let's turn our attention now to evaluating the three approaches from the point of view of spiritual practices and the process of being conformed over time to Christ.[43] An ethics of principles, the deontological approach, highlights the importance of moral norms and obligations, but neglects formation as a disciple over time. Karl Barth's approach to ethics is instructive in pointing up this deficiency. Barth places his ethics in the frame of faithful and obedient discipleship rather than rational deliberation. In the spiritual relationship we the faithful share in with God, God commands and the believer faithfully obeys. Barth says that a command may be distinguished from a law in that the former has an interpersonal directness and unique application that the latter does not have. That is, in issuing a command to an individual God gives a concrete directive that God expects to be followed. Barth states that the command of God is "the specially relevant individual command for the decision which we have to make at this moment and in this situation." He goes on to state that such a command is "a claim addressed to man in such a way that it is given integrally, so that he cannot control its content or decide its concrete implication."[44]

Although grounded in the ethical commands of Scripture, the divine command continually comes to us anew because God is radically sovereign and free to command new and surprising actions. In this way, Barth gives the impression that the Christian life is a series of radical decisions that do not link together in an overall pattern of discipleship.[45]

43. In relation to the analysis that follows, we acknowledge our indebtedness to William Spohn. In our view, he makes a very compelling argument for the strong compatibility between virtue ethics and spirituality. We follow his line in this section. See Spohn, "Christian Spirituality and Theological Ethics"; Spohn, "Spirituality and Ethics"; Spohn, *Go and Do Likewise*.

44. Barth, *Church Dogmatics* II.2, 662, 663.

45. Cf. Gustafson, *Can Ethics be Christian?* 160; Hauerwas, *Character and Christian Life*, 142; Lovin, *Christian Faith and Public Choices*, 27–28. There are, however,

He pays little attention to the emerging identity of the disciple and their abiding dispositions because he thinks that doing so supports the sinful human tendency to turn in on the self. As Stanley Hauerwas points out, such an approach has us focusing on the wrong concern: "The moral life is not first and foremost a life of choice—decision is not king—but is rather woven from the notions that we use to see and to form the situations we confront."[46] The Christian moral life is primarily about being formed in Christ-like character over time; ethics needs to attend to more than discrete events of decision and obedience.

The second type is the ethics of consequences. As we have seen, the right action is the one that produces the most benefit for the agent or the society. It is certainly the case that a concern with consequences crops up quite regularly in Scripture.[47] In the Old Testament we find a contractual theology articulated by the Deuteronomistic historian. According to this theology, blessings flow when the People of God are faithful to *torah*, and curses rain down when they fall from the requirements of the divine law. We find the judgment and reward theme also in the New Testament. Paul exhorts believers to think and act in ways that are pleasing to the Lord. "For all of us must appear before the judgment seat of Christ, so that each may receive recompense for what has been done in the body, whether good or evil" (2 Cor 5:10). Jesus famously used the metaphor of sheep and goats to communicate the message of a final reckoning (Matt 25:31–46).

Many ethicists downplay the significance of rewards and punishments for an ethical theory because they appeal to self-interest.[48] When spiritual theologies concentrate too heavily on outcomes, such as growing in personal holiness or avoiding divine judgment, they risk reducing the life of faith to a means of satisfying human needs. The focus, on this view, is on individual fulfilment and security when it should be on social transformation. Socially minded theologians argue that, since Christ's

---

alternative readings of Barth's ethics. Gerald McKenny, for example, contends that Barth does allow for moral deliberation. See McKenny, "Heterogeneity and Ethical Deliberation." McKenny argues that "ethical deliberation for Barth exhibits a heterogeneity between the weighing of reasons or values that count for or against various possible courses of action on the one hand, and the act of testing these possibilities in anticipation of the decision of God regarding them on the other hand" (206).

46. Hauerwas, *Vision and Virtue*, 2.

47. On this, see Spohn, "Christian Spirituality and Theological Ethics," 272.

48. Spohn, "Christian Spirituality and Theological Ethics," 272.

overall aim was to extend God's Reign of peace and justice, all Christian action needs to be tied into this overarching mission. For our part, we reject the dichotomy that some set up around the moral life. Our preference is for a both/and approach. The Christian moral life, we think, is both a journey into personal holiness and a commitment to work with God to shift socio-political systems and structures in the direction of Kingdom values.

An ethics of consequences appreciates only a part of discipleship. Certainly, Christians need to concentrate on doing good and alleviating human suffering. Love of neighbor is a principle that carries with it the need for continual evaluation of how it is being applied. The question of whether our decisions and actions are actually benefiting others in terms of the non-moral goods that have accrued to them needs to be asked time and again.

That said, pledging faith in Christ is not something we do mainly because we want to improve our moral decision-making. Faith is a response to prevenient grace and embrace of the call to a new covenant in Christ. God calls Christians to be faithful; we are not expected to act with such wisdom that we consistently secure the greatest good for the greatest number.[49] God is the primary agent in the project of extending the Realm of God; it is the duty of disciples to faithfully cooperate with God in this project.

Virtue ethics shifts attention from acting to being, to asking what sort of person I should become in response to God's gracious action in Christ. As we have seen, action follows from character. This focus on the Christian identity and character fits the radical response that Jesus demands at the beginning of Mark's Gospel: "The time is fulfilled, and the kingdom of God has come near; repent, and believe the good news" (Mark 1:15). Thomas Merton interprets hearing this call as committing to the nurture of what he calls "the true self." According to Merton, the essential aim of the spiritual life is union with God in Christ. To experience this loving union, Merton observes, is to experience profound joy: "The only true joy on earth is to escape from the prison of our own selfhood . . . and enter by love into union with the Life who dwells and sings within the essence of every creature and in the core of our own souls."[50] In drawing close to God, the Christian both comes to know the divine

---

49. Spohn, "Christian Spirituality and Theological Ethics," 272.

50. Merton, *Seeds of Contemplation*, 8.

will and is empowered to live it out. To know God and God's will is to come to your true self. To refuse the divine life and purpose is to contradict yourself. This self-contradiction that characterizes the false self is the result of sin. "To say I was born in sin is to say I came into the world with a false self. I came into existence under a sign of contradiction, being someone that I was never intended to be and therefore a denial of what I am supposed to be."[51] Every one of us, says Merton, is "shadowed" by an illusory person. It's an illusion to believe that we can live outside God's will. An attempt to do so puts a person outside reality, outside life.

In order to nurture the true self, it is necessary to be receptive to the divine missions.[52] God the Source (the Father/Mother), dwelling in your personal depths, communicates the Word and the Spirit to you. In this way, God lives in us not only as our Creator, but also as "[our] other and true self."[53] Merton turns frequently to Paul's expression to communicate this state of being: "It is no longer I who live, but Christ who lives in me." With this in mind, Merton tells us that Christ becomes our "superior self."[54] Christ has united the faithful one's inmost self with his own life. In this way, we become a new being, a new person in Christ. Mysteriously, Christ living in us remains himself, but at the same time he becomes our true self. From the moment that a person is united to Christ, says Merton, there is "no longer any contradiction" in the fact that they are different persons.[55]

Through the sanctifying power of the Spirit a person takes on a whole new identity; their heart is changed and the process of becoming ever more Christ-like is the central concern. The old attitudes, motivations, and dispositions fall away, and those that conform to Christ come in their place. Sinful dispositions are replaced with the fruits of the Spirit: "love, joy, peace, patience, kindness, generosity, faithfulness, gentleness and self-control" (Gal 6:22).

Christian spirituality becomes embodied in the lives of believers through intentional disciplines or "spiritual practices."[56] Every way of life is constituted by a set of practices, and Christianity is no exception.

51. Merton, *Seeds of Contemplation*, 11.

52. See Merton, *Seeds of Contemplation*, 14.

53. Merton, *Seeds of Contemplation*, 14.

54. Merton, *New Seeds of Contemplation*, 123.

55. See Merton, *New Man*, 168–169.

56. On the link between spiritual practices and virtue ethics, see Spohn, "Christian Spirituality and Virtue Ethics," 274–275.

In Wesleyan, Lutheran, and Reformed traditions they have been called "means of grace," since God communicates salvation through these practices. All such practices, despite their own particularities and emphases, have as their common aim and purpose promoting a way of life that forms Christian identity and conforms disciples to Christ. An authentic Christian community is characterized, shaped, and formed primarily by baptism, the Eucharist, and preaching of the Word, but also very significantly by hospitality, prayer, forgiveness, and generosity toward the poor and marginalized.

When spiritual theologies are defective it is because they lack one or more of the central practices of the gospel way of life. Although we may debate which practices are absolutely required and which ones ought to be given priority, there are certain features that clearly mark spiritualities as authentically Christian. Different communities and eras will stress worship over service or commitment to the poor over preaching the Word, but the core practices should all be represented. These practices are the defining characteristics of the Body of Christ.

Virtue ethics shows how spiritual practices are the point of connection between the story of Jesus and the Christian moral life. The spiritual disciplines form Christ-conformed attitudes and beliefs in the practitioner. Under the grace of the Holy Spirit, these beliefs are continually expressed in right action and dynamic habits of the heart are formed. A readiness to act for the good is inculcated in the disciple. A virtue supplies us with both insight and the will to do that which is right and good. Compassion, for instance, helps us recognize what suffering people need from us, and motivates us to meet that need.

Historically, spirituality has insisted that individuals and communities will not be transformed by the Spirit without committed practices. Spiritual experiences are uplifting and exciting, but absent regular, intentional practices there is no real spirituality. A peak experience inspires, provides fresh insight, and may renew commitment, but growth in moral and spiritual character requires a life of regular spiritual practices.

The notion of practices is assigned a central place in virtue ethics by Alasdair MacIntyre. MacIntyre argues that every way of life inculcates its characteristic virtues through practices. A practice in his understanding, simply put, is a socially constituted way of acting that has inherent value and which expands our human capacities.[57] Virtuous habits are

57. He discusses the connection between practices and virtue at length in his classic work, *After Virtue*. MacIntyre formally defines a practice as "any coherent and

learned from traditions and from personal example; they result from acting in certain ways with the right intention. Here we can clearly see the influence of the Aristotelian tradition of moral philosophy.

Spiritual practices are vitally important because they form individuals and the faith community in the story of Israel and the story of Jesus over time. This is not a process of behavioral conditioning; it does not happen automatically. However, engaging in these practices on a regular basis means that we are constantly exposed to attitudes of heart, values, patterns of thinking, and actions that are at the heart of the gospel. Over time Christian character becomes more firmly established.

SUMMARY

We have seen that a virtue in the Christian sense is a habit, a readiness to act, a moral character trait, that is established through Spirit-inspired, grace-empowered training. There has been a renewal of virtue ethics in Christian moral theology since the 1970s. Some writers have raised the question of the connection between ethics and spirituality. The argument we mounted, drawing on the important work of William Spohn, is that virtue ethics is a better fit with Christian spirituality than either deontological or utilitarian ethics. We contend that because growth in Christ-like character, rather than commitment to the categorical imperative, or highly developed moral decision-making, is the main aim of the moral life of disciples, it makes good sense to establish virtue ethics as the preferred option in a spiritual formation process.

---

complex form of socially established cooperative human activity through which goods internal to that form of activity are realized in the course of trying to achieve those standards of excellence which are appropriate to, and partially definitive of, that form of activity, with the result that human powers to achieve excellence, and human conceptions of the ends and goods involved, are systematically extended" (187).

10

REVISIONS

*What We Learnt from the Ministry Agents
and Parishioners*

WE ARE DEEPLY APPRECIATIVE of the time and thought that the participating ministry agents and parishioners gave to reflection on the process
and how it could be improved. All the focus group sessions were recorded
and transcribed. The project coordinator then read over them and com-
piled a list by country of all the suggestions for revisions. As you would
expect, there was some repetition in the ideas offered. A list of unique
suggestions was generated and discussed in a meeting of the team.

Before discussing the feedback received, it is important to respond
to what was *not* said. What we mean by this is that when participants
were asked about connections between the areas of spirituality, moral
character, and emotional well-being (See Appendix B, Q. 8), very few
could identify any specific ones. The comments tended to be very general
ones along the lines of, "Well, there is overlap between the areas for sure."
In our minds, we were offering a whole-person model of spiritual formation that moves past the "silo approach" that sometimes operates. This aspect of our model was highlighted in the information document handed
to participating pastors. They were asked to make this a central feature
of the final session. The ideal that we hold is the weaving together of our
growth areas as persons of faith into a seamless garment. The feedback
we received indicated only partial awareness of this aim. After reflecting
on this generalized inability to integrate the domains, the team decided

to modify both the moral character and emotional well-being prompts to include specific theological references. Here are two examples. The original version of prudence (moral character area) was this: "The ability to think rightly about what the ethical thing to do is in a particular situation. Usually, you are able to decide on a course of action that leads to a good result." The new version is this: "The ability to think rightly about what the ethical thing to do is in a particular situation. You are able to decide on a course of action that reflects God's Realm and the way of Christ." The original version of intellectual curiosity and imagination (emotional well-being area) was this: "Openness to new experiences, a tendency to daydream, to play with ideas, and to imagine novel solutions to problems." New version: "Openness to new experiences, a tendency to play with ideas, to imagine novel solutions to problems, to wonder about Mystery, and to reimagine the world according to God's love and justice." The purpose in making these revisions is to offer clues about how biblical theology can be correlated with ideas from moral philosophy and psychology. Obviously, all that can be managed in a sentence or two on a prompt card is a hint. However, it seems important to do this, given that it is evident that integration across the domains eluded most participants. By dropping these hints, the need to work on integration is reinforced.

We move now to a discussion of the feedback. The list of suggestions for change and improvement is reproduced below.

1. Encourage the facilitatiors to go through the process themselves before they administer it.

2. Add an image to the various themes addressed. Include a story and a relevant scripture verse (or verses).

3. Offer less material to reflect on; i.e., reduce the number of cards in each area (to reduce the likelihood of overload of information).

4. Extend the length of time beyond six weeks.

5. Shorten the length to four weeks.

6. Include family members in the process. This would provide the opportunity to grow together and to keep each other accountable for maintaining this growth.

7. Promote it for use by couples.

8. Prepare a simple document (or video) to give to participating parishioners to orient them to the process.

9. In a large congregation, equip leaders to work with individuals or a group.

10. Offer a group process to reach more people, or possibly as an extension after the six-week one-to-one with a pastor.

11. Have the parishioner select one card and the ministry agent one card each week. [Note: This arose out of the discussion at the Ridley College symposium that the project coordinator spoke at.]

12. Blank card needs an explanation on it.

13. Provide an opportunity to revisit some of the issues later.

14. Change "Psychological Well-being" to "Emotional Well-being." The former term is a loaded one for some. The latter is "softer."

In relation to suggestion 1, it was the judgment of the team that while this would clearly be useful, ministry agents already have a full dance card, so to speak, and we are reluctant to suggest adding to it. In addition, we recognized that ministry agents commonly have their own program of spiritual formation that they are pursuing. However, we do see this as a valuable resource for pastors whose practice it is to meet with other pastors on a regular basis. Often these gatherings are focused on administration, new ministry and mission ideas, and other practical issues. Sharing on the level of the personal and the spiritual would change the dynamic considerably; indeed, it would add a fresh and deeper dimension.

The team saw a great deal of value in the second suggestion. We had considered it ourselves, but we decided that we wanted a process with as few "moving parts" as possible. We reasoned that a simple process would be inviting for parishioners who typically think spiritual formation is for Christians in the "advanced class"—the ones who know their Bibles and/or Church teaching inside out and who are active in Bible studies and retreats. Indeed, in the focus groups we heard comments such as this: "I'm not one for Bible studies. I don't think I know enough for that. But this, this I thought I could do." We also heard a comment such as this more than once: "I didn't even know what some of the things on the cards meant. But it was great that I could go along to my pastor each week and just tell her that. It started a really good conversation." Finally, there were those who said that they hadn't prayed or read their Bibles for a very long time, but now they were engaging again. One of the great strengths of the process is that it is simple, straightforward, and therefore non-threatening. We would like to keep it that way.

It is also a very open process. The parishioner is invited to discuss the various traits, virtues, and practices in whatever way speaks to them at this point in their spiritual journey. Including a scripture verse or verses on the cards, and/or supplying various images that the ministry agent thinks speaks to the content of the card in some way, is directive. The gaze of the parishioner is led in a particular direction.

Having said that, we do recognize, of course, a potential "value-add" in including scriptural references. We have not added biblical verses, but we have included quite a few more gospel metaphors and concepts in the definitions of the moral and psychological virtues. While we held the hope and expectation that parishioners would open their Bibles as part of the reflective process each week, we do acknowledge that some might not have known where to start. Some pastors therefore may want to go further than we have and find verses that they think fit with the theme and print them on the back of the cards. They may also choose to supply various images and/or stories to spark reflection. Stories are for everyone; they have universal appeal. Images, on the other, speak to some more than to others. However, we do recognize that those who have a strong visual orientation would relish the opportunity to engage through images. Indeed, the consensus in the team discussion was that a ministry agent may like to include a prompt question each week along this line: "When you think of justice [to take this example], what image comes to mind?"

Some participants suggested a shorter duration, and some a longer one. One pastor thought that it would help parishioners avoid overload if the number of cards was reduced. However, the view expressed by a large majority in the focus groups was that we hit the "Goldilocks spot" with six weeks and forty cards. In relation to the latter number, it is important to bear in mind that we are not asking parishioners to fully process and discuss all forty issues! They pick only one or two cards to bring to each session.

Four participants took part as couples and shared their reflections with each other before attending the session. They expressed the view that the process not only strengthened their spiritual lives, it also enhanced their relationship. One South African pastor suggested that the program could be promoted for family use. The view of the team on this is that, while this is interesting feedback, it is not our intention to offer the program as means to build couple and family relationships. Obviously, we think that if some individuals choose to engage as a couple or family group, and subsequently find it has enhanced their relationships, that is a very good outcome. It's simply the case that we continue to be comfortable with it being primarily for individuals and for non-familial groups.

The conversations in some of the focus groups indicated that some of the parishioners were a little unsure as to how the process was supposed to run. We are therefore very happy to include an orientation not only for the ministry agents, but also for the parishioners (see Appendices C and D, respectively).

The suggestion that came up the most was incorporating a group process. Some parishioners, for example, expressed a desire to keep the experience going. They suggested that forming a small group might be a way to facilitate this. This comment captures well the view of those that see benefits in engaging with others: "I was thinking that it was going to be more of a group session. And I don't know if it can be. Because this is just concerning *your* character, *your* spiritual practice. But I get a lot out of group discussions, because . . . because . . . I enjoy hearing other people's opinion on something. I like getting another perspective . . . " ("Martha," Roman Catholic, Chicago).

Others said that they would like an opportunity to revisit the issues in the future (see suggestion number 13), and that a small group setting would allow for this. The project coordinator, as mentioned in the introduction, has facilitated the process with small groups. He found, among other things, that the depth at which most participants were prepared to share was quite limited. The advantage of a one-to-one conversation with a trusted pastor is that going deep is more likely. One of our participating ministry agents made a comment reflecting this experience: "I think that the tension between the intimacy of one-to-one versus the benefit of a group is an interesting point to wrestle with. Maybe it's a both/and."

We agree that it's a case of "both/and." The process is suited to both a one-to-one and a group process. In relation to the latter, there are certain principles that it is important for the group leader to work with. See Appendix E for guidance.

One suggestion that we consider also needs a fuller treatment than the others is the ministry agent picking one card and the parishioner one card each week. The idea was offered by Rev Dr Graham Stanton at a very interesting and helpful symposium on Christian formation in the parish that he kindly convened at Ridley College, Melbourne in March 2020. Ridley is an evangelical college within the Anglican tradition. The proposal connects with the principle that Christians are called to hold each other to account. There is potentially a difference between what a parishioner may *like* to talk about and what they *need* to talk about. That is, it is possible that a person chooses to side-step a confronting or uncomfortable issue in their Christian life. A pastor who knows their parishioner well may pick up on that.

Keeping each other accountable in discipleship is a strong theme for many evangelical Christians. We designed our process with an ecumenical scope in view. We sought to include Roman Catholics, Anglicans, mainline and evangelical Protestants, and more. Our team acknowledges the importance of traditions that all Christians embrace—scriptural ones—and the ones that evangelical Christians, among others, specifically draw from—e.g., Calvinist, Wesleyan, and Baptist. In the Scriptures we find the following counsel concerning holding each other to account. "Iron sharpens iron, and one person sharpens the wits of another" (Prov 27:17). "My friends, if anyone is detected in a transgression, you who have received the Spirit should restore such a one in a spirit of gentleness. Take care that you yourselves are not tempted. Bear one another's burdens, and in this way you fulfil the law of Christ" (Gal 6:1–2).

It is far beyond the scope of this chapter to survey the long and complex story of Protestant traditions of pastoral discipline and mutual Christian accountability. What is offered here is merely the flavor of some of these traditions. John Calvin strongly embraced this scriptural tradition. He refers to the Christian responsibility to apply God's Word to call the wayward to account. "For they have the word of God with which to condemn the perverse; they have the word with which to receive the repentant into grace. They cannot err or disagree with God's judgment, for they judge solely according to God's law, which is no uncertain or earthly opinion but God's holy will and heavenly oracle" (*Institutes* 4.11.2). Calvin thought it important to highlight that the motivation behind calling one's fellow Christians to account needs to be concern for their uplift and restoration, rather than pharisaic zeal for discipline: "For it often happens that in their zeal for correction men are betrayed into Pharisaical severity that casts the poor sinner down rather than healing him."[1] Contemporary evangelical author, Jerry Bridges, affirms Calvin's conviction. Bridges

---

1. Calvin, *New Testament Commentaries*, 31.

asserts that accountability and discipleship must be grace-based to avoid harsh legalism: "But there is something more basic than discipleship, something that actually provides the necessary atmosphere in which discipleship can be practiced. The one word that describes what we must continue to hear is gospel."[2]

Early Methodism featured bands and class meetings with a strong focus on accountability. The practice goes back to John Wesley's days at Oxford and the Oxford Club. The class meeting was viewed as the most effective means of supporting the journey into authentic discipleship. All Methodists, even those in a band, were required to meet once a week in their class to provide an account of their discipleship. David Lowes Watson points out that it was seen as "an affirmation of grace."[3]

When it comes to the early Baptist tradition of accountability, it is a long and convoluted story. In her research on it, Anne Klose does a marvellous job of reconstructing this narrative.[4] There is space here to mention just one aspect. Klose discusses the primitive Baptist covenantal ecclesiology. One of the most influential covenants of the early Baptists was that shared by the churches of Benjamin and Elias Keach. The articles were, she says, "both demanding and yet warmly relational in tone."[5] The community members promised to live a life in all holiness, humility, and brotherly love. They promised to "watch over" one another, not suffering sin in one another and being ready to "warn, rebuke, and admonish one another with meekness," and yet also confidentially to bear "with one another's weaknesses, failings, and infirmities with much tenderness."

The team strongly affirms this tradition of grace and a warmly relational style in maintaining accountability in a Christian community. We hold that the truth needs to be spoken, but it must be spoken humbly, gently, and respectfully. In a word, it needs to be spoken in love. Love resists the temptation to exert pastoral power and to act in an authoritarian manner.

The team members all have a strong background in pastoral counseling and are appreciative of the person-centered approach. However, we also recognize that part of helpful therapy is facilitating

---

2. Bridges, *Discipline of Grace*, 20.

3. Lowes, *Covenant Discipleship*, 51.

4. Klose, "Covenantal Priesthood."

5. Klose, "Covenantal Priesthood," 95.

self-confrontation.[6] What we offer is *not* a therapeutic model. Our focus is very much on spiritual formation (though in a broader sense than some might allow). The point in raising this is to indicate why we opted for the parishioner choosing their issues. We do understand that in some settings a more active role by the ministry agent is seen to be appropriate. Further, in a context where the pastor and the parishioner know each other well and there is a high level of trust, we see a place for pastoral facilitation of self-confrontation.

We also hold to the theological tradition which posits the Holy Spirit leading a disciple in discernment. Ignatius of Loyola offered *The Examen* (examination of conscience/consciousness) as a resource that focuses on our inner experiences of *consolation* and *desolation* as indicators of God's presence and leading in our lives. In contemporary language, the spirit orientations that Ignatius refers to are "ego-centered" and "God-centered" inclinations. Our driven, destructive ego-bound inclinations are self-serving and self-protective and close us off from wholeness and our authentic selves. These patterns of self-gratification and power block off healthy paths of authentic loving. Discernment brings these desires and reveals their true intentions, thus empowering us to do the loving things that God-centeredness awakens in us. The Spirit leads this process in women and men of good will and spiritual openness. The point about accountability is that sometimes a person needs a gentle and loving prompt to greater receptivity to the Spirit.

Suggestion number 12 is about including an explanation on the blank card in each set. It was amusing to listen to the confusion caused by the inclusion of a blank card. It was designed as a "wild card"; parishioners were invited through the blankness to bring their own pressing issue(s) if none of the other ten cards really spoke to them. Pastors were instructed to inform their parishioners about it in the first session. Clearly some forgot to do this, or the parishioner misunderstood what was being said. Some thought the blank card was an error by the printers and found it useful as a coaster to set their coffee cup on while they pondered the issues of the week! Others thought that the team was being thoughtful in supplying a card for them to jot their reflections down. Suffices to say that the message did not get through very often. We therefore suggest printing this message on the "wild card" in the pack: "Feel free to bring something for reflection not covered in this set. Fill in the blank.

6. See Pembroke, *Foundations of Pastoral Counselling*, 161–183.

In reflecting on . . . do I need to explore it further at the session?" (See Appendix A in which all the cards are reproduced).

The second to last suggestion has already been covered. It is incorporated into our response to the idea of adding in small groups.

The final thought on improvements is changing "psychological well-being" to "emotional well-being." The team agrees with this proposal.

Once again, we say a big thank-you to all those who participated in the pilot! We are especially appreciative of the feedback and the very helpful suggestions for improvement.

Allow us to conclude this book on a fresh approach to spiritual formation in local faith communities with the words that sit at the end of the orientation sheets: You will soon embark on an interesting and hopefully wondrous journey. May the befriending Spirit accompany you!

Appendix A

THE PROMPT CARD SETS

Note 1: The cards should be playing-card size.
Note 2: The card sets should be color-coded to avoid confusion.
Note 3: There are 12 cards in each set. The last is a "wild card."

Set 1: Spiritual Practices

In this set of cards, you are invited to reflect on your SPIRITUAL PRACTICES	In reflecting on this aspect of my Christian life, do I need to explore it further at the session? PARTICIPATION IN WORSHIP Honoring, praising, and adoring God. Enjoying God's company as we listen to and sing God's Word, break bread, and share the cup of salvation together.
In reflecting on this aspect of my Christian life, do I need to explore it further at the session? PRAYER A regular time of personal adoration of God, discernment, thanksgiving, and praying for others.	In reflecting on this aspect of my Christian life, do I need to explore it further at the session? SELF-EXAMINATION and CONFESSION In self-examination, we allow the Holy Spirit to open our hearts to what is true about us. In confession, we receive Christ's forgiveness and gift of peace.
In reflecting on this aspect of my Christian life, do I need to explore it further at the session? MEDITATIVE READING OF SCRIPTURE Reading the Scriptures with an open and listening posture. Taking our time over a Scripture passage, reading it expectantly and being fully alert to God's voice.	In reflecting on this aspect of my Christian life, do I need to explore it further at the session? SPIRITUAL RETREAT An extended period of time during which we quietly listen to God and enjoy communion with God. Taking time out from the demands of everyday life for spiritual renewal.

Set 1 continued

In reflecting on this aspect of my Christian life, do I need to explore it further at the session? SABBATH-KEEPING God's gift of a regular routine of rest. A time given to us to celebrate life and the world around us and to simply be with God. A time for *being* in the midst of a life of *doing*.	In reflecting on this aspect of my Christian life, do I need to explore it further at the session? SIMPLICITY The Son of Man had nowhere to lay his head. A simple life is letting go of the desire to own and to have things. Simplicity is founded on a spirit of generosity that sets us free.
In reflecting on this aspect of my Christian life, do I need to explore it further at the session? COMMUNITY Christian community exists when believers are open to the grace of God and live through love. In such a community, people relate to each other in compassionate, empathic, honest, and just ways.	In reflecting on this aspect of my Christian life, do I need to explore it further at the session? ECOLOGICAL SPIRITUALITY Caring for the earth is a way of expressing delight in, and a sense of God-given responsibility for, an endangered creation. By engaging in such care, we honor God and the gift of the creation.
In reflecting on this aspect of my Christian life, do I need to explore it further at the session? HOSPITALITY Christ came as both guest and host. He made a gracious offer of a safe, open, and warm space. In this space, people are free to sing their own song and to find their true self.	Feel free to bring something for reflection not covered in this set. Fill in the blank. In reflecting on . . . do I need to explore it further at the session?

Set 2: Spiritual Character

In this set of cards, you are invited to reflect on your SPIRITUAL CHARACTER	In reflecting on this aspect of my Christian life, do I need to explore it further at the session? LOVE Giving of myself for the good of others. Living in communion: giving to and receiving from others. Giving up power; embracing others rather than excluding; respecting others rather than dominating.
In reflecting on this aspect of my Christian life, do I need to explore it further at the session? FAITH Trust in the love and grace of God that has been made known to us by Christ. Trust that in the Word, God's Beloved One, there is a perfect witness to truth and life.	In reflecting on this aspect of my Christian life, do I need to explore it further at the session? JOY Rejoicing in the grace and love of God. Joy that flows from the knowledge that in the good times and in the bad, God is with us, those we love, and all of creation.
In reflecting on this aspect of my Christian life, do I need to explore it further at the session? HOPE Confidence that God is at work in our world bringing good out of evil; that no matter what happens in life God loves us, sustains us, and offers the hope of eternal life.	In reflecting on this aspect of my Christian life, do I need to explore it further at the session? PEACE Serenity flowing from resting secure in God's unconditional love, sustaining grace, and gift of Christ and the Holy Spirit.

Set 2 continued

In reflecting on this aspect of my Christian life, do I need to explore it further at the session? PATIENCE Spirit-enabled endurance in the face of strife and adversity; spiritual strength to bear up under the stresses and strains of life.	In reflecting on this aspect of my Christian life, do I need to explore it further at the session? GENTLENESS Relating to others and to self in a non-judgmental and nurturing manner; including those who are different, in the spirit of the One who welcomed all to his table; speaking a hard truth in a gentle way.
In reflecting on this aspect of my Christian life, do I need to explore it further at the session? KINDNESS Reflecting God's kindness to us; acting tenderly, benevolently, and hospitably toward others.	In reflecting on this aspect of my Christian life, do I need to explore it further at the session? SELF-CONTROL Awareness of personal desires and keeping in check those that need to be kept in check. This is not self-negation, but rather reining in desires that do not align with a Christ-like way of life.
In reflecting on this aspect of my Christian life, do I need to explore it further at the session? GENEROSITY A reflection of God's generosity to us; giving good things to others freely and abundantly.	Feel free to bring something for reflection not covered in this set. Fill in the blank. In reflecting on . . . do I need to explore it further at the session?

Set 3: Moral Character

In this set of cards, you are invited to reflect on your MORAL CHARACTER	In reflecting on this aspect of my Christian life, do I need to explore it further at the session? JUSTICE One of love's forms. A commitment to give to each and to all what is due to them. Doing your fair share in your daily activities and working for a fair share of burdens and benefits in the society.
In reflecting on this aspect of my Christian life, do I need to explore it further at the session? HONESTY The quality of being fair, sincere, and truthful. Consistently choosing truth, especially when that is costly.	In reflecting on this aspect of my Christian life, do I need to explore it further at the session? PRUDENCE One of love's forms. The ability to think rightly about what the ethical thing to do is in a particular situation. You decide on a course of action that reflects God's Realm and the way of Christ.
In reflecting on this aspect of my Christian life, do I need to explore it further at the session? FORTITUDE One of love's forms. If you have this virtue, you don't give into fear on the one hand, or to recklessness on the other. Doing what is right when faced with opposition and threat.	In reflecting on this aspect of my Christian life, do I need to explore it further at the session? HUMILITY Your general pattern is that you realistically assess both your gifts and your flaws. You happily live under God's teaching. You are prepared to acknowledge the good ideas or suggestions of others.

Set 3 continued

In reflecting on this aspect of my Christian life, do I need to explore it further at the session? COMPASSION Sympathetic concern for and understanding of the suffering of others, together with a desire to do something to alleviate that suffering.	In reflecting on this aspect of my Christian life, do I need to explore it further at the session? SOLIDARITY A firm, ongoing determination to seek the good for the society and each individual; opposition to all that is oppressive and helping everyone to live with dignity, to assert their rights, and to exercise their responsibilities.
In reflecting on this aspect of my Christian life, do I need to explore it further at the session? INTEGRITY The habit of refusing to compromise that which you believe to be true, to follow the crowd, or to do what will win praise; to be consistent and utterly trustworthy.	In reflecting on this aspect of my Christian life, do I need to explore it further at the session? ECOLOGICAL STEWARDSHIP The habitual practice of responsibly using and protecting God's gift of creation through conservation, political engagement, and sustainable practices.
In reflecting on this aspect of my Christian life, do I need to explore it further at the session? PEACEABLENESS A way of life in the spirit of Christ involving the refusal to use force to protect yourself, to use coercion to get your own way, or to violently resist evil when it is done to you.	Feel free to bring something for reflection not covered in this set. Fill in the blank. In reflecting on . . . do I need to explore it further at the session?

Set 4: Emotional Well-being

In this set of cards, you are invited to reflect on your EMOTIONAL WELL-BEING	In reflecting on this aspect of my personal life, do I need to explore it further at the session?
	AUTONOMY You appreciate the worth of both independence and interdependence; you listen to others in the Christian community and beyond, but you are not controlled or dominated by them; you do not need to constantly seek others' approval.
In reflecting on this aspect of my personal life, do I need to explore it further at the session? **SELF-ACCEPTANCE** Holding a positive attitude toward yourself; maintaining positive self-regard despite awareness of your weaknesses and shadow side.	In reflecting on this aspect of my personal life, do I need to explore it further at the session? **SKILL IN EVERYDAY LIVING** Handling people and tasks well in your everyday life. You set Christ's love and acceptance above any talent you may or may not have. You see your skill as a resource God can use in serving others.
In reflecting on this aspect of my personal life, do I need to explore it further at the session? **POSITIVE INTERPERSONAL RELATIONS** A capacity to relate to others in a warm, generous, trusting, empathic, and loving manner.	In reflecting on this aspect of my personal life, do I need to explore it further at the session? **PURPOSE IN LIFE** Knowing who you are in Christ and a good general sense of what you need to be doing with your life; having a clear set of goals; having a reason to get out of bed each day.

Set 4 continued

In reflecting on this aspect of my personal life, do I need to explore it further at the session? PERSONAL GROWTH You embrace opportunities to grow spiritually, morally, and in emotional intelligence; when situations present that you know will challenge you and help you to mature, you grab hold of them.	In reflecting on this aspect of my personal life, do I need to explore it further at the session? CONSCIENTIOUSNESS A capacity for self-discipline, reliability, hard work and perseverance in life's tasks and in the spiritual disciplines.
In reflecting on this aspect of my personal life, do I need to explore it further at the session? OPTIMISM Looking to the future, you expect more good events than bad ones in your life; you have confidence that through God's aid and your natural gifts you will overcome obstacles and succeed in personal projects.	In reflecting on this aspect of my personal life, do I need to explore it further at the session? BEING IN THE MOMENT (FLOW) You experience becoming completely absorbed in a task, and when you do, your brain and body are really firing; you are greatly enjoying what you are doing at that moment.
In reflecting on this aspect of my personal life, do I need to explore it further at the session? INTELLECTUAL CURIOSITY and IMAGINATION Openness to new experiences; a tendency to play with ideas, to imagine novel solutions to problems, to wonder about Mystery, to reimagine the world according to God's love and justice.	Feel free to bring something for reflection not covered in this set. Fill in the blank. In reflecting on . . . do I need to explore it further at the session?

Appendix B

QUESTIONS FOR PASTOR FOCUS GROUPS

Preamble

Word of welcome and thanks. Then make it clear that the conversation today is about the process and not the content of the conversations. That is, we wish to evaluate how helpful or otherwise the process that we have developed is in facilitating spiritual formation in the parish.

1. Has engaging in this process generated any new insights concerning the nature of your calling as pastor?

2. What did you find helpful in the process? What are its strengths?

3. What were some of the highlights for you over the six weeks?

4. Did any parishioners choose the blank card option? If so, what is your evaluation of the use of the prompt cards?

5. Was six weeks long enough for the issues to be adequately explored?

6. Would a longer period have been useful, or did you sense that on the whole the parishioners were happy to draw it to a close?

7. To what extent did you find the parishioners making connections between the domains of spiritual practices, spiritual character, moral character, and positive psychology in their conversations?

8. What was unhelpful in the process? What are its weaknesses?

9. How could the process be improved?

QUESTIONS FOR PARISHIONER FOCUS GROUPS

Preamble

Word of welcome and thanks. Then make it clear that the conversation today is about the process that was used and not how helpful or otherwise the pastor was. That is, we wish to evaluate how helpful the process was in raising significant issues in your journey of spiritual formation.

1. What impact has the experience had in relation to your ongoing journey of spiritual formation?

2. What did you find helpful in the process? What are its strengths?

3. What were some of the highlights for you over the six weeks?

4. How useful were the prompt cards in stimulating your thinking about your spiritual life?

5. Was it useful to have the blank card option?

6. Was six weeks long enough for the issues to be adequately explored?

7. Would a longer period have been useful to you? If so, what would you like to do in subsequent sessions?

8. To what extent did you find yourself making connections between the domains of spiritual practices, spiritual character, moral character, and positive psychology in the conversations?

9. What was unhelpful in the process? What are its weaknesses?

10. How could the process be improved?

Appendix C

ORIENTATION FOR PASTORS

Introduction

This six-session process that you are about to embark on with your parishioners addresses the whole person. They will be invited to reflect on four areas in their personal and spiritual lives: spiritual practices, spiritual character, moral character, and emotional well-being.

The first of the sessions is an orientation to the approach and the process. This is followed by four sessions on each of the areas mentioned above. They can be addressed in any order; it's up to the parishioner to choose. The final session consists of a closing conversation and prayer or ritual.

The parishioner is invited to work with sets of prompts for reflection; they are printed on cards of playing card size. You will note that each set has a blank card. This symbolizes an invitation for the parishioner to bring an issue or issues not covered in the prompts.

It's important to recognize that the three categories parishioners will address—positive psychology, spirituality, and personal/social ethics—are interconnected. The thinking is that it is not possible for you to be optimally helpful in companioning parishioners on their journey of spiritual development without addressing their moral life and their emotional well-being.

These categories are not three water-tight containers standing side-by-side; they leak into each other. For example, a lack of self-awareness and emotional well-being in a person often results in destructive interpersonal behavior rather than that which is good, right, and upbuilding. Stating the connection positively, emotional strengths are supportive of moral virtue. It's also clear that the way a person engages in their set of spiritual practices impacts on their personal psychology and their moral life.

While it is evident that there is interaction and overlap between the categories, it is also true that each of them has its own specific focus. In the psychological domain, we are concerned to enhance emotional well-being and positive relationships with others. The spirituality area involves us in reflection on prayer and meditation on God's Word, sacramental life, images of God, and the God-relationship. Finally, in the moral category we concentrate on virtue and character, on moral principles and rules, and on what is right and good. A significant feature of the closing session will be an invitation for the parishioner to do some integrative thinking. More on this below.

The Process

The process consists of six sessions (each 1 to 1 ½ hours). The first session is an orientation; it has a number of aims. The first is to give an opportunity for a conversation about expectations, hopes, and concerns. You will invite the parishioner to reflect on questions such as these: What would you like to see come out of this process and our conversations? What are you hoping for? What is it about what we are about to embark on that excites you? Are there things about it that you feel a bit anxious or uncertain about?

The first session is also the time, obviously, to talk about how the process will unfold over the next five sessions. This is laid out just below.

Finally, at the first session you invite the parishioner to select a set of cards to work with at the next session (it can be any one of the four).

The process is as follows. After the first session, the parishioner reflects on the set of prompts (covering, for example, spiritual character, or emotional well-being, etc.) that they have chosen. They then bring 1 or 2 of these cards to the second session. These cards form the basis for the conversation.

The style of the conversation is pastoral and informal in tone. The approach is not that of formal spiritual direction. It needs to have the feel of companioning, guiding, and facilitating. The pastor in this process is not set up as "the expert," though you clearly have quite a bit of expertise to bring. Mutuality in the working together is appropriate. It is envisioned that the parishioner will likely contribute to the spiritual formation of the pastor along the way (though this is not a stated aim).

At the close of the session, you invite the parishioner to consider doing some journaling as a way of reflecting further on what was talked about. This is an invitation only; the parishioner needs to feel free not to take it up. If s/he does opt for journaling, provide the minimal guidance set out below. The questions we suggest reflect three levels of "seeing" (on the model of John 20 and the relevant Greek words):

> In reflecting on the session just past ...
>
> What do you notice? What feelings and thoughts arise for you as you reflect on the conversation?
>
> What are you wondering about? What are you feeling curious about?
>
> Is there a "light bulb" moment for you? Is there an insight that seems especially important right now?

If the parishioner wants to reflect on what came to them in the journaling process at the start of the next session that is fine, but it is not expected. That is, there is no need to offer an invitation to do so.

At the conclusion of the second session, you invite the parishioner to select their second set of prompt cards to take away. They bring one or two cards to the third session to form the basis of that conversation. And so the process goes on.

The sixth session is a wrap-up. It's a time for both reflecting back and reflecting forward. You might ask questions such as: What was most significant for you along this journey? What did you learn? What are the issues that will stay with you? Where to from here?

The final session, finally, is an opportunity to reflect on the whole-of-person dimension in the process. Though each session has a particular focus, humans are whole beings; we can't be carved up into four sections. Emotional well-being, spiritual and moral character, and our spiritual practices are all inextricably linked. To promote integrative reflection, you may ask questions such as these: What connections have you noticed between the conversations in the four sessions? After our times together and your own reflection, how are you seeing your emotional life, your spiritual life, and your moral life as linked?

You will soon embark on an interesting and hopefully wondrous journey with your parishioner. May the befriending Spirit accompany you!

Appendix D

ORIENTATION FOR PARISHIONERS

Introduction

This six-session process that you are about to embark on addresses the whole person. You will be invited to reflect on four aspects of your personal and spiritual life: spiritual practices, spiritual character, moral character, and emotional well-being.

The first of the sessions is an orientation to the approach and the process. This is followed by four sessions on each of the aspects mentioned above. They can be addressed in any order; you get to choose. The final session consists of a closing conversation and prayer or ritual.

You will be invited to work with sets of prompts for reflection; they are printed on cards of playing card size. You will note that each set has a blank card. This symbolizes an invitation for you to bring an issue or issues not covered in the prompts.

It's important to recognize that the categories you will be working with—positive psychology, spirituality, and personal/social ethics—are interconnected. The thinking is that it's not possible for the pastor to be optimally helpful in companioning you on your journey of spiritual development without addressing your moral life and your emotional well-being.

These categories are not three water-tight containers standing side-by-side; they leak into each other. For example, a lack of self-awareness and emotional well-being in a person often results in destructive interpersonal behavior rather than that which is good, right, and upbuilding. Stating the connection positively, emotional strengths are supportive of moral virtue. It's also clear that the way a person engages in their set of spiritual practices impacts on their personal psychology and their moral life.

While it is evident that there is interaction and overlap between the three categories, it is also true that each of them has its own specific focus. In the psychological category, we are concerned to enhance emotional well-being and positive relationships with others. The spirituality area involves us in reflection on prayer and meditation on God's Word, sacramental life, images of God, and the God-relationship. Finally, in the moral category we concentrate on virtue and character, on moral principles and rules, and on what is right and good. A significant feature of the closing session will be an invitation for you to do some integrative thinking. More on this below.

The Process

The process consists of six sessions (each 1 to 1 ½ hours). The first session is an orientation; it has several aims. The first is to give an opportunity for a conversation about expectations, hopes, and concerns. You will be invited to reflect on questions such as these: What would you like to see come out of this process and our conversations? What are you hoping for? What is it about what we are about to embark on that excites you? Are there things about it that you feel a bit anxious or uncertain about?

The first session is also the time, obviously, to talk about how the process will unfold over the next five sessions. This is laid out just below.

Finally, at the first session you will be invited to select a set of cards to work with at the next session (it can be any one of the four).

The process is as follows. After the first session, you reflect on the set of prompts (covering, for example, spiritual character, or emotional well-being, etc.) that you have chosen. You then bring 1 or 2 of these cards to the second session. They form the basis for the conversation.

At the close of the session, the pastor will invite you to consider doing some journaling as a way of reflecting further on what was talked about. This is an invitation only; you need to feel totally free not to take it up. If you do opt for journaling, take note of the questions below.

> In reflecting on the session just past . . .

> What do you notice? What feelings and thoughts arise for you as you reflect on the conversation?

What are you wondering about? What are you feeling curious about?

Is there a "light bulb" moment for you? Is there an insight that seems especially important right now?

If you want to reflect on what came to you in the journaling process at the start of the next session that is fine, but it is not expected.

At the conclusion of the second session, you will be invited to select your second set of prompt cards to take away. You will bring one or two cards to the third session to form the basis of that conversation. And the process goes on.

The sixth session is a wrap-up. It's a time for both reflecting back and reflecting forward. The pastor might ask questions such as these: What was most significant for you along this journey? What did you learn? What are the issues that will stay with you? Where to from here?

The final session, finally, is an opportunity to reflect on the whole-of-person dimension in the process. Though each session has a particular focus, humans are whole beings; we can't be carved up into four sections. Emotional well-being, spiritual and moral character, and our spiritual practices are all inextricably linked. To promote integrative reflection, the pastor may ask questions such as the following: What connections have you noticed between the conversations in the four sessions? After our times together and your own reflection, how are you seeing your emotional life, your spiritual life, and your moral life as linked?

You will soon embark on an interesting and hopefully wondrous journey. May the befriending Spirit accompany you!

Appendix E

GROUP SPIRITUAL FORMATION: STRUCTURE AND PROCESS

Our spiritual lives are lived out in our personal quest for the Sacred. Ultimately, our responsibility before God is ours to manage and maintain. Yet, none of us grow in faith by ourselves or for ourselves, but require the presence of others to nurture, bless, and confirm our growth journeys. Scripture suggests that the participation of others is vital, not only for our maturation as persons of faith, but perhaps as importantly, to reveal Christ in our midst: "For where two or three are gathered together in my name, there I am in their midst" (Matt 18:20).

For the Christian, the road we walk is an interpersonal and relational road. Perhaps the most iconic Scriptural examples we find in the Bible are the road to Emmaus, and the path to Pentecost. The Emmaus journey captures for us the full range of our spiritual journey, from fear, despair, and sorrow, to seeing and knowing through the mutuality of sharing Christ among us. Christ became visible in and through the disciples' sharing. But Emmaus was not a complete journey to consolidate that Presence. The Emmaus Road led to Pentecost, where the full measure of the Spirit's awakening infused those present with the flame of love that seeks to burn in all of our hearts even now.

In being invited to grow in faith and Christ-likeness, we need structures and practices that nurture our growth in communal ways. Our personal responsibility for spiritual growth remains our own, but perhaps the contemporary privatization of faith has handicapped and limited our growth. Group spiritual formation can serve as a counterpoint to our isolation and privatization, and even provide an acceleration to our maturation.

But why might we seek a group process to support our spiritual formation?[1] To begin with, in meeting with others we learn to attend to the Spirit's Presence among us, not simply for ourselves, but as a shared experience. Second, we learn from the collective wisdom and strength. Third, and perhaps most importantly, we have a "mini-experience" of the body of Christ, by noticing God's Spirit at work in us in discernment, strengthening us in our journeys, and growing in love.

Parameters for Structuring the Group Spiritual Formation Process

Effective and enriching groups benefit from clear and reliable structuring to provide the container that holds the process. Without clear guidelines groups can easily wander into extraneous matters not related to the purposes of the group. The center-point to these purposes is to guide the group's efforts into a greater awareness of God's presence in our lives. When a group begins its work the potential focus areas can be introduced in an initial orientation session, where the prompt cards are explained and described. The group can select which domains to address at any given meeting, but the selection of the specific cards for personal reflection and sharing should remain the prerogative of the individual. Of course, more than one person can select the same card for their own personal work, but this overlapping, if it occurs, can deepen and strengthen the group sharing that occurs.

Group Size

Practitioners of group process report that group size is a critical element in group formation. Obviously, when a group becomes larger, participation lessens, or perhaps the more vocal members dominate and there is erosion of the necessary mutuality and growth-in-trust for the group. Evidence suggests that a range of 4 to 10 members is very viable, with perhaps 6 to 8 members as an optimum number, allowing for deeper immersion in the theme(s) of the sessions, while also retaining the intimacy of disclosure and sharing. If a group ends up with more than this

1. Edwards, *Living in the Presence*, 123-158. Edwards provides a valuable handbook for those wishing to strengthen their group leadership awareness.

optimum number of members, it is a good idea to divide into subgroups of 3 to 6 people, depending on how much time is available for the overall commitment. A good rule of thumb is that the smaller the timeframe available the smaller the group should be. When utilizing subgroups, it is necessary to secure adequate leadership for any additional subgroups.

Duration

The length of meetings requires clarity and discipline, with two hour sessions recommended. Modest adjustments on either side of the two hour suggestion can be considered, depending on the size of the group.

Groups that have 8 to 10 participants will need enough sessions to allow members to bring to voice the insights and challenges they are living in their spiritual lives. It is recommended that larger groups meet perhaps for 8 weeks, beginning with an initial orientation meeting, and a closing summary, with the remaining sessions organized around the four prompt-card focus areas: spiritual character, spiritual practices, emotional well-being, and personal/social ethics. Each focus area can thus have two dialogue opportunities. When working as a group, the structure can provide a rich and diverse engagement with the themes of each area, given the uniqueness of each individual group member. Smaller groups (4 to 6 participants) may well have sufficient time to address the desired focus areas with fewer sessions, but 6 sessions could serve as a minimum.

Recommended Guidelines

Gathering

Sharing groups seek to structure their time together in ways that strengthen and support the reflective process. Gathering in a circle signals the mutuality of the process, and the equality we share before God. Providing a symbol of centering in the middle of the room such as a candle, referring to a desire to be guided by the light of Christ, is useful. Gathering in silence before beginning recognizes that we gather with intentions that go beyond standard socializing; it highlights that we are entering Sacred Space in which the presence of God can be discerned.

Signals of beginning include ringing a bell and using a prayer of centering such as the Lord's Prayer or some other prayer mode selected by the group. Each subsequent meeting can be structured to include opening rituals that could include the prayerful reflection on the designated prompt-card themes of the week. Again, these are the ones chosen by the group as the basis for the personal reflections each member will undertake.

Weekly Practices

Spending time each week in prayerful reflection on the selected themes of the week will stir the heart and soul. As in any disciplined activity, these themes should be consciously noted and gathered up into awareness. Journaling lends itself well to such gathering so that our recollections during the week are not lost. These summaries need not be extended essays; they are brief notations with sufficient detail to serve as prompts for further awareness and insight.

When the group then meets, these reflections become the basis for the sharing that occurs. Certain "ground rules" should be identified in the orientation meeting, and referenced again if needed along the way, if the group drifts into extraneous or non-related themes. Among these ground rules would be a commitment to sensitive receptivity to one another, without judgment to any personal sharing that is offered. Respectful listening is the central requirement for this process. We commit to receiving the sharing of our group partners with gratitude.

When a member shares we are not required to respond, and when responding we seek to support the sharing by validating how the insight has touched us. Although we need not respond orally, we can respond prayerfully in silence. There should be no pressure on anyone to be helpful or to supplement what has been said. Sometimes, one or two questions from the group can draw out an implication from what has been said, or provide further clarification, but this is not essential. Our task as listeners is not to offer agreement or disagreement, but to share how our lives in God's presence are touched, confirmed, or challenged by what we have heard. Any sincere sharing by a group member should be met by gracious validation of the experience.

A danger that can sometimes appear in sharing groups is "cross-talk." Cross-talk includes the impulse to expand the sharer's contribution by "improving it" with one's own "deeper" insight. This is a form of "spiritual one-upmanship," with the temptation being that we treat spiritual growth competitively. Perhaps St Paul inadvertently set us up for such competition in I Corinthians 9:24, when he describes the call to "run the good race" in which only one runner seemingly receives the winner's garland. In Hebrews 12:1, we are given a different emphasis: to similarly run the race with endurance, but the image of a "great cloud of witnesses" cheering us on is also offered. In group spiritual formation we are not in competition in this race, but we have a cheering section for which the group is a reliable voice. On the road of life we are all at different legitimate points in our journey, and there is a profound grace that comes in recognizing the legitimacy of where we are spiritually in each person's "here and now."

Creating Space for Diversity

In any human community where comprehensive life themes are at stake, there will be differences of personality, temperament, values and principles for life. Even in a faith community where there are generally assumed common virtues and values, differences will emerge. These differences should not threaten us; on the contrary, they ultimately become the basis for our unity in Christ. The bright shining example for us of this commitment is Pentecost, as noted above. Pentecost marks the awakening of the Spirit's unifying presence among us, and our likely diversities will meet their Pentecost opportunity in the group.

A spiritual formation group is a powerful way to test and stretch our Pentecost receptivity. Pentecost is not a one-off moment of spiritual awareness, only to sink back into unawareness. Having a conscious awareness of our Pentecost responsibility toward honoring difference, can be named as an aspect of the commitment the group makes toward unity in Christ. "They will know you are my disciples by your love" (John 13:35).

One way to secure this respectful engagement is to include an intentional reflection at one or two specific times in the process, to review how the group is experiencing the creative awareness of differences. There is a liberation that happens as we respectfully name those differences in the light of God's presence in our midst. Providing a structure for such naming of difference facilitates important moments of learning and insight; the process also provides a vehicle for addressing unacknowledged tensions before they become a problem that can derail a group.

Space for Silence

Among the varieties of spiritual practices that a group might utilize, silence should be included as one element. Silence is the doorway that draws us into fuller awareness. Whether we are experienced practitioners or newcomers to silence, it creates a necessary buffer for chatter or restlessness and gently draws us toward Presence. Leaving room for collective silence, whether brief (a few minutes), or extended (ten or more minutes), creates an inner space where spiritual resonance can occur. Its ultimate intent, however, is to direct us toward God's presence as a way into the expansiveness of God in our midst. In being silent with others we are drawn into a prayerful life with God, to and for each other.

Commitment to Sharing

When we have spent time in personal prayer and reflection, we may feel the urge to share our experiences. These personal stirrings are not meant to be fully articulated position papers, but quite simply the subtle, even vague stirrings of our hearts and souls. Trusting ourselves to share them, and trusting the group to receive them, binds the group into a solidarity of seeking God's presence. In receiving the sharing of others we become aware of the richness of one another's spiritual lives, and the wealth of wisdom that resides among us. We get to see "grace in action" within the body of Christ. We gain direct evidence that we are not alone in our struggles and challenges.

One possible risk could surface at this point when we feel pressure to respond to what is being shared. Beyond the potential to become competitive with another's experience as noted earlier, there can be a danger in seeking to become sharp and precise in rational articulation or analysis in response to what has been shared. Seeking to categorize or define ideas can take us away from the mystery of God in us and in our midst. Sharpening up ideas is not the objective here, but rather a settling into the sufficiency of the grace that we receive in sharing.

Group spiritual formation is not intended to be a forum for exclusively sharing our powerful experiences, so that our so-called spiritual highlights can be revealed. The danger therein is that it creates a climate for displaying our "spiritual successes" only, as if the spiritual journey is one "victory" after another. In so doing, the everydayness or ordinariness of our spiritual life is missed or ignored. Spiritual discernment takes time. Seeking good feelings for their own sake takes us away from the richness and depth that is then missed in the more subtle movements of our spiritual journeys.

Insight

Among the blessings of group sharing, we gain insights about one another's experiences with God in the ebb and flow of our God-encounters as a living relationship. In talking about God, we seek to articulate our experiences, using the best images and ideas about God we can generate. These intentions are legitimate because they can help build a bridge to new awareness of God in ways we might have missed or ignored. A limitation, however, might be that we settle for a conceptual understanding of God and are satisfied with insight for its own sake; in this way we fail to move further into the realm of relationship with God. Beyond the ideas, insights, and feelings that come we would do well to remember that we seek to move toward the ongoing relationship with the Holy that is its living center.

Managing Anxiety

It would not be surprising if even willing participants in group spiritual formation experience some degree of anxiety about their participation. Particularly if an individual has not had experience with groups, there is likely another layer of concern about their capacity or worthiness for such an undertaking. Many of us already experience anxiety about perfection, performance, or needing to demonstrate mastery in everyday life, and furthermore spiritual self-disclosure is not something most persons are practiced at. Given that possible anxiety, it is important, even in the initial orientation encounters, for the group to identify some of the fears and apprehensions. What is vital to identify and claim early on is that spiritual growth work is meant to be an exercise in trust, that God's grace is sufficient to cover our gaps in knowledge, faithfulness, or rigor. The group is God's temporary vessel for holding our fears, anxieties, and hopes. In so doing we are finding new strength and affirmation in our life journeys toward greater God-awareness and Christ-likeness.

Final Key Consideration

What is vital for anyone choosing a group spiritual formation experience is gaining clarity about intentions. When the invitation to participate comes, it is important for the potential participant to discuss their
desires, hopes, and objectives with their pastor/group leader/facilitator.
Beyond receiving information about the broader process in its formal
details, it will be important to examine their deeper hopes for such an undertaking. An intentional journey of this type will change the participant
and prayerful reflection and discernment about purposes will provide a
necessary foundation for the process.

Bibliography

Aelred of Rievaulx. *Spiritual Friendship*. Collegeville: Liturgical, 2010.

Aquinas, Thomas. "Commentary on Nicomachean Ethics." In *An Aquinas Reader*, edited by Mary T. Clark. New York: Fordham University Press, 1988.

————. *Summa Theologica*. Translated by Fathers of the English Dominican Province. Cincinnati: Benziger Brothers, 1947.

Aristotle, *Nicomachean Ethics*. In *The Complete Works of Aristotle*, the Revised Oxford Translation, vol. 2, edited by Jonathan Barnes. Princeton: Princeton University Press, 1984.

Artress, Lauren. *The Sacred Path Companion: A Guide to Walking the Labyrinth to Heal and Transform*. Berkley: Berkley, 2006.

Augustine, *The City of God*. Washington: Catholic University of America Press, 1950.

Barth, Karl. *Church Dogmatics* II.2. Edinburgh: T&T Clark, 1958.

Beaumont, Stephen. "Pastoral Counseling Down Under: A Survey of Australian Clergy." *Pastoral Psychology* 61 (2011) 117–131.

Austin, Nicholas. "Spirituality and Virtue in Christian Formation: A Conversation between Thomistic and Ignatian Traditions." *New Blackfriars* 97 (2016) 202–217.

Beeley, Gregory. *Gregory of Nazianzus on the Trinity and the Knowledge of God*. Oxford: Oxford University Press, 2013.

Bentham, Jeremy. *An Introduction to the Principles of Morals and Legislation*. London: Athlone, 1970. First published in 1789.

Benner, David G. *Spirituality and the Awakening Self*. Grand Rapids: Brazos, 2012.

Bom, Klaas. "'Joy, Joy, Joy, Tears of Joy': A Contribution to Theological Anthropology." *International Journal of Philosophy and Theology* 78, no. 3 (2017) 215–33. DOI: 10.1080/21692327.2017.1302814.

Bourgeault, Cynthia. *Centering Prayer and Inner Awakening*. Lanham: Cowley, 2004.

Bridges, Jerry. *The Discipline of Grace: God's Role and our Role in the Pursuit of Holiness*. Colorado Springs: NavPress, 1994.

Browning, Don. *The Moral Context of Pastoral Care*. Philadelphia: Westminster, 1976.

————. *A Fundamental Practical Theology*. Minneapolis: Fortress, 1991.

Bruce, Frederick F. *Commentary on Galatians*. Exeter: Paternoster, 1982.

Brueggemann, Walter. *Hope within History*. Atlanta: John Knox, 1987.

Burton, Rod. "Therapeutic Spiritual Direction: Refraining Contemporary Pastoral Counselling." *Contact* 126, no. 1 (1998) 14–21.

Calvin, John. *Calvin's New Testament Commentaries Vol 10*. Grand Rapids: Eerdmans, 1996.

————. *Calvin's New Testament Commentaries Vol 11: Galatians, Ephesians, Philippians, and Colossians.* Grand Rapids: Eerdmans, 1996.

Campbell, Alastair. *Rediscovering Pastoral Care*, 2nd ed. London: Darton, Longman & Todd, 1986.

Capps, Don. *Life Cycle Theory and Pastoral Care*, reprint ed. Eugene: Wipf & Stock, 2002.

————. *Living Stories: Pastoral Counseling in Congregational Context.* Minneapolis: Fortress, 1998.

Caranfa, Angelo. "The Aesthetic and the Spiritual Attitude in Learning: Lessons from Simone Weil." *Journal of Aesthetic Education* 44, no. 2 (2010) 63–82.

Chandler, Diane J. "Introduction." In *The Holy Spirit and Christian Formation: Multidisciplinary Perspectives*, edited by Diane J. Chandler, 1–15. Cham: Springer International, 2016.

Charry, Ellen T. and Russell D. Kosits. "Christian Theology and Positive Psychology: An Exchange of Gifts." *The Journal of Positive Psychology* 12, no. 5 (2017) 468–489.

Charry, Ellen. "Positive Theology: An Exploration in Theological Psychology and Positive Psychology." *Journal of Psychology and Christianity* 30, no. 4 (2011) 283–292.

————. "The Necessity of Divine Happiness: A Response from Systematic Theology." In *The Bible and the Pursuit of Happiness: What the Old and New Testaments Teach Us about the Good Life*, edited by Brent Strawn, 229–248. Oxford: Oxford University Press, 2012.

Chase, Steven. *Nature as Spiritual Practice.* Grand Rapids: Eerdmans, 2011.

Chichester, Teddi. "The Word as Poet and Poem in the Christian Gospels." *Pacific Coast Philology* 52, no. 1 (2017) 31-53.

Chrysostom, John. "Homilies on the Gospel of Matthew." In *A Select Library of the Nicene and Post-Nicene Fathers*, Vol X, edited by Philip Schaff. Grand Rapids: Eerdmans, 1986.

Clebsch, William A. & Jaekle, Charles R. *Pastoral Care in Historical Perspective.* Englewood Cliffs: Prentice-Hall, 1964.

Clift, Jean Dalby & Wallace B. Clift. *The Archetype of Pilgrimage: Outer Action with Inner Meaning.* Eugene: Wipf & Stock, 2004.

Csikszentmihalyi, Mihaly. *Flow: The Psychology of Optimal Experience.* New York: Harper Perennial, 1990.

Curry, Helen. *The Way of the Labyrinth.* New York: Penguin Compass, 2000.

Darling, Mary A. and Tony Campolo. *The God of Intimacy and Action: Reconnecting Ancient Spiritual Practices, Evangelism, and Justice.* New York: John Wiley, 2007.

Davis, Darin H. and Paul J. Wadell. "Educating Lives for Christian Wisdom." *International Journal of Christian Education* 20, no. 2 (2016) 90–105.

Delaruelle, Jacques. "Attention as Prayer: Simone Weil." *Literature and Aesthetics* 13, no. 2 (2003) 19–27.

Descartes, René. *Principles of Philosophy*, Part II, § 24, translated by Michael S. Mahoney. Accessed from https://www.princeton.edu/~hos/mike/texts/descartes/desc-mot.html, January 15, 2019.

DeHoff, Susan L. "In Search of a Paradigm for Psychological and Spiritual Growth: Implications for Psychotherapy and Spiritual Direction." *Pastoral Psychology* 46, no. 5 (1998) 333–346.

Desert Fathers. *The Anonymous Sayings of the Desert Fathers*, translated by John Wortley. Cambridge: Cambridge University Press, 2017.

———. *The Paradise of the Fathers*, Vol 2, translated by Wallis Budge. Putty, NSW: St. Shenouda, 2009.

Dietz, Mary G. *Between the Human and the Divine: The Political Thought of Simone Weil*. Totowa: Rowman & Littlefield, 1988.

Dodd, Patton, Jana Riese, and David Biema. *The Prayer Wheel*. New York: Convergent, 2018.

Dunn, Marilyn. *The Emergence of Monasticism from the Desert Fathers to the Early Middle Ages*. Chichester: John Wiley, 2007.

Edwards, Jonathan. *The Works of Jonathan Edwards. Volume 2: Religious Affections*. Edited by John E. Smith. New Haven: Yale University Press, 2009 (1959).

Edwards, Tilden. *Living in the Presence: Spiritual Exercises to Open our Lives to the Awareness of God*. San Francisco: Harper, 1995.

Ellin, Jeanne. *Listening Helpfully*. London: Souvenir, 1994.

Erikson, Erik H. *Identity: Youth and Crisis*. New York: Norton, 1968.

Faricy, Robert. *Prayer*. Minneapolis: Winston, 1979.

Fleming, David L. *What is Ignatian Spirituality?* Chicago: Loyola, 2008.

Flett, John G. *Apostolicity: The Ecumenical Question in World Christian Perspective*. Downers Grove, IL: InterVarsity, 2016.

Foster, Richard J., *Streams of Living Water: Celebrating the Great Traditions of Christian Faith*. San Francisco: HarperOne, 2001.

Frankl, Viktor. *Man's Search for Meaning*, rev. ed. New York: Washington Square, 1984.

Franklin, Samuel S. *The Psychology of Happiness: A Good Human Life*. Cambridge: Cambridge University Press, 2010.

Ganiel, Gladys. "21st Century Faith: Results of the Survey of Clergy, Pastors, Ministers and Faith Leaders." Retrieved from http://www.ecumenics.ie/wp-content/uploads/Clergy-Survey-Report.pdf, August 4th, 2020.

Ganzevoort, Reinder R. and Jan Visser. *Zorg voor het Verhaal: Achtergrond, Methode en Inhoud van Pastorale Begeleiding*. Utrecht: Meinema, 2007.

Gerkin, Charles V. *An introduction to Pastoral Care*. Nashville: Abingdon, 1997.

Fredrickson, Barbara. "What Good are Positive Emotions?" *Review of General Psychology* 2 (1998) 300–319.

———. "The Role of Positive Emotions in Positive Psychology: The Broaden-and-Build Theory of Positive Emotions." *American Psychologist* 56 (2001) 218–226.

Graham, Larry. *Moral Injury: Restoring Wounded Souls*. Nashville: Abingdon, 2017.

Green, Joel. "'We Had to Celebrate and Rejoice!' Happiness in the Topsy-Turvy World of Luke-Acts." In *The Bible and the Pursuit of Happiness: What the Old and New Testaments Teach Us about the Good Life*, edited by Brent Strawn, 169–186. Oxford: Oxford University Press, 2012.

Greer, Rowan. "Pastoral Care and Discipline." In *The Cambridge History of Christianity*, edited by Augustine Casiday & Frederick Norris, 567–584. Cambridge: Cambridge University Press, 2007.

Gubi, Peter M., ed. *Spiritual Accompaniment and Counselling: Journeying with Psyche and Soul*. London: Jessica Kingsley, 2015.

Gubi, Peter M., ed. *What Counsellors and Spiritual Directors Can Learn from Each Other*. London: Jessica Kingsley, 2017.

Gushee, David P. *After Evangelicalism: The Path to a New Christianity.* Louisville: Westminster John Knox, 2020.

Gustafson, James, M. *Can Ethics be Christian?* Chicago: University of Chicago Press, 1975.

Hanh, Thich Nhat. *Walking Meditation.* Boulder: Sounds True, 2019.

Haight, Roger. *Christian Spirituality for Seekers: Reflections on the Spiritual Exercises of Ignatius Loyola.* New York: Orbis, 2012.

Harrison, Carol. *The Art of Listening in the Early Church.* Oxford: Oxford University Press, 2013.

Harrison, Nonna Verna. *God's Many-Splendored Image: Theological Anthropology for Christian Formation.* Grand Rapids: Baker Academic, 2010.

Hauerwas, Stanley. *Character and the Christian Life: A Study in Theological Ethics.* San Antonio: Trinity University Press, 1975.

———. *Vision and Virtue.* Notre Dame: University of Notre Dame Press, 1981.

———. "Character Convergence: The Prospect of Holy Living." In *The Holy Spirit and Christian Formation: Multidisciplinary Perspectives,* edited by Diane J. Chandler, 205–218. Cham: Springer International, 2016.

Heschel, Abraham. "The Sigh." In *Modern Spirituality: An Anthology,* edited by John Garvey. Springfield: Templegate, 1985.

Higgins, Michael and Kevin Burns. *Genius Born of Anguish: Life and Legacy of Henri Nouwen.* New York: Paulist, 2012.

Hitlin, Steven. "Values as the Core of Personal Identity: Drawing Links between Two Theories of Self." *Social Psychology Quarterly* 66, no. 2 (Jun 2003) 118–137.

Hobfoll, Stevan, Melissa Briggs-Phillips, and L. R. Stines. "Fact or Artifact: The Relationship of Hope to a Caravan of Resources." In *Between Stress and Hope: From a Disease-centered to a Health-centered Perspective,* edited by Rebecca Jacoby & Giora Keinan, 81-104. New York: Greenwood, 2005.

Hoenkamp-Bisschops, Anke. "Spiritual Direction, Pastoral Counseling and the Relationship between Psychology and Spirituality." *Archive for the Psychology of Religion* 23, no. 1 (2000) 253–263.

Houston, James M. "Seeking Historical Perspectives for Spiritual Direction and Soul Care Today." *Journal of Spiritual Formation and Soul Care* 1, no. 1 (2008) 88–105.

Immink, Gerrit. *Faith: A Practical Theological Reconstruction.* Grand Rapids: Eerdmans, 2005.

Johnson, Luke T. "Making Connections: The Material Expression of Fellowship in the New Testament," *Interpretation* 58, no. 2 (2004) 158-171.

Kainz, Howard. *Ethics in Context.* London: Macmillan, 1988.

Keating, James, ed. *Spirituality and Moral Theology: Essays from a Pastoral Perspective.* Mahwah: Paulist, 2000.

Keating, Thomas. *Open Mind, Open Heart.* Rockport: Element, 1986.

———. *Invitation to Love: A Way of Christian Contemplation.* New York: Continuum, 1992.

Keenan, James F. "Catholic Moral Theology, Ignatian Spirituality, and Virtue Ethics: Strange Bedfellows." *The Way* 88 (1997) 36–45.

Kennedy, Ted. *Who is Worthy?* Sydney: Pluto, 2000.

King, Pamela Ebstyne and Frederic Defoy. "Joy as a Virtue: The Means and Ends of Joy." *Journal of Psychology and Theology* 48, no. 4 (2020) 308–31. DOI: 10.1177/0091647120907994.

Klose, Anne. "Joint and Mutual Covenantal Priesthood: A Narrative of Community for Australian Baptist Churches," PhD diss., University of Queensland, 2013.

Krejcir, Richard J. "Pastoral Ministry is Tough Work." Retrieved from http://johnmark. net.au/kz/?p=252 on August 4th, 2020.

Krueger, Joachim. "Seligman's Flourish: The Second Coming," *American Journal of Psychology* 125 (2012) 121–124.

Lamontagne, Richard E. "Inner Sharing: Spiritual Direction and Pastoral Care." Unpublished Doctor of Ministry thesis, George Fox University, 2002.

Leclerc, Diane, and Mark A. Maddix. *Spiritual Formation: A Wesleyan Paradigm.* Kansas City, MO.: Beacon Hill, 2011.

Leidenhag, Joanna. "Demarcating Deification and the Indwelling of the Holy Spirit in Reformed Theology." *Perichoresis* 18, no. 1 (2020) 77–98. DOI: 10.2478/perc-2020-0005.

Liebert, Elizabeth. "Perspectives on the Ministry of Spiritual Direction: One Person's View." *New Theology Review* 16, no. 1 (2003) 44–65.

———. "Practice." In *The Blackwell Companion to Christian Spirituality*, edited by Arthur Holder, 496–531. Oxford: Blackwell, 2005.

Louw, Däniel J. *A Mature Faith: Spiritual Direction and Anthropology in a Theology of Pastoral Care and Counseling.* Louvain: Peeters & Grand Rapids: Eerdmans, 1999.

———. "Philosophical Counselling: Towards a 'New Approach' in Pastoral Care and Counselling?" *HTS Teologiese Studies/Theological Studies* 67 (2011), 7 pages. DOI: 10.4102/hts.v67i2.900.

———. *Mechanics of the Human Soul.* Stellenbosch: Sun, 2005.

———. *A Pastoral Hermeneutics of Care and Encounter: A Theological Design for a Basic Theory, Anthropology, Method and Therapy.* Cape Town: Lux Verbim, 1998.

Lovin, Robin W. *Christian Faith and Public Choices: The Social Ethics of Barth, Brunner, and Bonhoeffer.* Philadelphia: Fortress, 1984.

Lowes, David. *Covenant Discipleship: Christian Formation through Mutual Accountability.* Eugene: Wipf & Stock, 2002.

Luther, Martin. *Galatians.* Wheaton, Ill: Crossway, 1998.

Lutheran World Federation, "Nairobi Statement on Worship and Culture: Contemporary Challenges and Opportunities." *International Review of Mission* 85, no. 337 (1996) 184–88. DOI: 10.1111/j.1758-6631.1996.tb03477.x.

MacIntyre, Alasdair. *After Virtue: A Study in Moral Theory*, 2nd ed. London: Duckworth, 1985.

McClure, Barbara. "Pastoral Care." In *The Wiley-Blackwell Companion to Practical Theology*, edited by Bonnie J. Miller-McLemore, 269–278. Oxford: Wiley-Blackwell, 2012.

McGrath, Alister E. *The Intellectual World of C. S. Lewis.* Chichester: Wiley-Blackwell, 2013.

———. *Iustitia Dei.* 4th edition. New York: Cambridge University Press, 2020.

McLaren, Brian. *We Make the Road by Walking: Spiritual Formation, Reorientation, and Activation.* New York: Jericho, 2014.

McEwan, David. *The Life of God in the Soul: The Integration of Love, Holiness and Happiness in the Thought of John Wesley.* Bletchley Milton Keynes: Authentic Media, 2015.

McInerny, Ralph. "Ethics." In *The Cambridge Companion to Aquinas*, edited by Norman Kretzmann and Eleonore Stump, 196–216. Cambridge: Cambridge University Press, 1993.

McKenny, Gerald P. "Heterogeneity and Ethical Deliberation: Casuistry, Narrative, and Event in the Ethics of Karl Barth." *The Annual of the Society of Christian Ethics* 20 (2000) 205–224.

Manney, Jim. *A Simple Life-Changing Prayer: Discovering the Power of St Ignatius Loyola's Examen*. Chicago: Loyola, 2011.

Marcel, Gabriel. *The Mystery of Being*, vol. I. London: Harvill, 1950.

———. *Metaphysical Journal*, translated by B. Wall. London: Rockliff, 1952.

———. "Phenomenological Notes on Being in a Situation." In *Creative Fidelity*, translated by Robert Rosthal, 82–103. New York: Noonday, 1964.

———. "Belonging and Disposability," in *Creative Fidelity*, translated by Robert Rosthal, 38–57. New York: Noonday, 1964.

———. *Homo Viator: Introduction to a Metaphysic of Hope*. London: Victor Gollancz, 1951.

———. "Desire and Hope." In *Readings in Existential Phenomenology*, edited by Nathaniel Lawrence & Daniel O'Connor, 277–285. Englewood Cliffs: Prentice-Hall, 1967.

Meinert, John. *The Love of God Poured Out: Grace and the Gifts of the Holy Spirit in Thomas Aquinas*. Steubenville: Emmaus Academic, 2018.

Meland, Bernard. "Can Empirical Theology Learn Something from Phenomenology?" In *The Future of Empirical Theology*, edited by Bernard Meland, 283–306. Chicago: University of Chicago Press, 1969.

Merton, Thomas. *Seeds of Contemplation*. London: Burns and Oates, 1949, 1957.

———. *New Seeds of Contemplation*. London: Burns and Oates, 1961.

———. *New Man*. New York: Farrar, Straus and Giroux, 1961, 2000.

Miles, Rebekah. *The Pastor as Moral Guide*. Minneapolis: Fortress, 1998.

Miller, Samuel G. "Reciprocal Maturities: Spirit and Psyche in Pastoral Counseling and Spiritual Direction." *Pastoral Psychology* 40, no. 2 (1991) 93–103.

Moon, Gary W. "Spiritual Direction: Meaning, Purpose, and Implications for Mental Health Professionals." *Journal of Psychology and Theology* 30, no. 4 (2002) 264–275.

Moon, Gary W. and David G. Benner. "Spiritual Direction and Christian Soul Care." In *Spiritual Direction and the Care of Souls: A Guide to Christian Approaches and Practices*, edited by Gary W. Moon and David G. Benner, 11–28. Downers Grove, Ill: Intervarsity, 2004.

Moschella, Mary Clark. *Ethnography As a Pastoral Practice: An Introduction*. Cleveland, OH: Pilgrim, 2008.

———. "Positive Psychology as a Resource for Pastoral Theology and Care: A Preliminary Assessment." *Journal of Pastoral Theology* 21, no. 1 (2011) 5-1-5-17.

———. *Caring for Joy: Narrative, Theology, and Practice*. Theology in Practice, Volume 1. Leiden: Brill, 2016.

Mother Teresa. *Come be My Light: The Private Writings of the Saint of Calcutta*. Edited by Brian Kolodiejchuk. New York: Image, 2009.

Murphy, Nancey. *Bodies and Souls, or Spirited Bodies?* Cambridge University Press, 2006.

Nakamura, Jeanne and Mihaly Csikszentmihalyi. "Flow Theory and Research." In *The Oxford Handbook of Positive Psychology*, 2nd ed., edited by Shane J. Lopez & C. R. Snyder, 194–195. New York: Oxford University Press, 2009.

Neafsey, John. *A Sacred Voice is Calling: Personal Vocation and Social Conscience*. New York: Orbis, 2006.

Newsom, Carol. "Positive Psychology and Ancient Israelite Wisdom." In *The Bible and the Pursuit of Happiness: What the Old and New Testaments Teach Us about the Good Life*, edited by Brent Strawn, 117–136. Oxford: Oxford University Press, 2012.

Noyce, Gaylord. *The Minister as Moral Counselor*. Nashville: Abingdon, 1989.

Nouwen, Henri. *Reaching Out: Three Spiritual Movements of the Spiritual Life*. New York: Doubleday, 1975.

———. *Spiritual Direction: Wisdom for the Long Walk of Faith*. London: HarperOne, 2008.

———. *The Wounded Healer*. New York: Image Books, 1979.

———. *The Way of the Heart*. San Francisco: HarperCollins, 1981.

Nussbaum, Martha Craven. *Anger and Forgiveness: Resentment, Generosity, Justice*. New York: Oxford University Press, 2016.

Oden, Thomas C. "The Historic Pastoral Care Tradition: A Resource for Christian Psychologists." *Journal of Psychology and Theology* 20, no. 2 (1992) 137–146.

O'Keefe, Mark. "Catholic Moral Theology and Christian Spirituality." *New Theology Review* 7, no. 2 (1994) 60–73.

———. *Becoming Good, Becoming Holy: On the Relationship of Christian Ethics and Spirituality*. Mahwah: Paulist, 1995.

Oliver, Simon. "The Sweet Delight of Virtue and Grace in Aquinas's Ethics." *International Journal of Systematic Theology* 7, no. 1 (Jan 2005) 52–71.

O'Meara, Thomas F. "Virtues in the Theology of Thomas Aquinas." *Theological Studies* 58, no. 2 (1997) 254–285.

Pembroke, Neil. *Moving Toward Spiritual Maturity: Psychological, Contemplative, and Moral Challenges in Christian Living*. New York: Routledge, 2007.

———. *Foundations of Pastoral Counselling: Integrating Philosophy, Theology, and Psychotherapy*. London: SCM, 2017.

———. "Toward a Structured, Tri-Domain Model of Companioning in Christian Formation by Pastoral Agents in a Congregational Setting: A Preliminary Report on an International Research Project." *Journal of Pastoral Care and Counseling* 72, no. 2 (2018) 104–115.

Perrin, David B. *Studying Christian Spirituality*. London: Routledge, 2007.

Peterson, Christopher. "The Future of Optimism." *American Psychologist* 55, no. 1 (2000) 44–55.

Peterson, Christopher and Martin Seligman. *Character Strengths and Virtues: A Handbook and Classification*. New York: Oxford University Press, 2004.

Peterson, Eugene. *Working the Angles: The Shape of Pastoral Integrity*. Grand Rapids: Eerdmans, 1989.

Porter, Jean. *The Recovery of Virtue: The Relevance of Aquinas for Christian Ethics*. Louisville: Westminster John Knox, 1990.

Post, Stephen. "The Inadequacy of Selflessness." *Journal of the American Academy of Religion* 56, no. 2 (1989) 213–228.

————. "Communion and True Self-Love." *The Journal of Religious Ethics* 16 (Fall 1988) 345–362.

Rehnman, Sebastian. "Virtue and Grace," *Studies in Christian Ethics* 25, no. 4 (2012) 473–493.

Roberts, Robert C. *Spiritual Emotions: A Psychology of Christian Virtues*. Grand Rapids: Eerdmans, 2007.

Rohlheiser, Ronald. *Sacred Fire: A Vision for a Deeper Human and Christian Maturity*. New York: Penguin Random House, 2015.

Rohr, Richard. *The Naked Now: Learning to See as the Mystics See*. New York: Crossroad, 2009.

————. *The Divine Dance*. London: SPCK, 2016.

Schmidt, William S. "Transforming Pilgrimage." In *The Spiritual Horizon of Psychotherapy*, edited by William S. Schmidt & Merle R. Jordan, 65–76. New York: Routledge, 2010.

————. *Walking with Stones: A Spiritual Odyssey on the Pilgrimage to Santiago*. Trafford, 2012.

Schuhmann, Carmen & Annelieke Damen. "Representing the Good: Pastoral Care in a Secular Age." *Pastoral Psychology* 67 (2018) 405–417.

Sedgwick. Timothy. *The Christian Moral Life: Practices of Piety*. Grand Rapids: Eerdmans, 1999.

Seligman, Martin. *Authentic Happiness: Using the New Positive Psychology to Realise Your Potential for Lasting Fulfilment*. London: Nicholas Brealey, 2011. First published in 2002.

————. *Flourish: A Visionary New Understanding of Happiness and Well-being*. New York: Simon & Schuster, 2011.

————. "Can Happiness be Taught?" *Daedalus* 133 (2004) 80–87.

————. "Authentic Happiness." Penn State University website entry. Retrieved from https://www.authentichappiness.sas.upenn.edu/newsletters/flourishnewsletters/newtheory on July 24, 2020.

————. Positive Psychology Center homepage. Retrieved from http:// www.ppc.sas.upenn.edu, July 24th, 2020.

Seligman, Martin, and Mihaly Csikszentmihalyi. "Positive Psychology: An Introduction." *American Psychologist* 55, no. 1 (2000) 5–15.

Sheldrake, Philip. "A Mysticism of Practice: Ignatius of Loyola." Retrieved from https:// ost.edu/mysticism-practice-ignatius-loyola/ on November 17, 2021.

Sittser, Gerald L. "The Battle Without and Within: The Psychology of Sin and Salvation in the Desert Fathers and Mothers." *Journal of Spiritual Formation and Soul Care* 2, no. 1 (2009) 44–66.

Sleeth, Matthew. *Reinforcing Faith: What Trees Teach Us about the Nature of God and God's Love for Us*. Colorado Springs: WaterBrook, 2019.

Smith, Christian and Hilary Davidson. *The Paradox of Generosity: Giving We Receive, Grasping We Lose*. New York: Oxford University Press, 2014.

Snyder, Charles R. "Hypothesis: There is Hope." In *Handbook of Hope: Theory, Measures, and Applications*, edited by Charles R. Snyder, 3–21. New York: Academic, 2000.

Snyder, Charles R., Cheri Harris, John Anderson, Sharon Holleran, Lori Irving, Sandra Sigmon, Lauren Yoshinobu, June Gibb, Charyle Langelle, and Pat Harney. "The Will and the Ways: Development and Validation of an Individual Differences Measure of Hope." *Journal of Personality and Social Psychology* 60 (1991) 570–585.

Snyder, Charles R., Jennifer Cheavans, and Susie Sympson. "Hope: An Individual Motive for Social Commerce." *Dynamics: Theory, Research, and Practice* 1, no. 2 (1997) 107–118.

Snyder, Charles R., Jennifer Cheavans, and Scott Michael. "Hope Theory: History and Elaborated Model." In *Interdisciplinary Perspectives on Hope*, edited by Jaklin Eliott, 101–118. New York: Nova Science, 2005.

Sperry, Len. *Transforming Self and Community: Revisioning Pastoral Counseling and Spiritual Direction.* Collegeville: Liturgical, 2002.

Spezzano, Daria E. "The Grace of the Holy Spirit, the Virtue of Charity and the Gift of Wisdom: Deification in Thomas Aquinas' *Summa Theologiae* Volume 1." Unpublished PhD dissertation, University of Notre Dame, 2011.

Spohn, William C. "Spirituality and Ethics: Exploring the Connections." *Theological Studies* 58 (1997) 109–123.

———. *Go and Do Likewise: Jesus and Ethics.* London: Continuum, 2000.

———. "Christian Spirituality and Theological Ethics." In *The Blackwell Companion to Christian Spirituality*, edited by Arthur Holder, 269–285. Oxford: Blackwell, 2005.

Stairs, Jean. *Listening for the Soul: Pastoral Care and Spiritual Direction.* Minneapolis: Fortress, 2000.

Steindl-Rast, David. *Gratefulness, the Heart of Prayer: An Approach to Life in Fullness.* New York: Paulist, 1974.

Swinburne, Richard. *Are We Bodies or Souls?* Oxford: Oxford University Press, 2019.

Taylor, Charles. *A Secular Age.* New Haven: Harvard University Press, 2007.

Teresa of Avila. *The Interior Castle*, translated by Kieran Kavanaugh. Washington DC: ICS, 2020.

Tetlow, Joseph. *Always Discerning.* Chicago: Loyola, 2016.

Thibodeaux, Mark. *Reimagining the Ignatian Examen.* Chicago: Loyola, 2015.

Thiselton, Anthony C. "Wisdom in the Jewish and Christian Scriptures: The Hebrew Bible and Judaism." *Theology* 114, no. 3 (2011) 163–172.

Torrell, Jean-Pierre. *Saint Thomas Aquinas, Volume 2: Spiritual Master.* Washington DC: The Catholic University of America, 2012.

Turner, Victor & Edith Turner. *Image and Pilgrimage in Christian Culture: Anthropological Perspectives.* Oxford: Basil Blackwood, 1978.

Underhill, Evelyn. *Concerning the Inner Life.* Minneapolis: Seabury, 1926.

Van Dam, Gideon. *Dichter bij het Onuitsprekelijke: Over Geestelijke Begeleiding voor en door Pastores.* Ten Have: Baarn, 2004.

Van Slyke, James A. "Understanding the Moral Dimension of Spirituality: Insights from Virtue Ethics and Moral Exemplars." *Journal of Psychology and Christianity* 34, no. 3 (2015) 205–216.

Voetius, Gisbertus. *De Praktijk der Godzaligheid. Ta Asketika sive Exercitia Pietatis (1644). Tekstuitgave met Inleiding, Vertaling en Commentaar door C.A. de Niet.* Vol. 1. Utrecht: De Banier, 1996.

Ward, Benedicta. "Spiritual Direction in the Desert Fathers." *The Way* 24, no. 1 (1984) 61–69.

Ware, Corinne. *Saint Benedict on the Freeway: A Rule of Life for the 21st Century.* Nashville: Abingdon, 2001.

Weil, Simone. *Waiting on God.* London: Routledge & Kegan Paul, 1951.

———. *Gravity and Grace.* London: Routledge, 2002. First published in French in 1947.

West, Melissa G. *Exploring the Labyrinth: A Guide for Healing and Spiritual Growth.* New York: Broadway, 2000.

Westley, Richard. *Redemptive Intimacy.* New London: Twenty-Third, 1984.

Willard, Dallas. *Renovation of the Heart: Putting on the Character of Christ.* Colorado Springs: NavPress, 2002.

Williams, Rowan. *Being Disciples: Essentials of the Christian Life.* Grand Rapids: Eerdmans, 2016.

Witherington, Ben. *Grace in Galatia: A Commentary on Paul's Letter to the Galatians.* Grand Rapids: Eerdmans, 1998.

Wortley, John. *An Introduction to the Desert Fathers.* Cambridge: Cambridge University Press, 2019.